D0530744

Early Childhood Education:
A Developmental Curriculum

EARLY CHILDHOOD EDUCATION:

A Developmental Curriculum
(Second Edition)

Edited by

GEVA M. BLENKIN and A. V. KELLY

P·C·P
Paul Chapman
Publishing Ltd

Selection and editorial material copyright © 1996 Geva Blenkin and A. V. Kelly.
All other material © as credited.

Reprinted in 2002

Paul Chapman Publishing Ltd
A SAGE Publications Company
6 Bonhill Street
London EC2A 4PU

British Library Cataloguing in Publication Data

Early childhood education: a developmental curriculum. –
  2nd ed.
  1. Early childhood education 2. Early childhood education—Curricula
  3. Education, Elementary—Curricula
  I. Blenkin, Geva M. II. Kelly, A. V. (Albert Victor), 1931-372. 2′1

ISBN 1–85396–315–1

Typeset by Anneset, Weston-super-Mare, Avon
Printed and bound in Great Britain

D E F G H   1 2 3 0 9

The beginning of every task is the most crucial part, especially when our concern is with those who are young and vulnerable. (Plato, *The Republic*, 377b)

Contents

Notes on Contributors

This book is the product of staff who have, all save one, been involved at all levels in specialist early years work at Goldsmiths' College – in the training of specialist teachers for the early years (when such specialization was permitted), in work with Masters and Research Degree students and in a wide range of research activities. All the contributors have played a direct part in the development of the distinctive view of education and curriculum which is set out and analysed in what follows.

Geva Blenkin's work and interests lie in the field of curriculum studies in general and the early years curriculum in particular. She was formerly headteacher of an infant school in the East End of London. She is currently Director of the national early years research project, Principles into Practice: Improving the Quality of Children's Early Learning. Her publications include *The Primary Curriculum* and *The Primary Curriculum in Action*.

Pauline Boorman is a physical education specialist whose prime interests are in physical development and special needs in the early years. Her main concern is to persuade teachers to recognize that physical education has a central role to play in children's education and to plan their practical provision in such a way as to reflect this.

Celia Burgess-Macey is currently a part-time lecturer working on the PGCE course at Goldsmiths' College. She is also research associate with the Principles into Practice and Quality in Diversity research projects. She was previously adviser for early years and primary education in the Education Department of Lambeth Borough Council.

Kerry Crichlow is currently Equalities Adviser in the Education Department of Lambeth Borough Council.

Mari Guha's major interests are in the evaluation of children's development in the early years of schooling and in learning through the playful use of resources. These interests are well supported by her background in child development. She has taught in primary schools in Hungary and India as well as in London.

Victoria Hurst has a particular interest in the education of three- to five-year-olds and in the implications for teachers of current insights into their learning and developmental needs. She is currently engaged in research into teachers' strategies of self-evaluation in the primary classroom, and is both Director of the Quality in Diversity research project at Goldsmiths' College and Deputy Director of the Principles into Practice project.

Clare Kelly is currently working at the Centre for Language in Primary Education. She has worked extensively as a teacher of children in the early years. Her previous experience has also included a period as a lecturer in early childhood education at Goldsmiths' College.

Vic Kelly is Professor of Curriculum Studies at Goldsmiths' College. He has published widely in the field of curriculum studies, his major books being *Knowledge and Curriculum Planning* and *Education and Democracy*.

John Matthews is an artist with experience of working with children of all ages. His major research interest is in representation in early childhood, on which he has published several important articles and addressed a number of international conferences. He is currently Senior Lecturer in the Division of Art at Nanyang Technological University, Singapore.

Marilyn Metz has taught throughout the nursery and primary age-range and in initial teacher education and higher degree studies, at both Goldsmiths' College and the London Institute of Education. She is now a primary education consultant. Her main concerns now lie in the fields of mathematics education and the role of computers across the curriculum.

Roy Richards was Director of the Schools Council's Learning Through Science project (1978–84), and was also a member of the Council's Science 5–13 project (1968–72). He has lectured and run courses throughout the United Kingdom and overseas, including the USA and the USSR, has broadcast on schools radio and television and has been an adviser to the BBC.

Marian Whitehead is a Senior Lecturer in Education at Goldsmiths' College. She has responsibility for the MA course in Language and Literature in Education and makes a major contribution to the MA in Early Childhood Education. She is a deputy director of the Principles into Practice research project, and has published extensively on language development, literacy and literature.

Preface to the Second Edition

The first edition of this book, which set out to provide both a theoretical underpinning for, and a practical exposition of, the approach to education which seeks to promote the development of the individual as well as to support the needs of society, was well received both in the United Kingdom and in a number of other countries. Indeed, it became the first of a trilogy of publications, and, in company with *Assessment in Early Childhood Education* and *The National Curriculum and Early Learning* from the same stable, it has constituted a continuing statement of this approach to education during a period when it has been increasingly under threat.

Its focus on the early years of education has also proved to be of particular interest during a period in which extensive research has been revealing the importance of this phase of schooling so cogently that it has attracted widespread political attention.

Such attention, however, has not always been accompanied by a full appreciation of its implications for the planning of the early years curriculum, and in England and Wales that curriculum has been converted by legislation into a form which neither reflects the developmental aspect of education at this stage nor acknowledges the thinking on which it is based.

This second edition, therefore, has been substantially modified to take account of the changes in the practice of early childhood education which have been imposed by the advent of the National Curriculum for England and Wales. For those changes have sought to eliminate the approach to education as development which the first edition was concerned to explicate, and, indeed, to celebrate. And, in doing so, they have gone some way towards destroying the notion that early education is in some way special, that it has, in the words of the Hadow Report, 'its own canons of excellence', and certainly they have denied the associated claim of the first edition that the view of education as development is one which is applicable at all stages of the educational process, that education in a democracy is, or should be, more than a device for supporting the country's economy.

In this context, it is gratifying to realize that a book which seeks to maintain the contrary view, to keep it on the agenda of the educational debate, and, indeed, to maintain the existence of a genuine educational debate, has attracted sufficient interest and attention, not only in other countries, such as the United States, but also in the United Kingdom, to warrant a further edition. It is also important to note, however, that the eight or nine years since the publication of the first edition have seen that view placed increasingly under threat and made it immeasurably more difficult for teachers who are committed to the notion that children matter as individuals to reflect that philosophy in their practice.

This second edition is an attempt to support and encourage, even to inspire, such teachers in their continued endeavours to ensure that the experiences they offer their pupils do significantly promote their development and genuinely enrich their lives as individual human beings.

Geva Blenkin
Vic Kelly
September 1995

Introduction

This book sets out to explicate, and indeed to celebrate, a distinctive approach to education. It is an approach which the contributors (all but one of them, either currently or in the recent past tutors concerned with the early years of schooling at Goldsmiths' College) have for some years been developing both through their work with the teachers in local schools and through that with students, on initial courses of teacher education (before these were reduced in their scope by governmental controls), on in-service courses, and on higher degree courses at both the taught and research levels. It is a view of education which we regard as very important and as entitled to the fullest possible consideration. This it has not always had, and, indeed, the failure of current political policies for education to recognize its existence we find very disturbing – whether it is ignorance or apprehension on the part of those responsible for framing and implementing those policies which this failure reflects. As a consequence of those policies, and especially of the manner in which they have been imposed on teacher education in the United Kingdom, this approach to education is being put at great risk, its development certainly inhibited and possibly about to be arrested altogether.

We feel, therefore, that this is a most opportune moment to re-assert this view and to make public the thinking which has led us to it over a considerable period of time, before such thinking becomes lost in the imposed reversion to policies of a more restricted and simplistic kind. Recent research (Beruetta-Clement *et al.*, 1984; Sylva, 1992) has stressed the importance of early education, both for future educational progress and for social well-being, with such force that the politicians have taken up its advocacy. What is being ignored, however, in their resultant policies is that it is not just any form of early education which generates these benefits, but a form of education which is developmentally appropriate.

This notion of a developmentally appropriate curriculum requires careful and detailed analysis. And this approach to education, especially in the early years, needs to be given the kind of clear and coherent statement it has hitherto lacked, if only to ensure that it has to be given proper weight and taken full account of in any genuinely professional and open debate about educational provision and the school curriculum. It is this task which this book addresses.

Those features which are central to a concept of education must of course remain central whatever the age of the pupil. For, whatever our view of education might be, there would seem to be little logic in claiming that it should be fundamentally different in secondary schools from in primary, or in higher education from in schools, or in the early years from in the later stages of primary schooling. To concentrate on a specific age range, then, in any discussion of education requires some explanation and, indeed, justification.

What is distinctive, then, about early childhood education that warrants this kind of separate and clearly focused discussion? Its first distinguishing characteristic is that for a very long time – almost two centuries in the United Kingdom, for example – it has placed great stress on the vulnerability of young children, on their consequent need for a caring form of provision and, as a corollary of this, on the notion of education as development. Its practitioners have thus been encouraged both by their initial courses of teacher education and by their subsequent experience to see studies of child development as their most profitable source of helpful advice and counsel. Hence it has been particularly in relation to the early years of schooling that people have recognized the value of Piaget's work, and that is still the case now with the many developments of that work that recent years have seen.

A major weakness of this approach, however, has been that it has seldom been translated into coherent curricular terms. Curriculum has too often been viewed as concerned with subjects, with knowledge, with the content of education, and thus as applicable only at the later stages of education when these have – whether rightly or not – come to be regarded as central. It has not always been appreciated that the subject, or knowledge, base offers us only one form of curriculum, and that a developmental base needs to be translated into another quite distinctive form. The marrying up of what we have come to understand about the development of children and what we have also learnt about curriculum planning, and especially the role of subject-content within it, is long overdue. It is, however, vital to the making of adequate *educational* provision. And it is a major element of what this book sets out to tackle.

A second distinguishing feature of early childhood education, which is closely related to this, is that its theory and its practice have for a long time demonstrated a much stronger commitment to the Hadow/Plowden philosophy of education than is to be found at any other level of schooling. Some research in primary schools, especially that of the ORACLE team (Galton, Simon and Croll, 1980), has revealed the gap between the theory and the practice, the rhetoric and the reality of this approach to education. Such research, however, has been mainly confined to the education of children of seven plus, where it has emerged that teachers are not always totally committed even to the rhetoric of 'child-centredness'. Studies of the three to seven age range, while revealing the same kind of gap, have also suggested that teachers at this level are more strongly committed to this view and have thus been more disturbed by the evidence of the inadequacies of their practice and more concerned than teachers of older pupils to narrow that gap. This is one reason why that gap has been narrowing.

Another is the concern with and respect for studies of human development which we noted earlier. For these studies are advancing at a rapid rate as a result of recent work in this field and there are signs that that work is already having its impact on teachers of young children. Research currently being undertaken at Goldsmiths' College, for example, is revealing overwhelming evidence of the importance placed on an understanding of child development as crucial to the provision of a high quality curriculum for the early years (Blenkin *et al.*, 1995). We know a good deal more now than we did in 1967 when the Plowden Report (CACE, 1967) was published not only about how children develop, from the very point of birth, but also about how curricula may be designed, planned and implemented to support their development. These two kinds of understanding have been coming together to provide greater insight into the planning of educational provision at this level; the gap between the Hadow/Plowden rhetoric and the reality of teachers' practice in the early years has begun to close. It is the intention of this book, as indicated above, despite the contrary pressures of current official policies, to assist in that process.

The Hadow/Plowden philosophy lacked a secure theoretical base, and it must be that, more than any other single factor, which has led to the inadequacies of implementation that most studies have revealed. As we have just suggested, however, we are nearer to the achievement of an adequate theoretical base as a result of recent work both in developmental psychology and in curriculum theory. What is more important is that that work has led not just to the creation of a sound base for that philosophy of education, it has also changed the philosophy itself in significant ways. Both Plowden and, perhaps to a lesser extent, Hadow might be viewed as attempts at restating what has come to be called – pejoratively in many cases – the 'progressive' ideology of education. Recent work has taken us well beyond the somewhat simplistic notions which are encapsulated in that term – and which have been the focus of attention for its many critics. The idea of education as process, or as a series of processes of human development is a good deal more sophisticated than that of 'progressivism'. For it is founded on a clearer concept of the epistemological issues which the planning of education must raise, on a deeper understanding of the forms and modes of human development and of the kinds of experience which can promote – or hinder – it, and on a

fuller understanding of the complexities of curriculum planning. It is a
view which recognizes, in a way which the Plowden Report never
approached, that our educational planning will continue to be inadequate
while it begins from assumptions about the essential nature of certain
bodies of knowledge which schools must transmit and fails to question
those assumptions by asking not only what schools should be offering
their pupils but also, and much more importantly, why. This is a
question that teachers in the early years have long been more accustomed
to asking than those at other levels of the school system, primarily
because of that concern with child development we have already noted.
It is, for the same reason, one which they have answered in developmental terms, claiming that the justification for the content of our
curriculum must be sought primarily in what it contributes to the
development of our pupils. It is this that constitutes another claim to
distinctiveness.

The notion of education as a form of human development, then, is an
important one and deserves to be more thoroughly explored than it has
been in the past. It is our view that the best way to explore it is by considering its implementation in early childhood education. There is
another compelling reason for doing this in the present educational climate, especially in England and Wales. For current political pressures and
policies are forcing the school curriculum into other models. The demand
now is for planning education in terms of its content, even in the early
years, and for viewing and evaluating it in terms of its intended outcomes, its objectives, what it is for rather than what it is. Such approaches
are inimical to the concept of education as human development, since
their concern is with the development of knowledge, or with the economic development of society rather than with the development of the
human individual, or else it is a concern with individual development of
a unidimensional kind. To say that is not of course to imply that a developmental approach to curriculum is not concerned with knowledge or
that it is not aware of the importance of the social aspects of education;
it is, however, to indicate an important difference of focus. And the
danger posed by current political initiatives is that the essence of that
view of education, which we believe has been emerging with increasing
cogency in the early years of schooling, will be stifled and that something of great educational significance will therefore be lost. This is
another compelling reason for making the kind of statement this book is
designed to offer.

It is important, then, in order to explicate a coherent theory of education as a device for promoting human development, to indicate some
of the ways in which its very essence differs from content- or product-
based approaches to educational planning. It is also necessary, however,
to go further than that. For if the gap between theory and practice is to
be further closed, as in our view it must be, then any exploration of the

theoretical bases of this view of education must be related closely to issues of implementation. It is important to do this not only to ensure the interlinking of theory and practice but also to demonstrate the practicability of this approach to education. A. N. Whitehead (1932, p. 7) once said, 'Whenever a textbook is written of real educational worth, you may be quite certain that some reviewer will say that it will be difficult to teach from it.' The truth of this assertion is perhaps nowhere more apparent than in many of the responses the advocacy of a developmental approach to education and curriculum seems to elicit. Our intention here is to demonstrate not only its theoretical desirability but also its classroom practicability.

To achieve this the chapters in the book represent a gradual progression from more abstract and theoretical levels of discussion to the more practical and applied. We begin with an explication of the theoretical positions we regard as essential to the notion of education as development, proceed to a consideration of some of its more general implications for such things as the context for education, the role of play in education, the multicultural dimension of curriculum and the importance of the teacher–parent partnership, and then narrow the focus to specific areas of the curriculum and particular aspects of development.

Even when the focus is narrowed to particular curriculum areas, however, several crucial common themes emerge. The first of these is the importance of recognizing, and planning for, the links young children naturally detect and make between what (some) adults regard as discrete 'subjects' – mathematical, scientific and linguistic understandings being promoted by appropriate experiences in visual representation and physical movement, for example. Indeed, it is clear, from a vast array of research evidence, that all of these dimensions of development, along with the all-important emotional dimension, are, or can be with the right kind of provision, promoted by experience in any one of them. And, conversely, all of these dimensions of development can be inhibited by inappropriate forms of provision, and especially a concern to isolate them within 'subject' boundaries.

Second, the evidence in all of these areas points quite conclusively to the centrality of informal experiences in the early stages of development, and again, conversely, to the dangers of too great a formalization too soon.

Third, all of this has to be seen as adding up to quite comprehensive evidence of the complexities of all human learning and of the particular complexities of supporting that learning in its early, formative stages.

It is this that renders almost incomprehensible the contrary thrust of current policies in England and Wales for education in the early years (including current proposals for the under-5s), especially the insistence within the National Curriculum on subject divisions and the early formalization of learning. One cannot interpret these policies as a result of stupidity on the part of those responsible for formulating them; one can only look for more sinister, political explanations. To read the evidence, as it is set out in what follows, is to be convinced; to impose policies without reading that evidence is irresponsible, even immoral; to read the evidence and to reject it is to stand convicted of a deliberate attempt to impoverish educational provision in the early years and to deny the democratic right to fully educational opportunities to a large proportion of our young children.

One last point must be made in this Introduction. If, as was suggested at the beginning, the central feature of a concept of education must remain the same whatever the age of pupils we are concerned with, the only justification for focusing on the early years is that we can identify a concept of education there which is distinctive and perhaps more fully worked out, both in theory and in practice. It is, however, a concept which, if accepted, must have applicability at all ages and stages, so that what we offer here we would recommend to the consideration of all teachers, whatever the ages of their pupils. It is odd but true that the other point at which this approach to education is discernible is in the education of adults, not only in institutions of continuing education but also in the rarified atmosphere of the research degree. If it is to be found at the beginning, and, in a sense, the end of formal education provision, one has to ask what it is that is different about the middle that renders it inappropriate there.

In short, then, what we are attempting to elucidate in this book is the form of educational provision one must make at any stage of education once one accepts that the personal development of the pupil is at least as significant a concern as the knowledge to be purveyed or the economic or political ends to be attained, once one accepts that education in the full sense is not just about learning in the sense of the acquisition of knowledge, but is rather about that human development which properly planned learning can promote.

Such human development is too important to be left to chance.

Geva Blenkin
Vic Kelly

1

Education as Development

Geva Blenkin and Vic Kelly

There are no reasons, either conceptual or empirical, why the notion of education as development should be regarded as peculiar to, or as the sole province of, early childhood education. It is quite simply an alternative theory of education and, consequentially, an alternative basis for the planning of educational provision at every age and stage. As was pointed out in our Introduction, the main reasons for exploring it in the context of early childhood education are that it has been more fully worked out there as a theoretical perspective and that it is more often to be seen in practice in that sector and phase of the education service. It can of course also be found in practice in much of adult and continuing education but there its theoretical underpinning has hitherto been less well established.

This book will flesh out in detail many of the implications of adopting this view of education and this approach to curriculum planning. This chapter will launch that exercise by explaining the theoretical base of this view. It is crucial, however, that we begin both of these tasks with a clear recognition that its importance derives from the fact that it is, in a genuine and quite fundamental sense, an alternative view of education and of schooling – an alternative, that is, to that traditional view that is encapsulated in current policies for educational provision, especially in England and Wales.

It is our concern to demonstrate that there is such an alternative view, that it is worthy of consideration and that it cannot be rejected without a proper examination of what it asserts and what it offers. Furthermore, acceptance of its existence must also make it necessary to produce the kind of justification for current policies which one never sees; it must create the requirement that, if those policies are to be pressed upon us, they must be backed by cogent arguments demonstrating their superiority, rather than, as at present, merely by assertions which remain unquestioned and thus unsupported and unjustified. Indeed, those policies themselves can only be strengthened by a requirement that they be accompanied by supporting and justificatory evidence and reasons. For, pronouncements (Blenkin, Edwards and Kelly, 1992; Kelly, 1994). In most cases, however, it is not being used in the sense Lawrence Stenhouse wished to give to it nor in the sense in which we view it here, but again in what is the purely methodological sense of the processes or means by which children acquire the knowledge someone has decided they should acquire. It is in our view the developmental perspective on education and the consequent implications for its content which are crucial to our interpretation, so that 'development' is for us a clearer and more satisfactory term than 'process'.

The notion of education as development, then, has grown out of what was once called 'progressivism'; it has benefited from advances which have been made in recent times in our appreciation of the problematic nature and status of human knowledge, in our understanding of human development, and in our insights into the complexities of curriculum; it has drawn much that is central and valuable from the notion of education as 'process'; and it has blended all these ingredients into what must be recognized as a significant and alternative view of education and of the basis for curriculum planning. This alternative is advocated and offered, as indeed 'progressivism' was advocated and offered from the very outset, because of the many dissatisfactions which its proponents feel with the traditional view of education and its resultant approach to curriculum planning. It is to these dissatisfactions that we must now turn.

Dissatisfactions with traditional views of education

There are two major features of the traditional approach to educational planning that the notion of education as development is opposed to, and indeed represents a reaction against. The first of these is its instrumentalism, its concern with what Rousseau called the 'man-in-the-making' and its corresponding lack of interest in 'what he is before he becomes a man' (the sexism is Rousseau's). The second is the obsession of traditionalism with the content of education, education being defined, and planned, by reference to the knowledge-content to be transmitted and absorbed rather than, as the developmentalist would insist, the impact of that knowledge-content on the learner, its effect on and/or contribution to his or her development.

The emphasis on content

The traditional view of education, as it was first enunciated by Plato and as it is still advocated, too often without the same concern to justify it that one can see in Plato's work, is that it consists in some sense of initiation into certain kinds or forms of knowledge. This is the view that was argued very strongly by Richard Peters some thirty years ago (1965, 1966) and has been taken for granted and built on by many of his colleagues and followers since then (Dearden, 1968, 1976; White, 1973; Hirst, 1965, 1974; Hirst and Peters, 1970). It should be sufficiently familiar to readers, therefore, for it to be unnecessary to elaborate on it here. What must be stressed, however, is that it is based on a particular view of knowledge, a particular epistemology, a view which sees certain kinds or forms of knowledge as enjoying some mystical, God-given superiority of status quite irrespective of how we as human beings may view them, and independent of all human response to them, and thus as having some kind of inalienable claim to inclusion in any truly educational curriculum.

It is not the intention here to engage in this epistemological debate. What must be made clear, however, is that the view of education as development rejects the rationalist epistemological base as well as the educational prescriptions that it is claimed stem from it. And we must consider briefly why these are so rejected.

The view that some bodies of knowledge possess some kind of inherent intrinsic value is metaphysical (in the literal sense of being beyond any form of empirical demonstration) and very difficult to maintain in the light of the contrary evidence of the massive changes in knowledge of all kinds and in values of all kinds that the present century has witnessed, and the problematic nature of human knowledge that those changes have pointed towards (Kelly, 1986, 1995). Even the notions of what constitutes these intrinsically worthwhile bodies of knowledge and thus of which knowledge is central to educational provision have themselves changed. In this context, the view of knowledge as a human construct, and thus subject to constant modification, adaptation, evolution and change, represents a far more plausible and satisfactory characterization of what knowledge actually is. And the empiricist's view of knowledge as being dependent on empirical observation and limited to the hypothetical constructs we can temporarily erect on the basis of that observation has much more appeal and a far greater air of realism about it. It leads, however, to some dramatic consequences for educational planning, as we shall shortly see.

It is also a view of knowledge which makes possible the development of a concept of education which embraces its affective, emotional and social dimensions as well as the purely intellectual. The rationalist's view of knowledge as in some way absolute, leading as it does to a view of human values as similarly absolute, necessitates a rejection of the emotive side of human nature and makes it impossible to develop any coherent theory of this aspect of human existence. For the rationalist, 'man' is a rational animal, rationality is 'his' essence, and in a manner typical of essentialism (which has been largely discredited in mainstream British philosophy since the turn of the century) it derives many prescriptions from that analysis of 'man's' essence. By the very nature of that analysis, however, none of those prescriptions can include the emotional side of existence. As W. H. Walsh (1969, p. 32) once said in criticism of Kant's rationalism:

> The Kantian doctrine which makes practical reason in effect the godlike element in man and writes down the passions as belonging to his animal nature amounts to a form of dualism as objectionable as any to be found in Descartes. The unity of the human being is entirely lost in this account.

It is the inevitable and consequent loss of that unity in the educational planning which results from adopting this epistemological stance that is a major source of the rejection of it by those who see education as concerned with human development on every front. For the rationalist approach to educational planning has led to the alienation of many pupils from the experiences offered them in the name of education. There is no lack of evidence for the extent to which many pupils have rejected what has been offered them and thus effectively have left schools with no benefit at all from the time spent there. It is clear too from this evidence that this is a particular problem when there is a conflict between the values implicit in the knowledge-content which is being offered and purveyed and those inherent in the cultural background, social and/or ethnic, of the pupils to whom they are to be transmitted. It is an approach, therefore, which leads not only to alienation but also, and consequently, to educational inequality. This aspect of it, too, those who are concerned with human development find equally unacceptable.

It is also the case that a concern only with rationality leads to a lack of awareness of the individual or personal nature of educational development. Rationalism is concerned only with universals and its thrust must logically be towards sameness. We have already seen that it cannot cope with the emotional side of human life, and the corollary of that is that it cannot handle the notion of individual human differences – except in the somewhat trivial sense of differences in rate of and capacity for learning and the development of rational powers. Thus those who accept this view can, and do, talk of a common curriculum, defined in terms of its content, a single educational diet for all pupils, to be varied only in the rate and form of its dosage, not in any essential aspects of its content. There is only one road to the perfect form(s) of rationality and all pupils must follow that road at the fastest pace they can be whipped into. This again is a view the developmentalist cannot accept, since he or she sees education as centrally concerned with the development of individual abilities, talents or capacities and of a maximization of these in relation to the potential of every child. It is human difference which this view of education celebrates.

The last point that must be made here is that even those who have advocated this traditional content-based approach, from Plato to the present day, have done so because of a concern they have with the kinds of development which they believe education must lead to. Plato's main concern was with the development of the intellectual powers of his 'philosopher-kings'; the knowledge-content he advocated was merely a means to this development. And more recently, Richard Peters (1966) has written of education as 'the development of mind' and has joined with Paul Hirst (1965, 1974; Hirst and Peters, 1970) in making it quite clear that the concern is with the development of the child's ability to operate within the several forms of rationality which Paul Hirst has posited, so that again we can see that it is not the content itself which is the concern but the kinds of intellectual development it is thought to lead to.

There are two unsatisfactory aspects of this. The first is the bland assumption that these forms of development will automatically follow from exposure to certain kinds of knowledge and that this is the only knowledge content that will promote them. This is an empirical claim. Yet no attempt has been made, as far as we can see, to establish its validity. And the evidence of the alienation of many pupils to which we referred just now would seem to disprove the claim rather comprehensively.

The second unsatisfactory aspect of this assumption is that it leads to that very instrumental view of the educational process we identified earlier as the second major source of our criticism, that view of education as concerned with 'the man-in-the-making', with what the end-product of the process is to be rather than with the essential elements of the process itself. There are several aspects of this we must explore.

The emphasis on end-products

It is clear when one considers the combination of the essential instrumentality of this view with its parallel emphasis on knowledge-content how its prevalence and predominance in thinking about education have made it so easy for those who have recently wished to establish a political educational policy which stresses economic, vocational and, in general, utilitarian effectiveness as the prime concern and criterion. For they have been able to conceal that essential instrumentality behind a facade of concern for supposedly worthwhile bodies of knowledge. Yet instrumental these policies are, concerned not so much with the well-being and development of the individual as with those of society and, while no one would wish to argue that the well-being and development of society are not important, to make them the prime, even the sole, concern of education is to sell short a large proportion of the child population, for the reasons we have already listed.

There is a more subtle form of instrumentality, however, implied by that assumption to which we have already referred that education should, as Rousseau expressed it, treat the child as a 'man-in-the-making' and should always be 'looking for the man in the child, without considering what he is before he becomes a man'. The reason why this is seen as unsatisfactory by those who would adopt a developmental approach is that it shifts the focus of attention away from the child, this time not only on to the content of his or her education but on to the end-product, the notion of the kind of person he or she is to be moulded into. Much that is misconceived and misunderstood has been uttered about the concept of 'child-centredness' in education. As far as the developmental view is concerned, it is to be taken as implying that the child and his or her development are the first consideration in educational planning and that all else is secondary to that.

There are several reasons why the instrumental view is regarded as unsatisfactory. To begin with, its effect is to suggest that the end justifies the means, the doctrine of 'spare the rod and spoil the child' being rooted in this kind of education theory. Secondly, it is manifestly not the case, for reasons we have already considered, that two thousand or more years of this doctrine have achieved very much in relation to the education of most children. In fact, as we have also seen, its effect is more often counterproductive to its professed aims. Thirdly, in a manner completely consonant with rationalism generally, it is based on a concept of human perfection as an entity, as an end-state towards which we must strive, rather than recognizing that such a concept can have no meaning when divested of its rationalist epistemological base, but can only be viewed in terms of (to paraphrase John Dewey's words) 'the ever-enduring process of perfecting'.

In this context, it is worth noting that most of those features of education which have been identified as constituting the essence of the concept – autonomy, understanding, critical awareness and so on – are themselves not end-states to which we must strive but procedural principles by which it is suggested we should live and, as teachers, help our pupils to live. There is no such thing as an autonomous person, except in a totally trivial sense. The claim that education should concern itself with autonomy asserts nothing more than that we should help people to think for themselves as far as is possible for them and to go on extending the boundaries of that possibility until they die. For this reason, it is misleading to regard these aspects or features of education as aims; they must be seen as ever-present principles. It is the tendency of the traditional view to entice us into the former stance, by encouraging us to plan education by reference to some blueprint of its end-products, that is its most unsatisfactory feature for those who see education as development.

This problem is of course compounded when, as usually happens, those long-term aims come to be translated into, or used as the basis for the generation of, a hierarchy of short-term objectives. For education is then seen as a linear, step-by-step process by which we move slowly and inexorably towards the attainment of our aims – the 'Thirty-Nine Steps' model of educational planning. There are no doubt some simplistic forms of learning which can best be approached in this way, but education, especially if it is seen as a process of development, is a much more subtle and sophisticated process and must be based and planned at every stage by reference to intrinsic principles rather than extrinsic aims. One does not encourage the development of, say, literary appreciation in a child by some kind of step-by-step procedure with literary appreciation at its end, but by offering a series of experiences which from the very outset have literary appreciation as a major feature and a consistent principle of planning and provision.

The traditional view has too often and too readily added to the rationalist view of the sanctity of certain forms of knowledge a behaviourist form of psychology, reflecting a highly simplistic view not only of education but also of philosophy, of psychology and of their respective roles in educational planning. From behaviourist psychology has come the behavioural objectives model of curriculum planning (Tyler, 1949; Bloom, 1956; Mager, 1962; Kratwohl, 1964; Popham, 1969). This model, suggesting as it does, that once decisions about the content and the long-term aims of education have been made, these can be broken down into an almost infinite sequence of graded objectives, has fitted very well with the view of those who have claimed to have the answers to all questions of what that content and those long-term aims must be. It is thus a model which is much loved by those concerned to make and implement current political policies, as the briefest glance at the documentation which has emerged in recent years from HMI, DES, DFE, DFEE, SEAC, NCC, SCAA, and now OFSTED will reveal. The linking of the two, however, emphasizes the instrumentality of both, and this is a major reason why both approaches, whether separately or together, are rejected by those who wish to emphasize the developmental aspects of education. The concern has been, and with the advent of the National Curriculum for England and Wales now is, with what is to be taught and with the associated question of how it can best be transmitted. It becomes that much more difficult, therefore, to face up to the questions of why these things are to be taught or what are the educational implications of teaching them in this way. Yet these would seem to be questions to be faced long before we ask *what* or *how*, and they are questions the answers to which must be expressed in terms of procedural, developmental principles rather than extrinsic aims.

It is to these questions that those who have rejected the traditional approach have turned and it is to a consideration of some of the answers they have offered to them that we now turn.

The essential elements of the developmental view

Many of the essential elements of this view will have emerged clearly in the dissatisfactions with the traditional view which we have just considered. It is important, however, to be clear not only about why this view is opposed to the traditional approach to education but what are the major positive features of the alternative approach which it is advocating.

Perhaps the first point to be made is that, since, as we have seen, a major feature of this view is its rejection of rationalism's certainty about knowledge and thus about human values, it has to acknowledge from the outset not only that it is based on a recognition of the problematic nature of human knowledge but also that it adopts a particular value position, so that it is necessary to state clearly what this is.

Perhaps the least satisfactory feature of the traditional view, as it has been expressed both in theoretical discussions of education and in political policies, is its assumption that its values can in some sense be treated as given and do not need to be justified. It was this that led to the attack of those 'new directions' in the sociology of education (Young, 1971), and the criticisms offered by those who have explored 'the politics of knowledge'. For the claims made there were that the traditional approach represented the imposition of the values of a particular ideology on pupils and thus had to be seen as one aspect of the social control exercised by the dominant group in society. And it was this which led Lawrence Stenhouse (1970, p. 82), in his attack on the objectives model of curriculum planning, to insist that all curriculum planning must begin from a definition of 'the value positions embodied in the curriculum specification or specifications'.

It is of the essence of the developmental view that it does not believe that decisions about the nature of education or schooling can be taken by reference to some objective criteria of judgement, since its view is that no such criteria exist or could exist. It recognizes, therefore, that all educational prescriptions are made from particular value positions, so that, unlike most other views, it accepts the responsibility to declare *ab initio* what its value position is. It is not offering its notion of development as in any sense fixed, final or God-given; it is offering it as a contribution to what it sees must be a continuing debate, its concern being mainly that such debate should in fact continue, rather than be stifled by the presumed certainties of the traditionalists and/or the politicians.

The first premise of its value system is that the prime concern of education should be to develop to the maximum the potential of every child to function as a human being, that is, as a creature with the greatest possible control over his or her own destiny and thus with the widest practicable range of options and possibilities open to him or her. Its concept of education then is not as a device for the transmission of certain bodies of agreed knowledge and values or as a process of moulding people into some predetermined shape, it is of the enhancement of individual capacities, the widening of every person's horizons of appreciation and understanding, the maximization of everyone's potential, the development of everyone's powers of self-direction, autonomy, understanding and critical awareness. In general, it sees education as concerned, as Paolo

Freire (1972) has put it, to give people the power to see their own problems and situation in a reflexive perspective and to act on them for themselves and according to their own choices and decisions rather than to be 'dopes' whose destiny is decided for them by others. On this view education is a matter of empowerment, as in any genuinely democratic context it must be (Kelly, 1995).

Many principles, both theoretical and practical, follow inexorably from this first premise. For it follows first, 'as the night the day', that these forms of development cannot be brought about by the transmission of preselected content, along with the values implicit in that content, to largely passive recipients. Education, on this view, is a good deal more than mere learning. In particular, it requires the active involvement of the educand in the process of being educated, so that the concept of active learning is a crucial element in this theory. This concept does not imply gross physical activity, as is often naively assumed. Rather its concern is to stress the importance for development of the child's being actively and positively engaged with the content and processes of his or her learning in such a way that development of the kind envisaged does in fact occur. The contrast is with those forms of learning in which information is acquired and 'learnt' with no real impact on the learner's levels of understanding, the kinds of passive learning the Hadow Report (Board of Education, 1931, p. 93) once disparaged as 'knowledge to be acquired and facts to be stored' and which A. N. Whitehead (1932, pp. 1–2) once dubbed 'inert ideas', 'ideas that are merely received into the mind without being utilized, or tested, or thrown into fresh combinations'. For 'education with inert ideas is not only useless; it is above all things harmful – *Corruptio optimi, pessima*' (ibid., p. 2).

It follows further from this that the content of any child's education must consist of genuine, first-hand experience, since, if it does not, it will have very little real meaning and will fail to bring about real development. It is this that lies behind the claim that the curriculum should be based on the needs and interests of pupils, and no amount of conceptual analysis of those terms can counter the claim that, if it is not, then nothing to which the developmentalist would grant the name 'education' will occur. It is developmental needs that are the criteria of curriculum decision-making, since these, as we have seen, are the ultimate values of this form of educational theory, and those developmental needs, for the reasons we have just given, can only be met by reference to those things the child reveals a genuine interest in.

This is what is implied in the claim that we should make our decisions about the content of the child's education by reference to the child himself or herself rather than out of a concern solely for that content itself. This is what, as we saw above, the concept of 'child-centredness' entails. This is the basis upon which, as teachers, we must intervene in the child's learning and development. It has too often been assumed, perhaps, one must admit, with some justification in the light of the assertions of some theorists, that 'child-centredness' implies non-interference, non-interventionism, a standing-back to avoid interfering in natural growth, a literal interpretation of Rousseau's advice, 'From the outset raise a wall around your child's soul.' And this has, quite rightly, been a part of many attacks on this view. However, this represents a major misunderstanding by both some of its proponents and its critics. The notion of education as development makes clear that the role of the educator is to intervene appropriately to ensure that development does occur. For it is plain from the work of the developmental psychologists, and, indeed, from common sense, that development will not occur without such intervention, that natural growth in the cognitive sphere will, and often does, result in stunted growth.

It is here that John Dewey's notion of the experiential continuum is important and useful. For what that offers us is a criterion of judgement, a basis for intervention, which is not derived from some notion we might have about the eternal value of some form or forms of knowledge but from a basic concern with the continued educational growth and development of the pupil. We intervene to encourage and promote those experiences which are likely to be productive of further experiences and, conversely, to discourage and dissuade pupils from other less productive courses.

It must also be remembered that, as we suggested earlier, this view of education encourages us to take full account of and to develop appropriately experiences in the affective domain and not to limit ourselves to intellectual development. Indeed, as we shall see when we consider recent work in developmental psychology, it becomes increasingly difficult to justify any attempt to separate these out, since each is dependent for its promotion on an adequate consideration of the other. A major strength we would claim, then, for this approach to educational planning is that, unlike the traditional view, it is not restricted to the intellect but is capable of generating not only a genuine theory of emotional, social and, in general, affective development but also one which can harmonize these with development on the intellectual front (Kelly, 1986).

It will further be apparent that this will rapidly become an individual matter, that our selection of content and of experiences will have to be made in relation to the unique developmental needs of each pupil. This should not surprise us, since it would be very odd to find that children who differ greatly in their dietary needs, and, indeed, in the sizes of their shoes and clothing, were uniform in their requirements in respect of their educational development. It is only when one puts the demands of the knowledge-content of education itself first in the curriculum planning equation that one comes up with the crassly inane answer of identical provision for every child – a common National Curriculum and 'benchmarks' of agreed levels of achievement for all pupils at seven plus, eleven plus, fourteen plus and sixteen plus.

There are, however, several reasons why we must dissociate ourselves from any notion that what we are suggesting will lead to totally idiosyncratic and individualized curricula. The first of these is that, as we shall see shortly when we look at the implications of work in developmental psychology, the development of individuals depends to a very large extent on what they experience collaboratively in a shared social environment. The second is that there is a common element running beneath what we are proposing; it consists, however, of common developmental principles not of common subject-content.

The third reason is that, even within this kind of curriculum, it is not necessary to lose sight of the fact that there are certain bodies of knowledge, certain kinds of understanding and certain cognitive skills which it would be irresponsible, and in fact impossible, to ignore in the planning of educational provision. There are elements in the culture of society which cannot be dismissed from all reckoning. These will, however, be reflected in those very interests of the children we are suggesting should form the basis of their educational provision; they will be reflected too in the forms of development we are concerned to promote. It would be difficult, for example, to promote in children any kind of literary appreciation without reference to the conventions of literacy and the literature of their culture. An emphasis on the needs and interests of the children themselves, however, rather than on the assumed claims of certain bodies of knowledge to be transmitted or skills to be acquired, will ensure not only that the engagement with these elements of knowledge and of culture will be genuinely educative in the developmental sense, it will also ensure that we can be sensitive to differences of interest, and especially differences of culture. For there is a richness to be found in ethnic and cultural differences which itself has much to contribute to children's development. To quote Whitehead (1932, p. 10) again, 'the problem of education is to make the pupil see the wood by means of the trees'; it is an over concentration on the trees themselves that is counterproductive to a proper form of educational development.

We thus have a view of education which is a genuine alternative to the traditional view and which is distinctive primarily in respect of its attitude to the content of education. For it raises questions about that content which are not the instrumental, utilitarian questions that are of prime concern to the politician or merely the epistemological questions of the philosopher. The questions it raises about content are educational questions focusing on the role of content in promoting the development of the pupil; the concern is with learning through subject-knowledge rather than merely with the learning of subject-knowledge, with the growth of competence rather than merely the acquisition of skills and knowledge, with empowerment rather than social compliance.

It thus follows that the most important questions to be faced are those of what human development is, or what it might be, and how that may be promoted through our educational provision. The most productive source of data for such exploration, then, is the study of developmental psychology, and it is to an examination of the implications of that for this form of curriculum planning that we now turn.

The curricular implications of recent work in developmental psychology

We saw earlier that the traditional view of education has developed close links with behaviourist psychology. We suggested too that there were serious inadequacies in the appeal to this form of psychology, since, being derived for the most part from studies of animals, it adopts a simplistic view of learning, seeing it as little more than a form of behaviour modification, and thus, while seeming to provide useful methodological advice to those who are prepared to accept that notion of education, offers nothing to those whose concern is with the role of education in the promotion of the full development of human beings *qua* human beings.

It is important to note the limitations of this view and also to recognize its incompatibility with the idea of education as development. Many teachers, especially those who have received a massive dose of behaviourist psychology in their teacher education courses, profess a commitment to development but adopt the practices of behaviourism – individualized learning programmes, for example. This is a major source of theoretical, and thus practical, confusion. The fundamental principles of both the educational theory and the psychological theory which underpins it must be in tune if we are to avoid serious incoherence – in our practice as well as in our theorizing.

For this reason the alternative view of education, which we are attempting to explicate here, has looked for its support to the work of another school of psychologists, those whose concern has been with human learning and development as qualitatively distinct from that of animals, and who, within that context, have explored in detail the learning and development of children. For proponents of this alternative approach to education have, from the time of Rousseau himself, stressed the need for an ever-increasing understanding of the psychology of the child. And much of the exploration that has occurred in the field of developmental psychology can be seen as a response to that demand. Certainly, for fifty years or more, that work has been a major source of influence on the growth of this particular movement in education (Blyth, 1965; Blenkin and Kelly, 1981, 1987; De Vries, 1987).

It is important to note too that, unlike behaviourist psychology in its relation to the traditional view, the role of developmental psychology in this movement has been not merely to advise on methodology, although it has often been seen by those who support the traditional view in this light (Lawton, 1973), it has also contributed a good deal to the generation and elucidation of this new concept of education, not least by explicating for us what it might mean to set about promoting children's development. And, in doing so, it has provided 'progressivism' with the kind of rigorous theoretical base and hard practical focus that it has often been accused of lacking. The influence of studies in this field, then, can be seen to affect theory as well as practice, and to offer insights not only into how we might promote children's education and development but also into what it means to attempt to do that.

Perhaps the most important general message that is to be gleaned by educators from this work is that cognitive growth (the term 'cognitive' will be used here to denote all forms of human development, including the affective and even the psychomotor, since there is no single word – and that may tell us much about traditions in education – that can be used to denote the development of all aspects of the individual's 'mind') cognitive growth, then, unlike physical growth, does not proceed by dint of simple maturation. In the physical sense, embryos become foetuses, foetuses babies, babies toddlers, toddlers children, children adolescents, adolescents adults, adults 'senior citizens', and 'senior citizens' cadavers, by an inevitable process of physical maturation and deterioration – unless something untoward occurs to arrest this process. It is clear, however, that the same automatic development does not occur in the cognitive sphere. There are many people – too many one might argue – who are physically adult, even 'senior citizens', who remain, and have throughout their lives remained, intellectually speaking, children. Indeed, one of the main reasons for advocating the adoption of our view of education as development is a sense of dissatisfaction, even of disgust, that the education service still leaves so many people so obviously stunted in their cognitive development. Such cognitive development will only occur if the right kinds of educational experience are provided.

That is the first message of developmental psychology. The second concerns the nature of cognitive development, an understanding of which is crucial if educators are to be able to plan the kinds of experience that might forward it.

It might be helpful if we explore these interrelated questions in terms of three major themes which have emerged from recent work in the field of developmental psychology, themes which relate to decisions about, first, how the child's role in learning and development may be characterized, secondly, how that learning and development may be promoted, and, thirdly, how experiences may be selected and presented in order to support that learning. These three themes have been called 'the competent newborn', 'the growth of competence' and 'culture and cognition' (Blenkin, 1988), and we must look at each in turn.

The competent newborn

Advances in modern technology have made possible the investigation of the very beginnings of human thinking through explorations of the activities of very young babies. The most significant general finding of this kind of research is that the neonate is endeavouring to make sense of his or her environment and, further, to exercise some kind of self-directed control over it from the moment of birth (Bower, 1971). It is clear from these studies that human beings demonstrate intention-directed behaviour from the beginning. They can formulate plans, matching ends to means; they can combine actions into more complex activities; they can, in short, deploy skills to act intelligently and with the intention of achieving control (Bower, 1977).

It is also clear from these studies that children from birth need a stimulating and challenging environment if they are to engage in these intention-directed activities. Moreover, babies and infants are characteristically playful and their habit of trying out a range of actions through play is seen as related to their human urge to plan and control activities.

A further deduction which has been made from these studies of early thinking which has great significance for educational provision concerns the importance of social interaction and social perception for the development of the child from birth. By two weeks of age, for example, the child can identify his or her mother's voice and face (Bower, 1977). And recent studies have suggested that, certainly by the end of their first year, children are socio-centric, since they participate in, and even shape and direct, the preverbal interactions they become involved in with others (Bruner, 1981).

Even if one allows for the enthusiasm and possible consequent slight exaggeration of some of the researchers in this field, it is clear that from a very young age the child's intellectual life is a good deal more sophisticated than was once thought, and this must imply that the same is true of older children.

Studies of children have in fact confirmed this and have suggested that the limitations which Piaget's work once suggested we should place on our expectations of pupils are somewhat inaccurate and overdrawn (Donaldson, Grieve and Pratt, 1983). In particular, it has been claimed that Piaget's work did not take sufficient account of the social setting and, indeed, the interpretation placed by the child on the language of the adult researchers. Meaning is constructed by children in a social setting and that process embraces the people and the social interactions as well as the objects and materials in that setting. Hence the importance of language is stressed and the close link between the development of language and the development of thought; and it is further agreed that both depend on social interaction (Wells, 1981).

It is clear, then, from recent work that the human intellect is highly active from birth; that human playfulness is a vital means by which children gain control over their experiences and their learning; that a challenging environment is needed to promote this kind of development; that the social dimension of that environment is at least as important as other dimensions; and that the role of language is crucial in cognitive development.

All of this adds up to a comprehensive picture of the child as a learner and of his or her urge towards increased competence. It suggests that we should recognize the high levels of competence that have already been reached when children enter school. It supports the notion that children should be provided with a stimulating environment and opportunities for whatever experiences will extend those competencies. It should encourage us to attend also to the social dimension of that environment, and to recognize that the degree of the interaction it permits, especially in terms of the use of language, between child and child, and between teacher and child, is a vital element in promoting continued development (Vygotsky, 1962). And, above all, it indicates that we must start from where the child is, focusing on what he or she can do, or nearly can do, rather than on his or her incapacities, and not assuming that there is any kind of learning that has not already begun before the child enters school.

This then is the base from which we must look at the continued growth of competence.

The growth of competence

The feature of children's thinking which emerges again and again in recent research studies is the extent to which it is context-dependent. If the context makes sense to the child, and if the task or tasks which present themselves in that context enable him or her to use existing intellectual skills, then he or she will display not only a high level of competence but also the ability to extend those existing skills to meet new challenges.

These recent studies also confirm the view that children's thinking develops best when they are supported, as they talk and learn, by responsive adults. For the studies show that informal discussions and conversations with a supportive adult can enable the young child to operate at the limits of his or her understanding and to function in what Vygotsky (1978) has called a 'zone of proximal development'. Children's highest levels of thinking are usually revealed in informal conversations.

However, a major problem that is raised by these features of the child's thinking is that much of the learning necessary in schooling requires what Margaret Donaldson (1978) has called 'disembedded' thinking, thinking which is independent of context and which thus requires the child to ignore the contextual clues and concentrate on the language which is being used. This is especially evident in the teaching of mathematics and it has been offered as one explanation of the apparent paradox of the mathematical knowledge most children seem to bring to school with them and the difficulties so many of them experience with school mathematics (Hughes, 1986).

This kind of thinking is clearly difficult, not only for children but for adults too. The means by which the learner may move from 'embedded' to 'disembedded' thinking, therefore, has become a major focus of interest. And it has been suggested (Copple, Sigel and Saunders, 1979) that such a move depends on acquiring, first, the ability to develop internal representations of experience and, second, a facility for deploying these in such a way as to distance oneself from the context. Such abilities clearly do not develop spontaneously. If they are to develop, children need to be helped to reflect upon experience, to use their imaginations in relation to it and to create mental pictures of it. Hence they must be engaged in the kinds of practical activity which promote, encourage, even demand, representation – activities such as symbolic play or drawing or conversations about practical experiences. All these activities permit a degree of distancing from the immediate context and thus some generalization of thought. Direct questions about experience merely focus the child's attention back on to the context. The teacher's questions, comments, discussions and the activities he or she encourages the pupils to engage in must be such as to lead away from the context towards more 'disembedded' forms of thinking.

We must also remember, however, that the intention is not to move away from context-related thinking in the sense of leaving it behind for ever. For the key to abstract thinking is the ability to refer one's thinking constantly back to the concrete situation. There can be no such thing as totally abstract thinking. The teacher's concern, then, must be with helping children to build bridges which will take them both away from the context and back to it, so that abstract thinking and concrete experiences are permanently linked (Hughes, 1986). For this is the essence of fully developed thought.

Again mathematics offers ready examples of this process, and one can recognize the force of this explanation of why many children who, before they come to school, have no problems with the assertion that 'two bricks and two bricks make four bricks' begin to flounder immediately on being presented with the generalized and 'disembedded' or decontextualized assertion that 'two and two make four' or – more difficult still – '2 + 2 = 4' (Hughes, 1986). It is essential that children be presented with forms of learning which go well beyond the offering of this kind of propositional knowledge and which forward the growth of those intellectual competences by helping them to move away from the limitations of the immediate context of their experience and to make proper links between their informal and formal understanding(s). It is on this two-way process of transition, or translation, that the development of understanding depends.

A second and related aspect of the growth of children's competence which has emerged from recent research is the awareness of the need for greater reflection and self-consciousness on the part of children. As they become more competent, children become more able to reflect on their actions and, as their level of self-consciousness increases, so too does the degree of their control over their actions and thus over their learning.

This notion of reflective self-awareness, or 'metacognition' as the psychologists have called it, is also important, therefore, in the planning of the curriculum. Furthermore, it demands a completely different approach to that planning. For it is clear that, while thinking which is content-related is usually goal-directed, thinking which is more formal, 'disembedded' and largely context-free requires that the child be conscious of, and guided by, the processes of thinking themselves rather than the goals which have been set. It is for this reason, for example, that Margaret Donaldson (1978) has emphasized the importance of the child's becoming literate. There is more to this than access to a literate society or even to the wealth of that society's literature. It is equally, perhaps more, important because it involves thinking which is free of context, more controlled and less goal-directed. It thus enables the child to become more aware of the processes of his or her thinking, to become more reflective and self-aware.

The main thrust of educational provision, then, and the first consideration in curriculum planning, on this view, are the concern to facilitate the move towards formal, 'disembedded' and self-conscious thinking, which in turn will enhance the child's capacity for intelligent self-regulation.

It will be clear that such studies, as we claimed earlier, have not only offered us advice at the level of methodology; they have also provided greater insights than were available to us before into the very notion of education as development, or curriculum as process or, indeed, of 'progressivism'. We must not ignore, however, the implications they do have for methodology, for our approaches to education. For they clearly do offer great elaboration of the picture of the child as learner which we painted in the last section. If the child is seeking to make sense of his or her world from birth and to increase his or her control over it, then these studies reveal not only what is involved in these processes but also some of the ways in which we can assist and promote them. For these studies confirm that an informal, interactive style of both teaching and learning is vital if we are to ensure that the child's learning is meaningful, that it is in fact part of the process of development. They also show, however, that this is not sufficient in itself, since development depends more crucially on the growth of a capacity to think meaningfully in more abstract settings, independently of contextual clues, so that we must help children to move closer towards this kind of thinking.

It may be argued that the central purpose of education, if not of schooling, is to promote this ability to think in these more formal, 'disembedded' and reflective ways. The main task for teachers, then, is to help children to make translations from the material contexts of the experiences provided for them to more abstract forms of reflection and thinking. Much of school learning requires this latter kind of thinking anyway, and if teachers do not find ways of helping children to make these translations, through informal conversations, for example, as we saw above, where they can support or 'scaffold' children's thinking and talking (Vygotsky, 1978), many children will continue to find the tasks demanded of them at school literally meaningless and alienating. What is even more serious is that the development of their ability to think in these more abstract forms will be left to chance and thus may well not occur at all. It is clearly this that has led to that disturbing fact we noted earlier, the inability of so many of the adult population to think at a properly adult level.

On this analysis, then, the role of education, and more specifically of the teacher, is to promote the development of these more complex forms of thinking. Much that will come later in this book will elucidate ways in which teachers might set about this task. Let us remind ourselves here, however, that, in general, success will hinge on providing opportunities for children to make internal representations of experience, to engage in genuine conversations about their experiences and thus to be required to generalize about them, and to develop cognitive skills such as that of literacy which will support this ability to think in a context-free manner, to become deliberately conscious of their thinking and thus to learn to exercise intelligent self-regulation. Above all, however, we must remember the need to provide a solid base of concrete experiences, since it is only from this that we can begin to help them make the transition, and, as we stressed earlier, it is only by constant reference back to this, to work out or check their thinking, that the children themselves can move forward.

It will be apparent, however, that the nature of these concrete experiences will be a crucial factor in promoting this kind of development. For, as Dewey once said, not all experiences are equally educative. In a manner reminiscent of Dewey, and certainly not incompatible with, indeed complementary to, the advice we noted earlier he offered teachers for the making of such judgements, the developmental psychologists have argued that we should offer children the kinds of experience, and the kind of context for their curriculum, which will facilitate symbolic thought, that this should be our main criterion of selection. It is to this that we now turn in the third, and final, section of our discussion of the contribution of this work to our understanding of education as development.

Culture and cognition

The psychologist's concern is to gain greater understanding of how children think. He or she is not, *qua* psychologist, involved in questions of the forms of curriculum or the kinds of experience they should be offered. It is clear, however, that many prescriptions of the latter kind are to be found, implicitly, or even sometimes explicitly, in this work, and one or two have positively accepted responsibility for the generation not only of a theory of development but also of a theory of instruction, without which, Jerome Bruner (1966, 1968, p. 21) claims, any theory of development will be 'doomed to triviality'. Such a theory of instruction will of course concern itself with the kinds of experience we ought to be presenting to children, in short, with the nature and content of the curriculum; and it is with a consideration of the advice developmental psychology has offered on this that we conclude this discussion of its contribution to curriculum planning.

Bruner's own theory of instruction was based on the belief that individual development is dependent on an ability on the part of the learner to create representations of the world, an ability which we saw earlier is regarded as crucial to formal, 'disembedded' thinking. Bruner (1966, 1968) further claimed that there are three ways of accomplishing these representations – through action, through imagery and through symbols; and consequently that instruction should be planned according to three parallel modes – the enactive, the iconic and the symbolic. His later work on very young children and their interactions with their care-givers has led to a recognition of a further mode of instruction, the interpersonal mode.

The child's ability to make representations is influenced by internal factors such as his or her existing competence at symbolizing experience and his or her preferred style of making these representations. It is also affected by external factors, including, most importantly, the public mode of symbolizing experience in use in the society in which the child is living and learning. As children make and learn to make representations, then, two factors are in interaction, one personal, the other cultural.

It is this cultural aspect of experience and development which is of great significance in educational planning and offers the main source of selection of the content of education. Many have argued, of course, that the content of the curriculum should be a selection from the culture and that schools have a responsibility for transmitting the best of a society's culture (Lawton, 1975), in short, that considerations of culture are of importance only to the selection of the content to be transmitted *via* our curriculum. This is another aspect of that traditional view of education we considered earlier. Bruner, however, is offering us a totally different view of the role of culture in education. For he sees culture as educationally important not because in itself it offers us a content to be transmitted but because it influences the child's cognitive growth by providing modes of representation in a public form and by offering cultural amplifiers – amplifiers of action, amplifiers of the senses, amplifiers of thought processes. Culture provides the public structure through which the meaning of experience can be shared and through which it can also be internalized. It facilitates our understanding of experience through these modes of representation and also promotes their development within the individual child.

Hence the role of culture in the planning of education is not that it provides bodies of knowledge and values to be transmitted but that it enables the choice of experiences which will at the same time reflect the public and cultural forms of representation and support and promote the development of each pupil. 'The educational process consists of providing aids and dialogues for translating experience into more powerful systems of notation and ordering' (Bruner, 1966, 1968, p. 21). This of course is why developmental psychologists have evinced so much interest in language, since in all human cultures language is a prime medium for making public our representations of experience.

In Bruner's view, then, culture should be seen as providing experience of public modes of representation and thus enabling the child to structure his or her personal modes of representation. It is thus a further aspect of the support the child needs in the move between context-based and context-free thinking.

For Bruner, of course, these modes of representation are not stages through which we pass and which we leave behind. Rather they present and offer us alternatives which we may choose according to our own preferred style or the nature of the experience we are attempting to represent or a combination of both. It is this that we have foreshadowed in our assertion of the need to see education as the process by which this kind of choice, and thus the control and self-direction it leads to, can be enhanced. He also stresses, as we have, that these competencies will not be acquired simply by a process of maturation.

This is one of the points which is picked up by Elliot Eisner (1982) in his development of these themes. For he argues further that in Western culture at present it is even likely that schooling is having the opposite effect and is in fact counterproductive to the development of children's cognitive powers. For schooling systems of the traditional kind tend to overemphasize experiences which lead to discursive and numerical forms of thinking and learning, and consequently reduce the opportunities for developing the ability to represent a wide range of sensory experience and thus for conceptualizing this experience.

Eisner goes on to argue, therefore, that we should make a more extensive study of the uses people make of the forms of representation employed within a culture, so as to appreciate the many dimensions of experience and the many ways in which meaning is secured. The very existence of this variety should alert us to the importance of these many forms or modes and thus should encourage us to attempt to ensure they are more properly reflected in the experiences we offer pupils in schools. He is concerned that we should start our educational planning from a more sophisticated view of human development and, in particular, one that does not separate the psychomotor and the affective from the cognitive, as we saw earlier those traditional views of education as the transmission of knowledge-content must inevitably do.

He also suggests that it is not enough merely to recognize the existence of different forms of representation, that this in itself is not sufficient to explain human development. For he argues that, in the process of the conceptualization of experience, each form can be treated in one of three ways. Experience, he claims, can be represented as a replica (mimetically), as an expression of the deep structure underlying the experience (expressively) or in a manner which conforms to the meaning assigned within a particular culture (conventionally). Thus, in addition to the concept of modes of representation, he offers us the notion of different forms of treatment. And he offers many examples of how culture is shaped by public versions of both.

This kind of discussion of culture, then, and its role in educational planning offers teachers many insights into the kinds of experience that can and should be made available in schools if the development of children is to be promoted.

Recent work in developmental psychology has thus offered us deeper understandings of how the child's learning and development may be characterized, especially through its studies of how very young children attempt to make sense of and gain control over their environment; it has revealed many of the key features of how this kind of development can proceed and thus how it may be promoted, especially in relation to the zone of proximal development (Vygotsky, 1978) and to the move towards more 'disembedded' and self-conscious forms of thinking; and it has led to greater clarity over the role of culture in educational planning and, in particular, over the basis upon which we might select the kinds of experience and curriculum content to offer children in order to support and forward this development.

It can be seen, therefore, how this work has added considerable substance and backing to the alternative view of education we are discussing here. For it points to ways in which we can develop a genuinely 'child-centred' approach to education without having to adopt a policy of non-interference; it offers us advice on how we can select the content of children's education by reference to the children themselves rather than to criteria derived from the content itself; and it thus complements those more theoretical arguments we examined in the earlier sections of this chapter and combines with them to produce a theory of education which focuses on what education does or can do for children rather than on what it can do for society or for the development of human knowledge. In short, it provides a compelling and coherent underpinning for the view of education as development.

Before we conclude this initial discussion of education as development, however, we must emphasize that such an approach to education must be considered in its professional as well as its theoretical context. For teachers are professional practitioners and, by implication, act, whether they are conscious of it or not, in relation to a theoretical stance. The professional procedures which are chosen by or imposed upon teachers, therefore, will either protect or put at risk any aspirations they may have for the curriculum.

Developmental theories and professional procedures

If teachers are to ensure that the educational experiences they offer their pupils genuinely support their development, and, indeed, that the curriculum itself continues to develop, it is essential that they are enabled to make professional translations from theory to practice and also that they devise ways of reflecting on their practice in the light of that theory. This two-way process of translating ideas into practice and reflecting upon the results of such translations is, as we noted above, at the heart of genuine professional practice. For, on the one hand, it is the main safeguard for the theory and practice link and, on the other, it is a process which yields evidence of the kinds of development that have occurred in the children's learning and in the teacher's practice.

To make such translations and reflections effectively is not a simple or straightforward task. If they are to do this successfully, teachers need the support of structures or frameworks which have been devised to provide them with helpful insights into the various aspects and consequences of their professional performance. The two most important of these structures, as we have argued in a companion to this book on assessment in the early years (Blenkin and Kelly, 1992), derive from the decisions they make and the procedures they adopt in relation to evaluation and assessment – the evaluation of their planning, provision and practice, and the assessment of their pupils' performance and development. For it has been shown that the procedures adopted by teachers for assessment and evaluation purposes will have a crucial impact on the curriculum that is established in practice (Blenkin, 1980). It is essential, therefore, for teachers to decide not only between the models of education and curriculum that are available, as we have shown throughout this chapter, but also between the different procedures for assessment and evaluation. And it is important that they adopt those procedures which will promote rather than constrain their work as educators, those procedures which will match their chosen model of curriculum.

The choice of procedures for assessment and evaluation, however, has been seen by many, both within and outside the profession, as a purely technical decision. Some have acknowledged that it is a complex professional matter, but they have seen the complications in a technical sense only and have focused, as a result, on methodological issues. They have assumed that the procedures should be the same for all teachers and have outlined the main problems as, first, that of disseminating the information to teachers and, secondly, of ensuring that what is currently available is used well.

Procedures for assessment and evaluation, however, are never value-neutral, since each one is derived from a particular view of the nature of teaching, of learning and of education. And the practical approach will differ according to the stance which is taken on such issues. Examples of these characteristic differences abound in the literature. Teachers who espouse a behavioural view, for example, will structure their procedures in relation to the pre-specification of broad aims which will then be translated into detailed objectives. Their main emphasis will be on testing the product or endstate of the educational encounter and in some instances this will be the only consideration.

In contrast, those who subscribe to a content model of curriculum will use an analysis of the knowledge and skills to be learned as the main point of reference for assessment procedures. This is an approach which has been popularized, for example, by programmes such as *Mathematics for Schools* (Fletcher, 1970). Teachers who adopt this second approach may decide, as we noted earlier, to translate their analysis of content into curriculum aims and objectives, in other words, to merge two distinct procedures. Indeed, this merging of the two approaches was recommended by HMI in its *Curriculum Matters* documents (DES, 1985a), and is now encapsulated in the National Curriculum for England and Wales and its programme of regular testing. The main structure which shapes this subject-centred approach, however, is derived from an analysis of the content of education, and it is that content, therefore, which is the main emphasis.

The procedures for assessment and evaluation which derive from a developmental view, however, lead to a third distinctive approach. For here the main structure will be framed in relation to the development of both the children and the teacher as they share experiences. The resultant approach will resemble the action research model, an approach, for example, which was adopted in a recent study of children in reception classes (Barrett, 1986). Teachers who take this approach will draw upon the observational techniques and strategies offered by developmental psychology to provide them with insights into their work in the manner advocated by Piaget (1969) and developed by later researchers (Sylva, Roy and Painter, 1980; Wood, McMahon and Cranstoun, 1980; Donaldson, Grieve and Pratt, 1983, and so on). Their structure will be created to ensure that 'the progress of teacher and child alike is being checked' (Bierley, 1983, p. 181), and its first reference point will be their view of development.

Of course, all three of these distinctive approaches to assessment and evaluation incorporate the three dimensions of the curriculum. In other words, all three are concerned about curriculum planning, about the content of the curriculum and about the promotion of children's learning. The differences stem from the status and priority given to these three dimensions. For there is no doubt that, as each is given prior status and consideration, three very different approaches to teaching and learning, and thus to assessment and evaluation, will ensue, as reference to the examples of professional practice which were cited above will confirm. It is for this reason that teachers should adopt those structures and procedures for assessment and evaluation which will support and match their view of education. And it is for this reason that tensions, and indeed distortions, are now emerging where teachers wish to pursue a developmental approach to education and the curriculum but are being constrained to accept content and objectives based forms of public testing of their pupils (Blenkin and Kelly, 1994).

The establishment of appropriate structures for assessment and evaluation is, of course, complicated by the fact that such procedures are not only of interest to teachers themselves. Teachers are, quite properly, accountable to the parents of their children, to their employers and to the wider community. The means of calling teachers to account had remained flexible and open in England and Wales for several decades. Formal procedures have now been introduced by central government, however, and the assessment of both pupil and teacher performance and the evaluation of the curriculum - in particular, the content of the curriculum – is now intended to provide those outside the profession with evidence for the accountability and appraisal of teachers and schools.

On the other hand, assessments and evaluations will continue to fulfil the professional function which we have outlined earlier. It is important, therefore, that they continue to be made by teachers themselves and provide insights into professional work which will indicate both to teachers and to others the developmental achievements of the children and the curriculum.

There are, of course, potential dangers in using assessment and evaluation in these two different ways. Although the two purposes can function in parallel, it has been shown from past experience (Gordon and Lawton, 1978) that the professional purpose of assessment and evaluation is placed at risk if the external, accountability purpose is strengthened. It has also been argued (Stenhouse, 1975; Kelly, 1977, 1982, 1989; Eisner, 1982) that this will be particularly so if the view of education which shapes the external procedures for assessment and evaluation which are adopted contrasts sharply with that which is encapsulated in the procedures adopted within the school and the model of curriculum which is favoured.

It has become increasingly clear that the political structures which have been devised for purposes of teacher appraisal are not supportive of a developmental approach and have the effect of weakening such an approach, since not only do they not match it, they also run counter to it. For the emphasis is on assessment in relation to prespecified aims and objectives (DES, 1985a), and HMI have advocated the establishment of 'benchmarks of achievement' in required subjects and skills for seven-, eleven- and fifteen-year-olds. And the current policy in England and Wales is to test the performance of all children in these required areas at the ages of seven, eleven, fourteen and sixteen (DES, 1987). In short, the main thrust of current policies is towards content and objectives-based procedures rather than those derived from developmental considerations.

In a political climate where the demands for more and more tangible evidence of achievement are being made, it is important that all teachers maintain and strengthen their professional procedures for assessment and evaluation. This is particularly true, however, but also particularly difficult, for those teachers who are committed to a developmental approach. The procedures which have been adopted and imposed by central government are not only unsupportive of the work of such teachers, they also fail to give teachers and others any heightened insight into the development of the individual children in their care. Unless this aspect of their work is conducted successfully by teachers, however, it is likely that educational practice will be distorted by requirements to use other means of showing evidence of achievement, regardless of whether or not such means are educationally justifiable or meaningful. For it is only by employing appropriate professional strategies that teachers will ensure that the theory of education as development becomes effective educational practice.

Conclusions

It is our view that this is a highly compelling theory of what education can and should be. Our prime concern at this juncture, however, as we said at the beginning of this chapter, is not so much that it should be accepted as that it should be acknowledged and understood. For, at the very lowest, the acknowledgement that it represents a perfectly viable view and offers the basis of a perfectly workable education policy will at least require that those who reject it in favour of different approaches and policies must explain why they find it unacceptable and why they prefer their alternatives. That would at least establish or re-establish a debate about educational policies and priorities, and thus would mark a significant step forward from the present scene which is characterized by what at best must be seen as a massive ignorance, within and outside the teaching profession, of the potential of education, and, at worst, may be regarded as a deliberate policy of ignoring this potential and the existence of soundly based alternative views of education, for what, as we suggested in the Introduction, can only be interpreted as political purposes of a sinister kind.

There is a consistent, a viable, a practical, a convincing theory of education here. If these characteristics have not emerged clearly in the theoretical exploration of this chapter, it is hoped they will do so in subsequent chapters which will develop its main themes and explicate these by focusing on particular aspects of both the theory and the practice of education as development.

Suggested further reading

Blenkin, G. M. and Kelly, A. V. (1987) *The Primary Curriculum (2nd edition)*, Paul Chapman, London.

Bruner, J. and Haste, H. (1987) *Making Sense; the child's construction of the world*, Methuen, London.

2

Creating a Context for Development

Geva Blenkin and Marian Whitehead

The principles which were discussed in Chapter 1 provide a theoretical perspective on the work of teachers who espouse a view of education as development. This perspective has an important part to play in supporting those teachers, as it enables them to reflect upon their work with children and, in doing so, to evaluate the success of that work in an informed manner. To have a coherent theoretical perspective on practice is, without doubt, an essential dimension of a teacher's professional success.

These same principles, however, also have implications for curriculum planning and implementation, and it is this second dimension of successful practice that we are concerned to focus on in this chapter. The changes in research and understanding which have been highlighted imply that curriculum and curriculum planning for the early years should take account of all the rich complexity of child development in these crucial years. The curriculum needs to encompass and sustain children's growth in self-knowledge and social awareness and provide ways of developing autonomy in learning. Thus expanded concepts of curriculum planning are needed which will support children's development in these ways.

The significance of this enriched view of the early years curriculum and the danger of its neglect have been powerfully argued in a research report on starting school (Barrett, 1986). This view is also seen as 'basic to the basics', in a pre-school curriculum guide (Curtis, 1986). However, advocates of this approach to curriculum planning for the early years of education can take little pleasure in the fact that the approach has been advocated for at least half a century (Isaacs, 1930, 1933; Holmes, 1977) and is still 'more honour'd in the breach than the observance' (*Hamlet* I, iv, 16).

In our view, this disparity between principle and practice stems from a failure to translate theory into appropriate curricular terms. We begin, therefore, with the premise that, if it is to guide practice effectively, the developmental theory of education must be linked to a compatible theory of the curriculum.

Too often, however, curriculum theory has been neglected and practice has suffered as a result. For, although teachers may understand and support the developmental view and may, therefore, judge their work in accordance with its principles, they are likely to be disappointed by the gap between their aspirations and the reality of their practice unless they have given due regard to planning a developmental curriculum.

Neglect of this important aspect of professional theory has been widespread, of course, and does not apply only to those teachers whose views are developmental. For serious study of the curriculum is still in its infancy in Britain. The educational debate during most of the twentieth century has concentrated on the provision and organization of the schooling system. The justifications for choosing between different forms of organization were couched in theoretical terms which were derived from related fields of study such as philosophy and psychology. Influential as the insights gained from these sources have been, the distinctive forms of curricula which are implied by each have rarely been clarified. And this has been a major weakness of education theory.

In the past, it has been left to busy practitioners to devise appropriate plans and practices and, not surprisingly, they have often failed to do so. Many misinterpretations have occurred and the effects that such distortions have had on classroom practice have been well documented in studies of teachers at work (King, 1978; Willes, 1983; Tizard and Hughes, 1984).

During the past two decades, however, the curriculum has moved to the centre of the educational debate. This shift of attention occurred first within the profession and was largely a result of the curriculum development movement of the early 1970s (Stenhouse, 1980). Many of the researchers who were involved in the early Schools Council curriculum projects, for example, claimed that more sophisticated models of educational planning were needed than those that were available at the time. They argued that it was too simplistic to plan the curriculum by reference to pre-specified aims and objectives, an approach which had been introduced from America and was used widely by these project teams. The researchers showed how damaging the effect of this approach could be and argued that it put education at risk (Stenhouse, 1975). A range of alternative approaches began to emerge as a result of their work and, through the experience of these researchers, it became clear that each different style of planning was related to a distinct educational ideology (Kelly, 1986).

As professional understanding began to deepen, however, a second significant shift of attention occurred which halted this trend. For politicians also began to recognize the importance of the curriculum and have sought to increase their control over education by legislating for a national curriculum and by defining how it should be planned. With this political intervention has come a return by many to the confused and simplistic view of curriculum planning that worried the researchers referred to above.

Often curriculum is now equated with the content of education and defined only in terms of subjects and skills. And, from this narrow perception, it is assumed that curriculum planning is a purely technical problem which centres on solving how teachers can ensure that pupils acquire the knowledge and skills that are deemed to be desirable. Indeed, as we saw in Chapter 1, this technical procedure is now linked to assessment and to the appraisal of teachers. The conceptual and ideological aspects of curriculum planning are again being disregarded and, because planning is viewed merely as methodology, it is once again being assumed that a perfect technique can be found which will suit all teachers and can be applied to all aspects of the curriculum.

Uncritical planning of this kind is having an impact upon the work of teachers in early childhood education which is even more serious than the *laissez-faire* attitudes of the past. For it is promoting the idea that they must devise tidy, conveniently controlled programmes of instruction. And these programmes, being under the strict control of politicians, or even of teachers themselves, are, by implication, leaving the child out of control. This tendency runs counter to a main tenet of developmentalism – that the child should be in control of his or her learning – and leads us to argue that this is the main way in which the early years curriculum has become vulnerable to distortion, because it is imposing skills and subject-based objectives on to its learner-centred and developmental philosophy.

The notion that aspects of the curriculum can be pieced together in a prescribed recipe and that planning can follow a technical model is seductive in its simplicity, but it is also misleading. For the dimensions of educational planning are interdependent and should be directed at helping teachers to refine their judgements in action rather than providing them with a tight prescription for that action. In our view, nothing stifles education and the child's development more than attributing to curriculum planning technical rather than humanistic characteristics.

It can be claimed, therefore, that the recent focus on the curriculum has had mixed effects. On the one hand, it is to be welcomed as it has led to an increase in the understanding of professional theory and has made successful practice more attainable. On the other hand, however, it has increased the constraints on education, as it is the political rather than the professional views of planning that are currently in the ascendancy.

It is against this background of contradictions and confusions that we set out, in this chapter, to clarify how planning can be undertaken in a manner which is compatible with developmental principles. An acceptance of these principles, of course, calls for an immediate rejection of the simplistic and linear approach to planning that is outlined above. For the developmental view is, in essence, interactive rather than deterministic, based as it is on the idea that, as education promotes individual development, the role of the educator is to intervene in the individual's experience appropriately and in a manner which will ensure that development occurs. This means that the teacher cannot settle with absolute certainty all the decisions that need to be made about the experiences which will promote the child's development before the practical activity of teaching begins. It also means that evaluation cannot be left until the end of that activity.

To accept this, however, is not to argue that no planning can take place before teaching begins, or, worse, to believe that no planning can take place at all. It is to recognize and accept that planning must be subtle in style, must make reference to more than the content of experience and must enable teachers to be responsive to children.

In the course of the chapter it will be shown, therefore, that such planning depends not only on an expanded concept of the curriculum but also on an understanding of the nature of cognition and symbolic representation and that, to complement these understandings, a re-evaluation of the teaching role is necessary. We must begin, however, by outlining the key reference points of a developmental model of curriculum planning.

Dimensions of curriculum planning

The material environment

The most neglected and misunderstood dimension of the planned curriculum is the creation of an environment or setting in which education is to take place. Although it has long been accepted, in nursery and infant schools at least, that children need to work with practical materials, the provision of such materials is often seen by teachers as a problem of resourcing which requires skills of organization and management but which is peripheral to the real task of curriculum planning. Indeed, it is not unusual for some teachers to believe that making provision for play or for teacher-structured tasks is a necessary chore only because the majority of young children need to be occupied if the teacher is to be free to concentrate on teaching 'the real curriculum' to the few.

Neglect of this aspect of the curriculum has also led many teachers, particularly those who teach older children or adults, to consider that the classroom environment is of no importance at all. This view is still widely held, despite the fact that studies have shown the undesirable effects on learning of the hidden curriculum which pervades when the classroom context is disregarded (Barnes, 1976). These effects are usually more profound than those of the curriculum that has been consciously planned and they often work against and undermine teachers' intentions about the kind of understandings that pupils will acquire.

The general disregard of this dimension of the curriculum leads us to emphasize that a coherent and worthwhile approach to curriculum planning must be focused on the creation of the context or setting in which teaching and learning occur. To be appropriate for young children, that context must offer a framework for the development of competencies and understandings while not allowing these desirable goals to detract from the quality of children's present lived experience. In practice, researchers have shown that a strong respect for children's ongoing development, thinking and being appears to be the very best preparation for literacy (Payton, 1984; Wells, 1985b), numeracy (Hughes, 1986) and scientific understanding (Richards, Collis and Kincaid, 1986). And there is every reason to believe, as later chapters will show, that such respect for the present context enables other ways of thinking and knowing to be promoted and sustained. The pedagogical environment has a profound effect upon what children are able to do and the kind of thinking in which they can engage (Eisner, 1983). It is for this reason that curriculum planning for the early years of education is specifically about resource-based classroom environments.

Such planning extends far beyond a concern merely with the artefacts and the arrangements which are placed within those environments. It embraces judgements, for example, about the potential of resources for extending experience; judgements about both their inherent potential and their suitability for use by a particular group of children. It entails the creation of a climate or an atmosphere within the classroom which will enable human relationships and co-operation to be fostered in such a way that pupils can become competent and confident learners within a community. And it demands of the teacher the ability to create an environment which will stimulate children's curiosity, will set high standards of quality in a range of experiences and will, at the same time, support and extend learning. We will return later in the chapter to the practical implications of planning an environment that will incorporate these main characteristics. At this stage of our discussion, however, we must stress its importance as the first reference point of the curriculum.

The second dimension of curriculum planning that must be focused on is of equal importance and is equally neglected. For, although planning an appropriate environment is crucial, the early years classroom can provide effectively for the development of productive ways of thinking and knowing only to the extent that it provides for children's growth in self-knowledge and awareness, in social understanding and in personal autonomy. Again we would claim that the planned curriculum should be concerned with the promotion of these capacities at every stage of the schooling system. In the context of this discussion, however, we will concentrate on what such planning entails if it is to promote them in young children.

The interpersonal context

In the early years curriculum, growth in self-knowledge and awareness is frequently linked with, and thereby limited to, the survival skills of dressing, feeding, washing and toilet management. While granting our basic rooting of sense of self in these successfully achieved skills, we would want to broaden the theme of self-awareness to include two other aspects. The first is the part played by playful encounters with materials, persons, ideas and situations in an educational setting and the second is the significance to development of coming to terms with 'not knowing' and 'not doing'.

Play is an aspect of curriculum planning which suffers from being both all-pervasive and yet too vaguely acknowledged as 'a good thing'. In this particular context we wish to highlight the importance of planning for play by showing the ways in which playful encounters may sustain and develop children's self-knowledge and awareness.

The essence of playful encounters, as we will see in Chapter 3, is freedom from predetermined goals or outcomes and when this freedom applies to the handling of materials, ideas, language and situations, children also discover how they feel about themselves. It is as if access to the traditional range of materials, props, settings and persons in the classroom constitutes a rehearsal. If children can try out a range of roles they can practise a range of feelings such as helplessness and power, misery and vindictiveness. Evidence of this can be observed in the extremes of behaviour which characterize young children's play roles as 'parents' and 'teachers', 'little babies' and 'sick patients'. It is significant that these emotional re-enactments and explorations are conducted within the pretend frameworks of particular human and social contexts. Feelings in context are about appropriateness, self-knowledge and control. This sort of play is not, therefore, the wildly undisciplined or formless pastime that unperceptive critics might suggest. Similarly, the playful handling of natural materials and created or 'found' props is not undisciplined. Certainly materials and toys can be explored and tested to the point of destruction by young children, but such explorations establish the nature of materials and the limitations and structure imposed by that nature. In these activities young children may be seen to be laying the groundwork for the more controlled use of materials and play situations to symbolize or represent their feelings and understandings about the world and their relationship to it.

At this point it is helpful to consider a specific example such as children's responses to the poems and stories which are presented as part of the early years curriculum. For playful encounters may be a useful way of thinking of the complexity and mystery of children's responses to literature. In a sense we can only launch the stories and metaphors on their way; we do not know exactly what happens to them as they are taken over by young listeners. But one thing is fairly certain; literature provides children with further resources for exploring and symbolizing their inner worlds of instincts, desires and fantasies. Literature extends the emotional range of the one life we all have, teachers as well as pupils. Rewarding evidence of this involvement and extension is found in the young child's joy when Max tames the Wild Things (Sendak, 1967) or when nursery children tell their teacher that Red Riding Hood 'shoulda killed the wolf' (Bruner, 1984). And many similar examples of young children extending the range of their self-knowledge and awareness can be found in all aspects of the curriculum when playful encounters are planned for or encouraged.

Another important but rather neglected aspect of self-awareness is the knowledge of failures, inadequacies and ignorance. There is a wealth of evidence to show that children from every kind of socio-economic background are curious and questioning in their approach to learning at home (Clark, 1976; Wells, 1981; Tizard, Mortimore and Burchell, 1981). There is also evidence, however, that they are unlikely to adopt this style automatically in school. Indeed, Willes (1983) argues that, partly because of the way that the pupil role is perceived by children – a perception which is based on what they have learned from parents, peers and often from teachers themselves – their spontaneous behaviour in school is more likely to be passive and responsive largely to teacher direction. One reason for seeing their role as a pupil in this way is that success and the ability to do things correctly have tended to be overemphasized in school and children, therefore, are reluctant to take risks in their learning, as they are fearful that their inadequacies will be revealed. And yet if non-achievement cannot be accepted and lived with, for the time being, further learning may be impeded by fear and anxiety. The confident learner at any age is prepared to risk failure.

Barrett (1986), in a research report on starting school, draws attention to the significance of children's feelings about 'not knowing' in their first experiences of formal schooling. Children need to feel and to know that it is safe and acceptable to 'not know', and they also need opportunities and help to articulate or express what they do not know. Barrett points out that much of the so-called 'bad' behaviour in reception classes is really confusion caused by feelings of 'not knowing'. She argues that planning which will enable children to accept and live with their inabilities to understand and perform is vital to the early years curriculum. In reaching similar conclusions about this dimension of the curriculum, Katz suggests that it may be helpful to teach children 'tactics and strategies by which to inform teachers where they are, how they are constructing the problem, what confuses them and how they understand' (Katz, 1977, p. 61).

Curriculum planning for the early years should include, therefore, more opportunities for showing and telling about feelings aroused by 'what I can't do', or 'what frightens me'. These opportunities can be fostered in talking, drawing, painting, modelling, movement, PE and fantasy play. But the ethos of the classroom and the human relationships fostered there will determine the degree of genuine humility and respect for true learning which 'not knowing' produces.

Closely linked with the validity of 'not knowing' in classrooms is the status of 'not doing'. If we could rid ourselves of the tradition of always being busy producing things in schools – answers as well as end-products – we might see that educational establishments should be full of 'not knowing' and periods of reflective 'not doing'. Young children need blocks of unpressured time and space in which to reflect upon feelings and experiences in order to 'internalize' or make them part of their own world picture or representation. If we provide time, space and opportunities for children to practise motor skills, expressive arts or numeracy and literacy, we should also provide many opportunities for thinking, day-dreaming and observing.

At the practical level, as we will see later in the chapter, this requires the organization of the classroom environment so that spaces and areas can be made into quiet 'dens' or 'hides' where children may get away from adults. These spaces should be, in addition to quiet, attractive areas for looking at books, plants, objects and living creatures. All such areas are ways of planning for the development of 'inwardness', reflection and self-knowledge in the early years curriculum. They are only effective, however, if adults do respect and allow for children's need to be alone, to stand and stare and, apparently, to do nothing. Similarly, the provision of materials for a range of marking, colouring, moulding, modelling and sticking activities should not be devalued and limited by adult demands for an end-product or object to take home or stick on a wall. Finding out about materials, exploring a range of sensory experiences and thinking and reflecting are major human achievements but they are not measured in crude terms of productivity and 'busy-ness'.

We have argued in some detail that a curriculum which promotes playful encounters, which enables children to come to terms with the things that they can't do or understand and which allows them time for rest and reflection, will support the development of self-knowledge and awareness, as this aspect of learning is usually given scant attention in planning by teachers. The social nature of learning and the negotiation of relationships are far more obvious aspects of the early years curriculum. The development of a sense of self, however, is closely bound up with a sense of others, their needs and their sometimes conflicting impingement on our own personal space and identity.

A close observation of young children in schools soon reveals that, as they assert their own feelings and desires, they have to cope with the reality of the demands of others. In fact it is quite clear that the social world plays a large part in shaping our roles and identities and, indeed, our cognitive strategies (Shields, 1978). Curriculum planning in the early years is most helpful if it aims to promote and organize shared and collaborative learning experiences, with instruction that is rooted in partnerships of learning and directed at what, as we saw in Chapter 1, Vygotsky (1962) has called the 'zone of proximal development'. It is quite obvious that the shared use of limited collections of toys, apparatus and other resources gives rise to opportunities for discussing, planning and organizing fair and reasonable availability for all. But the real value of this curriculum opportunity is to be found in the degree to which the children are genuinely involved in the social experience.

Collaborative learning across the curriculum and at all stages of education is only successful if it reflects appropriate beliefs about teaching and learning. For example, early literacy should be planned in such a way that children and teachers work together on joint enterprises such as shared writing and the creation of books. Reading will need to be presented as a shared exploration of a text with the more experienced and skilled reader, child or adult, reading first or alongside the beginner. Much of the meaningful reading and writing in the classroom will arise from contacts with the community and expeditions into the environment surrounding the school. Mathematical and scientific investigations will be focused on the problems which groups of children pose for themselves and attempt to solve. In all these collaborative ventures more powerful and interesting questions and answers can arise from the diversity of the children's personal styles and cultural assumptions.

It is worth noting too that planning for collaborative learning in such a manner provides the developmental base for two other important aspects of the early years curriculum. For if social development is conceived of and planned for in this way, it allows, on the one hand, for a natural extension to the children's families and promotes, therefore, the positive involvement of parents in education. It also, on the other hand, enables a curriculum to be established which challenges stereotypical views on such issues as gender, class and race by emphasizing the positive and enriching aspects of diversity. These two aspects will be explored fully in Chapters 4 and 5, but at this point it is important to stress that planning which seeks to involve parents and a curriculum which emphasizes cultural pluralism can only be successful when both are linked to the child's social development and when they are focused, therefore, on meaningful social encounters.

Curriculum planning which is directed at the educational development of children as individuals in a social setting will also nurture the growth of autonomy in learning. A crucial feature of confident self-awareness is independence in managing oneself and one's environment. In early childhood education the well-organized, resource-based classroom is again the major factor in promoting this feature of autonomy. Materials, space and time can be planned to maximize children's experiences of self-help, of sustained sequences of activities and such valuable opportunities as getting into a mess and cleaning up and restoring order.

It is clear from our discussion so far that the second dimension of curriculum planning – planning which is undertaken to promote the child's growth in self-knowledge and awareness, social understanding and personal autonomy – relates to and builds upon the first dimension – the planning of a resource-based classroom environment. And both dimensions enable the teacher to create an effective educational context. For whilst one aspect provides for the more physical features of the planned environment and the experiences within it, the other emphasizes the interpersonal aspects of those experiences. Each is crucial to a curriculum which will support children's development because each emphasizes the planning of present-day experiences for children which build on their current understandings and will support further development. And this concern with the potential of experience for supporting further development means that both are connected to the third dimension of planning, that which is concerned with the promotion of competencies and understandings.

Aspects of formal learning

This third dimension brings us much closer to a consideration of what has been traditionally regarded as curriculum planning for, at its simplest level, it relates to planning which will enable children to learn specific skills and knowledge. It is more obviously concerned, therefore, with the content of education, but more especially with the child's response to that content. And in the early years of schooling this has usually meant planning for the teaching of numeracy and literacy. A note of caution needs to be sounded, however, in order to ensure that this third dimension of planning is not restricted in this way. For if the teacher is limited to extending only those experiences which support the learning of 'the basic skills', many valuable experiences will be ignored and opportunities for development consequently curtailed.

The developmental curriculum, as we saw in Chapter 1, derives from a view of knowledge and learning which emphasizes feeling as well as logical thinking and which values a wide spectrum of symbolizing activities – not just those of words and numbers. When we define which experiences are worthy of extension we are also, in Eisner's terms, 'defining the opportunities the young will have to experience different forms of consciousness' (Eisner, 1982, p. 52). It is important, therefore, that the opportunities we offer to children in the early years classroom are multisensory and allow for the representation of thought and experiences through such modes as the visual, auditory, tactile, graphic, linguistic, motor and logical–analytical.

These broadened views of curriculum planning may seem daunting to the professional educator who has been accustomed to plan for a traditional schooling and has been encouraged by political, social and economic pressures into promoting narrowly defined views of thinking and knowledge which, in effect, concentrate on basic conceptions of literacy and numeracy. It should be remembered, however, that such pressures now mean that young children encounter dangerously limited experiences in school (DES, 1982a; DFE, 1995a; SCAA, 1995a). This narrowing of focus may seem tidy and convenient for the teacher, but 'the more convenient a method of instruction is for the teacher the less convenient for the pupils. The only right way of teaching is that which is satisfactory to the pupils' (Pinch and Armstrong, 1982, p. 115). It must be emphasized that an education concerned with full human development and potential must amount to more than the impoverished or unbalanced curriculum which results from planning for the teacher's and not the child's convenience.

Planning this third dimension of the curriculum for the early years, therefore, will need to be focused on developing varied and diverse ways of making meanings, rather than on narrowly conceived subject-content. It is, in fact, thinking itself and the symbolic ways of developing and expressing thinking which education, and not just early education, should be concerned with. Experiences of a wide range of representations are the essential means by which children are enabled to move from their first personal concepts to public modes or symbols. Transforming a private experience into a public one (Eisner, 1982) is at the heart of education, art and culture, and may be expressed in words, pictures, music, sculpture, religion, mathematics, science and so on. Children need ample time and opportunities to experience all of these modes, hence the importance of creating an educational context to provide these. Professional planning, however, will need to find ways of extending such experience by encouraging and developing the expressive forms of telling and listening, story and book sharing, music and drama, play and movement, collecting and sorting, counting and estimating, drawing and writing, building and modelling.

Superficially, this long list might appear to consist of routinely conventional early years 'activities' or, perhaps, comforting occupations for easing children into schooling. But that would be a dangerous misunderstanding. These forms of representation and symbolic modes are tools for thinking and, as such, are central to education. Access to a rich range of resources and experience of diverse symbolic forms make it possible for children to formulate their own problems and questions and pursue their own hypotheses, using the languages and the techniques of public ways of knowing to extend their understandings and, in the process, to increase their competence and confidence.

A broadly planned early years curriculum, therefore, should pose many challenging situations for children. And, in attempting to meet these challenges, the children will come to experience the fact, as was highlighted in Chapter 1, that much school-based or formal knowledge demands context-free or 'disembedded' thinking. Planning this third dimension of the curriculum should, therefore, be focused on helping children to create 'bridges' or strategies which will link their common-sense views to the more abstract demands of formal thought (Hughes, 1986). For, unless such links are made, children may be mystified rather than challenged by the experiences offered them in school.

The children's success in dealing with 'not knowing' is dependent on their ability to build on and re-use their current everyday knowledge. Curriculum planning which aims to facilitate this making of links between formal and informal ways of knowing will focus, therefore, on what children already do well and on what their homes and communities contribute. School-based knowledge may be predominantly context-free or 'dis-embedded' but it originates in the context-dependent thinking of infancy, a style of thinking which continues to be used and valued by all of us. It is the common-sense 'taken-for-granted' knowledge of our homes and communities. It is the knowledge of how 'our group' has always done things and reflects how 'we' see the world and the values 'we' live by. This informal knowledge should not be disparaged, for it is the prime way in which cultures provide symbolic languages and public expression for our private inner worlds of feelings, fantasy and imagination. Hence the need to plan for a rich variety of experiences in such areas as song, story, poetry, ritual, religion, costume, games, foods, arts, crafts and dance. In many of these aspects of curriculum teachers will need to seek the active involvement and support of the children's parents and communities, for few of us are 'inside' the life of more than one culture.

Informal knowledge must be valued also because it is the foundation of young children's understanding and the framework within which they negotiate and make sense of the learning opportunities provided by teachers and schools. It is probable that the really significant learning experiences of early childhood occur in this process of forging links or connections between encounters with formal school learning and existing informal community knowledge. The process is often described as 'heuristic' because of its similarity to the process of scientific discovery. Young learners behave like scientists; they are involved in experimenting, hypothesizing, reflecting, revising and predicting. We can observe these cognitive strategies if we watch or listen to young children doing such common-sense things as cooking, dressing, gardening or tidying up in school. We are quite likely to be told, 'My Nan's got one of those', 'We don't do it like that', 'I mustn't eat that', 'I do different writing at my other (Saturday) school.'

Valuing what children already do well involves supporting these strategies of making connections and discoveries in the more formal areas of the curriculum too. Later chapters of this volume highlight these processes at work in, for example, early literacy, early representation and drawing, early science and mathematics and in children's responses to narrative and literature and to physical activities and dance.

The list is not exhaustive but it highlights another aspect of this third dimension of curriculum planning. For at this stage, the teacher needs to make decisions about the kinds of competencies and knowledge that will be provided for and extended, decisions about what will constitute the more formal aspects of school learning. Each of these later chapters, therefore, not only shows how planning must focus on the connections that can be made between informal and formal ways of knowing within different areas of human experience, but also shows how, through these experiences, the children's development can be positively promoted. Each chapter argues, in short, that if children are involved in particular kinds of activities – investigations of a scientific or mathematical kind, for example, or those experiences which enable them to become competent in writing or computing – their development can be enhanced.

Three caveats must be emphasized, however. First, the orientation of the planning of such experiences must be developmental. Learning to read, for example, may not in itself enhance the child's development. It may, in fact, produce the opposite effect if the child is passive in that learning (Blenkin, 1983). Any aspect of the curriculum that the teacher chooses to include or to promote must be in tune with developmental views of teaching and learning and must be planned, therefore, by reference to developmental principles.

In addition to planning appropriately, the teacher must be cautious, secondly, about defining such experiences too rigidly and, in doing so, directing the children's attention too narrowly. For, if experience is perceived too narrowly by the teacher, his or her attention may be distracted from the real meanings that are preoccupying the children. This, in turn, may cause experience to be too much under the teacher's control or too fragmented to be meaningful to the children. And this is most likely to occur if the teacher is using a subject or skill rather than the children themselves as the first reference point in planning. If it is thought by the teacher, for example, that young children must have experience of making constructions with waste materials or playing with technical toys only because they must learn about design and technology, much of the value of such experiences is likely to be missed by the teacher and hence lost to the children themselves. For, in reality, when the children use such resources they are just as likely to be fascinated by mathematical problems of inclusion or shape, or preoccupied with fantasies about such things as space travel, or involved in any number of other aspects of the experience, all of which may provide the teacher with opportunities for the enhancement of their learning in ways which are as valuable as those gained through experience of design and technology. The teacher must view such activities from the children's viewpoint and must extend experience, therefore, by reference first to the developmental needs of the particular child or group of children rather than by looking first to the demands of a particular subject or skill.

This takes us to the third caveat that must be stressed. For, in this approach to curriculum, the inclusion of particular skills and knowledge can never be justified in absolute terms. The developmental approach is rooted in a belief that human knowledge and skilfulness are themselves developmental and so the teacher can never settle with absolute certainty which skills and knowledge must be included in schooling. The only recourse open to the teacher, therefore, as we have argued throughout this chapter, is to seek justification in terms of the potential of that particular experience for promoting the child's competence and understanding, a potential which lies in each individual's response to experience and not in the experience itself. It is for this reason, as the writers of later chapters will show, that emphasis is placed on the children's learning through experience or their growth in competence rather than on the learning of the knowledge and skills themselves.

It is also from this concern with children's development rather than with the content of schooling that the most convincing arguments for including certain skills and knowledge, in our view, stem. For such arguments derive from educators' insights into what children already do well and from a recognition of the strategies that children are disposed to use in our culture as they strive to make sense of their world. They are arguments, in short, that define the content to be promoted in terms which build on what children themselves already do and are interested in.

One such argument is developed by Egan (1986), who is concerned with the centrality of narrative or story form in the early years of individual development. In what he describes as the mythic mode, young children derive meaning from the world by interpreting the new and the unknown in terms of their known inner worlds of fantasy and imagination. This, of course, puts a high priority on the role of narrative, story and poetry in the early years curriculum and this area is elaborated upon in Chapter 6. In the context of this discussion, however, it is important to emphasize that Egan's argument for making narrative a central pivot of planning stems from his view that it is from story-like strategies and encounters that children derive the emotional and moral tone of their education. Narrative is not simply a chronicling of events in time, it is an evaluation of behaviours, motives and events. And, similarly, this third dimension of curriculum planning, the dimension which is concerned with extending experience, is an enterprise which is intrinsically concerned with organizing and selecting meaningful, valued and worthwhile experiences for the young child which both build on the young child's strengths and, in doing so, extend his or her grasp of the unknown.

In our discussion so far, we have outlined the three main dimensions or reference points which must be focused upon and attended to when planning a developmental curriculum. In doing so, we have emphasized that educational planning is human in character rather than purely technical and it cannot, therefore, be reduced to a simple technique or methodology. It depends, instead, upon the professional ability of the teacher; upon the teacher's ability to plan and sustain an educational context, for example, and upon his or her ability to make informed judgements about the kinds of experience that will promote each child's learning. And alongside this professional understanding must go the teacher's ability to create such a context in reality and to act upon such judgements in practice. It is to a consideration of some of these practical implications that we must now turn.

The physical context:
resources, organization and management

If the emphasis of the developmental approach to curriculum planning is upon the importance of the context within which education is to take place, then the first practical considerations must relate to the creation of an environment within which the children will be stimulated to learn. The underlying principle which should guide the establishment of such an environment is that it must enable the children to be active in learning – enable them to develop their capacities to act upon the materials which are provided and the situations which they meet in a purposive way and, at the same time, to develop their abilities to inquire and to be independent in the choices that they make.

These conditions will not be established if the activities are too tightly controlled by the teacher and if there are too many adult-imposed structures on the materials that are available. The overall conception of the classroom, therefore, must be informal in arrangement, in use and in atmosphere. The teacher must plan for a classroom organization which, within the space available, stresses openness – opening choices for both the teacher and the children.

What is essential to making this way of working available for the children is a room planned as a workshop, resourced with all the appropriate tackle and gear and designed with distinct areas of curriculum focus. Thus, this rationale demands an art and craft workshop area, challenging outdoor play facilities and gardens, literacy and literature bays, areas for mathematical and scientific investigations, space for fantasy and role-play, access to music resources and to displays which stimulate and extend the children's ongoing interests and investigations. The materials that are established within these areas might include a selection from natural materials (sand, water, clay, etc.), construction materials (bricks, boxes, technical toys, etc.), materials for expression and craft (pencils,

paint, fabrics, etc.), materials for drama and role-play (sociodramatic play
areas, miniature worlds, puppets, etc.), living things (plants and animals),
reference materials (displays, book collections, audio-visual resources,
etc.). And these must be maintained carefully and stored in such a way
that the children have access to them at all times and can make use of
them in a flexible manner and in ways which suit their particular purposes and are appropriate to their needs. This is the rich reality which
should emerge from curriculum planning for the early years and it is
poorly served by tatty book corners, literally 'messy areas', pathetic
home-corners and asphalt playgrounds.

Teachers should be familiar with both the nature and possibilities of
the materials available and also with their limitations. And this familiarity can only come in some cases from their own first-hand experience of
using the resources. It should be noted also that, although we can be confident that certain resources will both absorb children and enable certain
kinds of development to occur, teachers should always be open to considering other basic provisions which might hold the potential for new
educational experiences. Who could have envisaged twenty years ago,
for example, that having a computer with a Logo program and a word-
processing program, or concept keyboard, as part of the basic classroom
provision would support children's development in the way described
by Seymour Papert (1980)?

All these toys, resources, tools and materials are, of course, to be shared
by a large number of children which, in early education, is a new experience for each child in the class. This is a positive learning opportunity,
it should be seen as such by the teacher and it should be incorporated
into the planned curriculum. Time should be spent, therefore, on routines
such as room maintenance and catering, for these routines are an essential part of learning to live in a community. Making such routines central to the early years curriculum has the additional benefit of posing real
problems and meaningful challenges for the children. Tidying activities
such as fitting boxes and bricks back into the correct storage containers
or shelves at the end of a day's work can be every bit as demanding, if
not more so, on the children's awareness of shape, space and matching,
as structured tasks such as puzzles which require the child to fit stylized
wooden ducks into spaces on a block of wood. Similarly, counting and
calculating who is in school and who will need food and drink are much
more purposeful and meaningful than deciding how many balloons are
held by a balloon-seller sketched in a maths book.

Planning the classroom environment must place a high priority, therefore, on time, space and provision for trying things out in active and experimental ways. This involves the undirected handling of materials,
opportunities for talking collaboratively and speculating about actions and
observations, plus time to reflect and contemplate silently. Needless to say,
this active involvement with materials and situations will not happen if

there are no elements of intrinsic challenge, excitement and aesthetic appeal in the resources. Young children clamour to know 'Who made it?', 'What's inside it?', 'Where did you find it?', 'How does it work?'. This passion of intellectual curiosity is not aroused by colouring-in outline pictures, copying from a work book or locating the whereabouts of Peter and Jane. It comes from the teacher's willingness and ability to make available a range of materials, objects and artefacts, to display these in a manner which will provoke interest and appeal, and to encourage children to take notice of and investigate their surroundings in a focused way.

The creation of such a setting depends, in part, on the teacher's display skills and aesthetic judgements and the importance of these professional abilities should not be underestimated. For the overall visual impact of the classroom has a profound influence on both the children who work there and the adults who visit it. This point is emphasized in a report on design in education (Design Council, 1987) where it is argued that planning the classroom involves elements of design which must be dealt with effectively by the teacher if the resulting environment is to be inviting, stimulating and conducive to learning. The report goes on to argue that teachers should not only develop design skills themselves but should also involve the children in these same processes. Children's experience of design problems can be extended in many ways through such activities as mounting exhibitions, making books, creating gardens and building working models. But the teacher will need to support the children's efforts by intervening appropriately in order to enlarge their awareness of how an effective result might be achieved.

Establishing appropriate resources and organizing the use of them within the overall design of the environment are two important practical considerations which must be attended to by the teacher when establishing the physical context. A third consideration is perhaps more elusive but is, nonetheless, important. For, as children move in purposeful ways around well-planned classroom workshops they will also need large blocks of time in which to initiate, sustain and extend their work. It is salutary to meditate on what we as adults would achieve if we were told to clear away our activities every hour, or even forty-five minutes, or were regularly forced to watch a television programme or attend a public meeting at short notice and without consultation. But this must be the reality of the school day for most young children!

In order to establish working relationships with the children of the kind that will encourage them not only to use the materials provided, but also to create, experiment, explore and above all to talk with each other and with their teacher about their experiences, the teacher will need to reduce the rigidity imposed by prescribed timetabling and grouping of children to a minimum. For it is the judicious planning of time and grouping as well as space and resources that will create an appropriate physical context for development.

It does not follow, however, that having established an appropriate physical context, the right kind of atmosphere and relationships will automatically ensue. A flexible approach to the use of time and informal attitudes to the grouping of children relate also to the interpersonal dimensions of planning and we must consider more closely the practical implications of these.

The interpersonal context: experience, interaction and the negotiation of meaning

A serious weakness of much of the early years planning undertaken at present by teachers, including much of the planning for Key Stage 1 of the National Curriculum, is its tendency, in practice, to concentrate on issues and problems which are not of children's making and demand answers to questions which children find meaningless. This disturbing tendency is exaggerated when programmes of disconnected skills are foisted on the early years curriculum and even described as 'enrichment' programmes. In practice they result in occupying children with trivial and pointless activities such as painting and glueing pasta, joining up dot-to-dot outlines of letters and numerals, or producing assembly-line Easter chicks, Chinese New Year lanterns or whatever! The real and insidious danger of this skills compromise is that, far from answering the attacks of the anti-early years education lobby, it results in a failure to educate young children because it fails to develop and extend their existing abilities and understandings and their continuous attempts to make sense of their world.

The significance for learning of those aspects of the classroom context which encourage children's personal involvement and satisfaction has been a central claim of learner-centred education. However, it is seriously eroded whenever skills, objectives, National Curriculum subjects, or 'jobs' must be completed by young children before they are allowed to go back to their own absorbing play and investigations. Furthermore, the very fact of relegating learner controlled experiences to the fringes of curriculum planning and to the leftover times of the school day signals the low value placed on such learning. We should all be driven by sheer common sense, if nothing else, to ask ourselves why the involvement of young children in self-motivated play and learning is so absorbing, while the completion of teacher-imposed tasks often demands so much insistence and prompting. Perhaps the plaintive question, 'Can I choose now?' which is heard so often in classrooms should be carved over the entrances to primary schools – an apt replacement for 'Girls', 'Boys' and 'Mixed Infants'! The activities the children choose are our best starting point for appropriate planning and for teaching us how to teach them. Barrett (1986) comments that the most sustained involvement she observed was in those 'play' or 'real' situations where individuals were representing or re-creating something they already knew and wanted to do. The situations observed by Barrett included tidying up, pretend cooking in the home-corner, painting, writing, drawing, building and playing in the sand. This makes a sound start for planning an appropriate early years classroom, and we would wish to extend the list with opportunities to cook for real, to handle malleable materials, to investigate the properties of water, to explore a garden area, to build with blocks (Gura, 1992) and to dress up in a collection of drapes, clothes and accessories. As has just been suggested, these situations allow children to re-create something they already know and want to do. We would also highlight the important cognitive activities of sorting, ordering and understanding which occur as the children represent and 'go over' in playful repetition events, language, ideas, movements, feelings and emotions.

Provision for experiences which promote satisfying feelings is not just a well-intentioned 'good thing'. Our thinking is permeated by feeling: 'the formation of concepts depends upon the construction of images derived from the material the senses provide' (Eisner, 1982, p. 34). As we argued earlier in the chapter, in order to 'know', we form concepts or representations which are based on images, pictures in the mind, and rooted in sensory experiences and social attachments. The early years of education should be particularly rich in situations which value and extend knowledge derived from perceptions of the world and relationships with other people. For this reason, it is quite central to the early years curriculum to plan experiences which support the exploration of feelings and relationships. Provision for rehearsing the patterns of relationships between parents and children, teachers and pupils, brothers and sisters, mothers and fathers, friends and enemies, customers and shop assistants, are a traditional part of classroom role-play but feelings and relationships are also re-enacted in miniature-world play, music and dance, stories and poems, modelling, painting and drawing.

The approach that we are endeavouring to describe requires that the teacher should seek to establish the kinds of relationship with every child in the class that encourage individuals to have the freedom to use materials, the experience of sharing and co-operating with others and the confidence and inclination to sustain and consolidate inquiries. The teacher may need to re-evaluate his or her role in order to establish such relationships with the children, and the aim should be to enable children to learn in the classroom, rather than to organize the room for the convenience of the teacher. This shift of focus and emphasis might be best described as teacher de-centring. For the teacher must be able to see problems and experiences from the child's point of view and must collaborate with the child on the task in hand until he or she can make sense of it.

Three practical strategies will support the teacher in this kind of collaboration. First, adequate time must be spent with each child in a variety of situations and economic means of recording the resultant observations and knowledge of each child must be established. These records will, of course, be framed in the manner that was discussed in Chapter 1 and be derived from developmental techniques of observation and assessment.

Secondly, the teacher must accept and understand each child's background so that it is possible to mediate between the child's experiences at home and at school. It is important, therefore, as will be shown in Chapter 5, that the teacher should work in co-operation with parents, recognizing the crucial and positive role that they too play in the child's education. The relationships established with the children must be of essence friendly and warm, and the teacher must start from 'where each child is', respecting as valuable the home background of every child.

Thirdly, the teacher must add to this warmth an intensity of relationship. The provision of a stimulating classroom environment with a warm, accepting teacher is clearly insufficient 'to engage the learner's mind and to help that mind as it attempts to improve and develop understandings of its experience' (Katz, 1995, p. 144). Katz argues that each child needs to feel or sense that what he or she does – or does not do – really matters to the teacher and this she sees as requiring more than warmth in the relationship. Her thesis is that optimum intensity of relationships between children and their teacher (that is, relationships which are both warm and intense) causes young children to develop their capacities for intentional behaviour and that this 'helps children to organize their own behaviour, to set, pursue, realize and achieve their own purposes' (op. cit., p. 147).

Clearly all three of these strategies overlap and all are partly dependent on the teacher's sensitivity towards children, a quality which cannot be planned for in the deliberate way suggested above. It is equally clear, however, that the teacher's manner and personality can only partly explain the successful development of this approach in practice. For these strategies also depend on a deep understanding of children, their development and the experiences that will promote that development.

Our discussion of the practical implications of adopting a developmental approach to the curriculum, therefore, highlights once more the fact that it is upon such professional expertise that successful practice depends. And in later chapters, when more focused explorations are made of developmental approaches to aspects of the curriculum – to the development of cognitive skills, for example, or the child's growth of understanding within particular spheres – we will see again that aspects of the teacher's professional understanding must interrelate if the child's development is to be advanced.

If the developmental view of education is to be promoted, therefore, a crucial factor will be the quality of the teachers. In this respect we would endorse the government's claim that 'the teacher force ... is the major single determinant of the quality of education' (DES, 1983, p. 1). In most other respects, however, we would disagree with the government's ideas and policy on how teaching quality can be achieved in early childhood education.

Teaching quality – an alternative view

Education, as opposed to teaching, is a highly sophisticated activity. To teach someone something can be a relatively straightforward matter; hence many people in many different contexts do it more or less successfully all the time. Our view of education, however, is of a much more complex process or set of processes. To educate, that is, to attend to and promote the development of immature minds and persons in the ways that this book sets out to describe, requires far more than mere teaching. It calls for qualities, skills and levels of insight and understanding of a special kind, and for a far more sophisticated form of preparation than the term 'teacher training' would suggest.

Furthermore, the continued development of education depends upon the continued development of teachers, so that, if we wish to forward curriculum development in a genuine sense, we must do this by promoting the continued professional development of teachers. And, if we are to do that, we must provide them with many different kinds of support, pre-eminent among which will be appropriate forms of in-service education.

But central to all provision for teacher education, at both initial and in-service stages, must be a concern to promote professional expertise. It must, therefore, focus on and advance all those skills and understandings which will enable teachers to attend more successfully to children's developmental needs. This has been a central thesis of our chapter for, in our view, this is the only route by which teaching quality will be assured.

In asserting this we recognize that present government controls are directing teacher training courses at all levels, including those courses which are designed to prepare teachers for nursery and first schools, along an entirely different route. The emphasis on traditional subject-content is increased, it is a requirement that this content is studied in its own right at undergraduate level and that only then can it be linked to method courses where students will learn to teach their chosen subjects. It is this emphasis on content and methodology which is the main feature of the recently established criteria for the approval and, indeed, the accreditation of teacher education courses. It is an emphasis which promotes the view that the teacher is 'a carrier of knowledge with transmission skills' (Goddard, 1985, p. 35). It requires that 'teachers are seen in the context of the subjects they teach, and knowledge and understanding of educational issues and pedagogy are relegated to a very poor second' (ibid.). It ignores the relevance to teachers of a study of children's learning and development, and grossly underestimates the intellectual demands of a proper study of professional theory and practice. It runs counter to what a recent survey has shown experienced early years professionals consider to be essential to the effective preparation of early years practitioners (Blenkin and Yue, 1994). In short, it fails to recognize what constitutes professional expertise.

The concern of current courses is with the *what* and the *how* of teaching. The essential *why* questions, which are asked so characteristically by those teachers who see the pupils' developmental needs as their prime responsibility, are ignored or even discouraged. And the result of such training is likely to lead to a diminution in teaching quality rather than to an improvement.

More productive ways of preparing teachers for their complex role as educators, however, have been developed during the past two decades and this has led to courses which have been designed specifically to promote the many features of professional expertise explored in this book. Although these courses are not permitted to continue in the UK at present, they serve as a valuable professional resource because they are based on a redefinition of the teacher's role in developmental terms. They have contributed, as a result, to professional understanding and practice, especially in the field of early childhood education, in two main ways. They have demonstrated, first, the elements of study and expertise which are derived from and are essential to a developmental position. They have also shown the ways in which courses and other forms of support can be directed at promoting those skills and understandings that are required by teachers if they are to establish a developmental curriculum.

A detailed description and analysis of one such course has been undertaken elsewhere (Blenkin and Kelly, 1983). We end our chapter, therefore, by summarizing the main features of professional expertise which are highlighted in that account. For these features are essential, in our view, to effective curriculum planning in particular and to teaching quality in general.

Professional expertise depends, first, on the teacher's ability to interweave the broad elements which contribute to professional understanding. Before we identify each of these elements their inter-relationships must be stressed. If the teacher does not recognize and deal with this interdependence it is likely, as we saw earlier, that his or her practice will be distorted. For an adult who is expert in mathematics, for example, without appreciating mathematical activities from the child's viewpoint, or understanding the role of logical and spatial relationships in the development of children's thinking, or being able to evaluate the impact that structured schemes and planned activities will have on children's learning, can be positively harmful to their education. Similarly, a teacher's understanding of child development does not, in itself, ensure that children's development will be promoted in the classroom. It must be accompanied by other kinds of understanding. Each element of professional understanding is equally demanding, both academically and practically, so that each should be afforded equal time and attention in any provision that is made for teacher education. All such provision, however, should take account of the prime requirement of teaching quality and should ensure that the teacher's expertise is not only developed in a balanced way, but also that the important elements of professional understanding are integrated and that a coherent approach is adopted as a result. It is only in this manner that expertise of a proper kind will be promoted.

Having emphasized the importance of this overall coherence in the development of professional understanding, we now turn to the second requirement of teaching quality; that is, to the identification of the elements themselves.

There are three broad elements of professional expertise – in professional skills, in the theoretical understanding of educational issues and in the knowledge of appropriate educational content. Each element, in our view, makes an important contribution to coherent professional practice and each, therefore, merits a closer examination.

We suggested earlier that there are many skills needed by the teacher and that these go well beyond the creation of teaching materials. Professional skills would include the ability to make perceptive observations of the work of children, their reactions and their interactions. Allied to this is the teacher's ability to make helpful and constructive evaluations of his or her own performance in the classroom and that of others. The depths of insight that are needed for such skills can only come from studies of the curriculum and of child development which go far beyond considerations merely of subject-content and methodology. The development of these skills is crucially dependent, also, on sustained contact with young children and on professional work undertaken in a variety of settings.

We argued earlier that the child's growth in competence takes time and depends upon certain conditions. It depends, for example, on appropriate experiences and upon the teacher's skilful intervention in those experiences so that helpful guidance can be offered to the child. Exactly the same conditions and processes are vital to the student teacher's growth in professional competence. Indeed, they are vital to teacher development in general. If we are to ensure that teachers develop the range of professional skills that we have outlined in this chapter, from those skills that are practical in nature to those that are based on informed judgements, it will be necessary to provide them with ample opportunities to work with children, to observe the work of other teachers and students and to be observed themselves. It also necessitates their regular contact with a

tutor or tutors whose task is to assist in enhancing their levels of observation and resultant powers of evaluation. Much has been achieved in
recent years by the development in this direction of some professional
studies courses which have been provided at both initial and in-service
levels of teacher education. In fact it might be argued that a more relevant form of intellectual rigour has entered the arena of teacher education
by this route than by any other, although unfortunately this has still to
be understood and appreciated by those currently judging the effectiveness of teacher education from the outside. There is no doubt, however,
that professional skills depend both upon a wealth of opportunities for
practice and upon a proper evaluation and analysis of that practice. And
rigorous analysis depends, in turn, upon the theoretical understanding
of educational issues which takes us to the second element of professional
expertise we wish to identify.

This second element may require that the teacher looks to related
disciplines – to philosophy, for example, or to psychology. But the relevance of such theoretical study must be clear to the teacher in exactly the
same way that school experiences must be meaningful to the child. Again
it is important that developmental principles are applied to teacher education as well as to education in general. Professional practice must be
linked with theory, therefore, in order to ensure that relevance is preserved.

This theory and practice link also provides the clue for the appropriate kind of approach to the theoretical elements of courses for teacher
education. Education theory must address itself to issues that are real,
especially in the eyes of teachers and student teachers. To say this does
not mean that only those issues that the teacher already recognizes as
real can be tackled. It does mean, however, that it must be possible to
demonstrate the relevance of any issues that are raised. In short, the only
useful direction of theoretical study is from a genuine educational issue
outwards to whatever is of value that any other discipline can contribute
rather than from the researches of those other disciplines *inwards* to education.

This approach to education theory is demonstrated in later chapters
when, for example, it is shown how linguistic theory has offered insights
into the teaching of reading and writing and how developmental psychology has informed approaches to the teaching of such diverse areas
as mathematics and art. But it must be emphasized that the right kind of
intellectual rigour in the study of education derives, first, from a proper
study of educational practices and from the teacher's ability to theorize
in a properly rigorous way about that practice.

The third element of professional expertise demands that teachers must
acquire a deep understanding of the knowledge-content that is to be
shared with the children. Much that we have said in this chapter may
suggest that we believe that this is not important. We must dispel, therefore, any such misapprehension. To stress the importance of planning

education in developmental terms is not to argue, as later chapters will also show, that its content is not important. It is to claim, however, that its subject-content should not be the first and central concern. Certainly, all teachers in nursery and first schools need a deep understanding of language development, of literature and of mathematics. But to lay heavy stress on one or two subjects is to limit seriously the teacher's scope in relation to the promotion of children's development. For it reflects an emphasis on the continuing value and importance of the subject or subjects concerned in their own right, and thus encourages the imposition of those subjects on children regardless of the kind of impact they may have on them.

It must be noted also that it is no longer feasible to justify subject study in terms of what used to be called the 'personal development' of the student teacher. It is fatuous to claim that the study of education, if conducted in the manner described above, is not intellectually demanding of teachers. What could be more demanding than trying to understand the workings of the human mind and how human learning and development can be promoted? The development of the student can be more than adequately attended to by such properly rigorous professional studies. The justification of any subject component within education, therefore, can only be found in relation to its role in the development of children. And this implies, in turn, that a good deal of attention needs to be given to the problem of finding a suitable form for the knowledge-content to be studied by teachers in early childhood education. It is knowledge-content approached in this way that provides the third element in professional understanding, and it is this approach rather than the knowledge-content itself that leads, in our view, to teaching quality.

Teaching quality depends, finally, on enabling teachers to develop special interests and spheres of expertise. For once a solid foundation has been laid along the lines outlined above, this can be built upon and issues of particular interest can be pursued in greater depth. There is an increasing need in schools of all kinds for teachers with special kinds of expertise. Sometimes these special kinds of expertise will be in curriculum areas such as language development or mathematics or science. Increasingly, however, there is a need for teachers with expert understanding of other kinds – understanding of children with special needs, for example, or of home–school liaison and parental involvement in education or, indeed, understanding of the complexities of curriculum (as opposed to subject) development. The concept of specialism should not, therefore, be limited to areas of subject specialisms only. So to limit it is to reveal a disturbing narrowness of educational vision. For an informed profession depends on shared expertise across a broad range of professional concerns.

These, then, are the elements which we regard as vital to teaching quality and essential, therefore, to any provision for teacher education.

Support for teacher development at both initial and in-service stages must take account of all these aspects of professional expertise, particularly if it is to produce teachers who can meet the demands of education as we view it. For if teachers are to be helped to develop such qualities as will enable them to support the development of each of their pupils as an individual, they must be assisted towards this in an appropriate manner. They will need, therefore, teacher-educators who possess the ability to plan and develop teacher education programmes which display and encourage exactly the same qualities as they are endeavouring to promote in their students. Creating a context for educational development requires a redefinition of the teaching role at all levels.

Conclusions

Teachers who are persuaded by the theoretical justifications for viewing education as development which were outlined in Chapter 1, and endeavour to embrace, as a result, the developmental approach, are entitled to ask how this theory can best be translated into effective educational practice. It has been our main purpose in this chapter to answer this question and, further than this, to answer it in a manner which is, itself, in an important sense, developmental. For we have set out not merely to describe 'good' developmental practices but to establish the links or, in developmental terms, 'create the bridges' between those theoretical principles and the approaches that complement them in professional planning and practice.

And this has led us to one overriding conclusion. The planning of education must be human in character rather than technical, it must be an art rather than a science, if it is to promote the personal understanding and competence of both the child and the teacher. It must be shaped more by the need to create genuinely human interactions and negotiations of meaning than by the demands of any educational content, even when that content is being selected to promote develement. It is for this reason that the creation of an appropriate context for development is of such crucial importance.

If the appropriate context for education is created, in both its material and its interpersonal aspects, it becomes possible to plan for and to promote the child's development through the more formal aspects of school learning. It also becomes possible for the teacher of young children to create those important opportunities for play, to deal successfully with such vital issues as multicultural education, and to develop effective ways of involving parents in their children's learning at school. The fundamental importance of this context for development will be referred to constantly, therefore, as these educational issues are explored more fully, and particular aspects of the curriculum are focused upon in more detail in later chapters of this book.

Suggested further reading

Hurst, V. (1991) *Planning for Early Learning*, Paul Chapman, London.
Katz, L. G. (1995) *Talks with Teachers of Young Children: a Collection*, Ablex
    Publishing Corporation, Norwood, New Jersey.

3

Play in School

Mari Guha

A playful preamble

We don't know what play is, nor do we know why anybody plays, but when we do it, we like it. We can't agree what exactly people do, when they play. But we certainly recognize in ourselves whether it is play or not play that we are engaged in. Children seem to have the same strong awareness: 'now I am playing, now I have stopped playing'. A 'state of play' is not only felt by the player internally, it seems also to communicate clearly to the observer. When people watch others 'playing', they share some kind of tacit understanding: they agree readily that play is play, it is plain to see.

There is a dilemma here: if we don't know what play is, how can we recognize it? Why is it so difficult to arrive at a generally acceptable definition of play, when at the same time it seems relatively easy to identify play as it occurs in daily life. Are we going around in circles? It is no wonder that researchers despair: 'Play is a remarkably elusive concept of fluctuating scientific popularity' (Burghardt, 1984). Elusive, yes, but with a long and impressive history. Aristotle wrote about man's ability to 'idle well' and Plato emphasized sports. The scientific interest in play came much later. It was triggered by Darwin (1871, 1872), and it has produced an intensive literature over the last hundred years. The interest continues today. There are numerous, often contradictory definitions and theories of play. They are too numerous to be usefully surveyed here. There are no easily identifiable sets of actions which could reliably be called play. To write about play is 'to define rainbows and hunt for pots of gold' (Burghardt, 1984). This chapter does not attempt the serious business of selecting an acceptable definition, it does not attempt to address contradictions. The starting point is that play exists, we know it when we see it, we know it when we do it. This chapter looks at play in relation to education in the first school and asks two questions: Should children be allowed and even encouraged to play in school? If so, when, during the school day, should play take place?

This chapter, then, is a playful hunt for answers; it will no doubt lead to new dilemmas. But if we stumble upon any 'pots of gold' we should consider them seriously.

The argument against play in school

There is little dispute about the natural occurrence of play in early childhood, or about its value for the individual child. The value of play in school, however, has been in the centre of much debate in the past and that debate is still with us today.

That children naturally play is a truism. It is taken for granted, so much so that it threatens to obscure a clearer understanding of what, in fact, the children do when they play. Because play is so widespread and frequent in the early years, it has come to stand for almost everything children do when freed from routine life-maintaining functions. The unease researchers feel about such an umbrella concept is reflected in Hutt's attempt to distinguish between some of the different aspects of what may loosely be described as play (Hutt, 1966). She suggests that a distinction needs to be drawn between exploration and play. Exploration, in her view, is not play, it is serious, concentrated, and it is aimed at finding out details as thoroughly as possible. Only after this intense exploratory phase is completed does play occur. In the first phase the child appears to ask the question: 'What does this object do?', and in the second phase: 'What can I do with it?'. Now the mood changes, becomes more relaxed, the actions become diverse and varied and the child may laugh; this is what could properly be described as play. Both phases have value for the child and Hutt points out, in particular, that the second playful phase may have strong links with the development of later creativity and original thinking.

Modern research has made great strides in teasing out the strands of learning and complex developmental processes which may occur in play. However, the issue here is not about play as such but about play in school. The argument against having play in the primary school may be put as follows.

Play is part and parcel of children's natural behaviour, embedded in their spontaneous day-to-day living. It forms an important part of pre-school and out of school early learning. The school has to acknowledge it and build on it, but the school's function is different. Although the learning which accompanies day-to-day living and play may be uniquely valuable for the individual, it also has several drawbacks. It is haphazard, fragmentary and, because it is unplanned, it may lack direction. It may pull the learner's attention to irrelevant details, it may lead children to make arbitrary, accidental, false connections. Some critiques suggest that the very relaxed nature of play, which is no doubt enjoyable, does not help the child to develop the grit and perseverance to pursue a difficult goal with sustained effort. It is all too easy, too much time is wasted in play.

School, on the other hand, is a special place with a special function. It is an educational institution which evolved because it became necessary to 'supplement' (for want of a better word) the learning that may occur 'naturally'.

These arguments are valid. School learning is different from spontaneous learning in the pre-school years. School learning is organized, it has clear-cut goals, it should be efficient, and it aims to benefit both individual children and the society in which they live.

Why then do we argue for the inclusion of play in the school curriculum? Inclusion – this needs to be stressed – is not substitution. Play cannot take the place of well planned, directed instruction. But play can enhance enormously the success of a well planned curriculum. In other words, it would be a great shame for schools to lose the spontaneous energy, vigour, curiosity and enthusiasm which is so obvious in young children's play. In addition, the actual learning that takes place, the cognitive achievements accomplished, the rate of learning in the early years is staggering. There must be links between play and the quality of this early learning. We educationalists would be the losers if we ignored the possible lessons to be learned. What follows is an attempt to look at some of these lessons

The love of learning:
lessons to be learned from babies

Educational theories may be complex and sophisticated, but, no matter how elaborate the system of explanations, at the root we must find some assumptions about the basic nature of the child. This mythical 'child' is a curious changeling: a noble savage (Rousseau), a plant waiting to unfold (the Kindergarten Movement), or like an electric iron – in search of homeostatic equilibrium (Cannon, 1932), a creature in the grip of instinctual urges (Freud), or, according to more recently fashionable metaphors, the child is comparable to a miniature architect/designer who is engaged in the continuous pursuit of constructing and reconstructing his or her 'model of the world'. For the teacher the choice of the perspective is important. A great deal in educational theorizing and educational practice hinges on what one takes to be the 'nature of children'.

The questions could be phrased as follows. Is the child's natural orientation to the world in harmony or in conflict with the educator's aim? Is the love of learning the result (Gagne, 1969) or the very basis of education? Or perhaps both? These broad questions have direct bearing on our topic: play in school or out of school? If children spontaneously enjoy learning, and this spontaneous learning takes place in play, then play must link with education. If, on the other hand, children have to be led to 'love learning' through carefully structured steps, and only after mastering the constituent skills will they be able to enjoy what they have learnt, then spontaneous play may be a waste of precious time. Or do children need a bit of both?

The recent explosion of research, focused on babies, puts us in an enviable position as regards the search for answers to these questions. It has taken nearly forty years for the exciting findings of infancy research to filter through and begin to have some impact on educational thinking. We are now in a better position to speculate about how babies' minds work, and this must affect our assumptions about the 'nature of the child'.

A particularly beautiful demonstration of the 'love of learning' involved babies as young as two to three months (Papusek, 1969). To start with, the experimenters established that babies love looking at flickering lights. These lights were then so arranged by the experimenters that they could be 'turned on' by the babies themselves, as a result of the babies' own movements. This could be as simple as turning the head to the right. Babies soon discovered which movement turned the lights on, and they repeated this several times. However, the rewarding spectacle soon lost its magic. The babies stopped bothering about the lights, they were getting bored with them. They paid relatively little attention to the lights, turning them on every now and then as if to check that they still worked. However, when the scheming experimenters changed the situation so that the lights *did not* come on with the well-established movement, the babies burst into activity, with full attention and renewed energy. The babies now got very excited. They tried and tried until they accidentally found that now it was another movement (turning to the left) which made the lights work. Once this was established, boredom set in again. Similar experiments were tried with mobiles. The mobile was attached by a string to the baby's left arm first, then the string was moved to the right arm, then it was attached to the left and, later, to the right foot. Each time the baby invested maximum attention in the mobile when the mobile did not do what it was expected to do.

What was going on here? These tiny babies appear to contradict the reinforcement or reward theories of learning. The 'reward' (the bright, flickering lights, or the movement of the shiny mobile) holds the attention only when the babies find it unpredictable in some way. Once they have figured out what needs to be done to make the lights appear, or the mobile move, once the connection between the babies' own efforts and the consequences they have on the world outside are well established, the babies get bored. Is 'getting bored' significant? Boredom, the capacity to get bored, seems to be a wonderful human gift. Boredom and curiosity are two sides of the same coin. Boredom is perhaps the clearest indication that the human mind is active, that it is not the slave of external stimuli. The capacity to get bored with things which are thoroughly familiar must mean that the mind wants to move on, it searches and scans the world, it looks for what else there is. Babies seem unable to resist the urge to go past the already familiar towards novelty, in order to take in more of the world.

It appears that there are lessons to be learnt from babies. Commenting on the above experiments and the related research literature, this is how Bower (1974, p. 8) sums up the lessons:

> Examination of the behaviour shows that it is not random. The infant seems to be testing hypotheses and trying out sequences of movements in order to discover which one operates at the moment . . . It thus seems that the pleasures of problem-solving are sufficient to motivate behavioural and mental activity in young infants.

These babies seem to engage in 'problem-solving' for its own sake. They seem to be saying: we are born with a functioning nervous system and it is good fun to use it. Research into infants' capabilities has been particularly rich in the last few decades and has resulted in a healthy respect for babies. It led Bower (ibid.) to conclude enthusiastically: 'Problem-solving seems a most unlikely form of motivation to attribute to infants; however, there are a number of experiments which make this conclusion inescapable.'

Therefore, it is argued here that the 'love of learning' is part and parcel of children's 'basic nature': that learning is what they *spontaneously* want to do. The spontaneous love of learning in young children is by no means some kind of vague inclination. It produces results. Nobody could deny that the learning achievements of the pre-school years are immense. Most complex of these achievements is probably the acquisition of the mother tongue. How the child accomplishes this in approximately the first three and a half years of life is something that has bewildered many and continues to be at the centre of much research today.

This view of the child who starts out in life with the 'love of learning' brings us back to the implications for teachers mentioned above: how does school learning relate to the child's spontaneous love of learning? Could schools build on the assumption that the love of learning is there in every child? Could this be taken as the starting point? Could schools capitalize on children's natural inclinations? Is there a danger that by ignoring or underestimating children's spontaneous love of learning, we throw away the most valuable asset they bring with them? And what is the role of play in all this? These questions are not new, but it is pertinent to raise them again.

Perhaps much of the teachers' time and energy in schools could be better used. Instead of concentrating on pre-specified learning objectives and then spending a great deal of effort in 'motivating' children to want to attain these specified objectives, we ought to look more carefully at the conditions in which pre-school children achieve their impressive learning success. Once we take the young child's early achievements seriously and pay attention to the messages of modern infancy research, the examination of the role of play in early learning becomes a central issue.

Play and learning

Young children spontaneously learn and young children spontaneously play. That there may be a connection between the two, between play and learning, was powerfully argued by Bruner in his famous paper 'Nature and uses of immaturity' (1972). He suggests that there may be a link between the evolutionary success of human adaptation and the long period of human childhood. The habitats to which humans are capable of adapting are not only hugely varied, they are also unpredictable. Humans have evolved into a species capable of changing their environment to suit themselves. Bruner sees a direct link between the success of human evolution and play, success is maximized for humans by the long period of childhood. In other words, the function of the long period of childhood is to create the conditions for play. Play is the vehicle for the kinds of complex learning on which the human condition depends.

In particular, there are three features of play which seem to affect significantly the capacity to learn: play is relatively pressure free; play is often symbolic; and much of play is interactive, social. Let us examine each in turn.

Why should learning benefit from the pressure-free aspect of play?

The proposition that play is 'non-serious' is generally agreed. An often mentioned corollary suggestion is that play has no extrinsic goals – 'it is inherently unproductive' (Garvey, 1977, p. 10). This should not be confused with the notion that the player does not set himself or herself play-goals. Indeed, players do, and within the bounds of the play, these goals are taken very seriously. There may be considerable effort and energy put into pursuing play-goals. Play is described as non-serious because the consequences of success or failure in play are very different from the consequences of success or failure in the real struggle for survival. When things are for real, one feels hungry without a dinner, but one could easily switch from cooking a play-meal to something more interesting or more urgent. That play is enjoyable is also generally agreed. Carl Groos (1901) in fact argued that the enjoyment of play is derived from feeling free: life is serious and the liberty of play signifies relief from pressure.

Bruner (1972), however, takes the argument further and suggests that the long period of human childhood evolved specifically to protect the young from fending for themselves, from facing life 'seriously' – precisely to allow for playful exploration. It is of great importance that the young should feel secure and protected to be able to take risks in play. It is, in particular, the playful exploration of variations between means and ends, which leads to the kind of creative flexibility the best of human thinking is capable of. Bruner suggests that without such play, tool-use may not have evolved. Species lower on the philogenetic scale spend a smaller proportion of their lifecycle protected by parents, there is little or no play, the adult life follows rigid patterns, the information needed for survival is carried in the genepool of the species. In humans this is reversed. For us novelty seeking becomes pleasurable for its own sake, for us adaptation is open-ended. The long period of protected childhood, which provides us with opportunities to play and shelters us from being overwhelmed by the risks we try out, encourages us to approach the unknown.

This evolutionary argument seems to accord well with the newly emerging picture of individual development. It fits in well with the view that the child's basic nature lies closer to the model of the 'architect/designer' than to the other models we noted above. Fagen (1984, p. 170), in a more recent influential paper, revisits Bruner's earlier theory and puts it in the dual perspective of ontogeny and philogeny:

> The idea that organisms, unlike machines, actively construct their own environments suggests that play helps intelligent animals develop the skills of active environment building in a changing, uncertain, incompletely defined world. . . . The simplistic view of development as optimized progress toward an ideal adult endpoint ought to give way to less Panglossian views more in keeping with the messiness of nature. The idea that behavioural development, unlike automobile assembly or computer programming, is not a mechanical process directed towards an ideal adult endpoint suggests that the study of development in general and play in particular needs to consider what Jerome Bruner (1972) has termed 'the uses of immaturity'.

The more direct trade-off between learning and object-play has been investigated by several researchers (see Smith and Simon, 1984). Some studies demonstrate links between creativity, divergent thinking and exploratory play (Hutt and Bhavani, 1972; Lieberman, 1977; Li, 1978; Pepler, 1982). Others looked at various aspects of problem-solving and play (Sutton-Smith, 1967; Sylva, 1977; Zammarelli and Bolton, 1977; Smith and Dutton, 1979; Simon and Smith, 1983). Children who made use of play showed improvement in problem-solving, in mathematical concept formation and performed better on various Piagetian conservation tasks. Some of the studies have been criticized on methodological grounds (Smith and Simon, 1984); the bulk of the research, however, supports the proposition that exploratory play in a pressure-free environment provides opportunities for the development of flexible thinking.

More naturalistic observations, particularly in pre-school settings, led many practitioners to intuitive support of the role of play in learning. There may, however, be qualifying conditions: some play may not facilitate learning. There may be situations when play does little for cognitive development (Tizard, 1977; Sylva, Roy and Painter, 1980). We shall discuss later the issue of 'good' and 'not so good' play.

Why is symbolic play important?

The second feature of play to be put into focus here is that play is based on 'pretend'. It dissociates the real from something that is not real, it makes a distinction between play and non-play. Thus players create alternatives to reality, they create symbols. In Bruner's (1972) view the most distinctive feature of the human species is that it creates and uses culture. Symbols are the building bricks of culture, symbols are what cultures are made of. In make-believe play the child transforms reality, as that make-believe play has to be seen as a form of representation. Either the player simulates an action in play *'as if'* it were real, or the player tries out new combinations with sequences of events, actions and situations in a *'what if'* fashion. Symbolization proceeds from performing an action or using an object in pretence, 'as if' it were something else, and moves on to creating alternative stories to reality: 'What if I, or someone, or something, did this and this?' The significance of make-believe play is powerfully argued by Bretherton (1984, p. 36): 'I suggest that the ability to engage in "serious" mental trial and error ("what if I did it this way rather than that way") and the ability to engage in make-believe are two different facets of the same representational function.' And she adds:

> I suggest that the ability to create symbolic alternatives to reality and to play with that ability is as deeply a part of human experience as the ability to construct an adapted model of everyday reality. Indeed, the successful building of accurate models may often involve prior play with a number of alternative possibilities.

> (ibid., p. 38)

It appears that in such pretend play children exercise their ability to think, to form abstractions. In make-believe play they begin to direct their thoughts at will to reflect, take apart, jumble up and rearrange, in abstract, symbolic form, bits and pieces of their expanding real world. Children have a powerful urge to fantasize, to reinterpret reality at will. It is an urge we seem not to outgrow.

The third aspect of play to be discussed is that play often involves others, it is greatly enjoyed in pairs or in groups. The social significance of play and through play the significance of the social world in the development of children goes to the heart of the major debate about the nature of intellectual development. It is well known that the two most influential theorists of child development, Piaget (1962) and Vygotsky (1962), approached the role of social interaction from different vantage points. Piaget is often accused of underestimating the importance of the social context (Fisher, 1980), and Vygotsky is seen as stressing it:

> The primary difference between the two theories is their localization of the
> 'site' of the construction of knowledge. According to Piaget, the child is the
> architect of his or her knowledge about the world ... Vygotsky's position shifts
> the emphasis from the child-as-architect and instead attributes primary impor-
> tance to the social context in the process of cognitive development.
>
> (O'Connell and Bretherton, 1984, p. 338)

Although O'Connell and Bretherton (1984) argue that the views of Piaget
and Vygotsky are less polarized than it would seem superficially, there
has been a shift in recent years towards what has been termed a 'script-
model' of knowledge (Mandler, 1979; Nelson, 1981). According to these
theorists young children acquire knowledge through participation in
social interaction.

Research into early infancy suggests that from the very start babies take
particularly keen interest in their social world. This fascination goes well
beyond the purely functional – needing to be fed, cleaned and kept warm.
Even a physically contented baby finds people more interesting than
objects or toys. It is argued that the first construction of meanings and
primary intentionality develops from the child's early interactions with
care-givers, 'because mothers *impute* meaning to "behaviours" elicited
from infants that these eventually do come to constitute meaningful
actions as far as the child himself is concerned' (Newson, 1979, p. 94).

Social play in infancy, play between mother and baby, has been extensively studied and has become a paradigm for the exploration of the
development of early communication, the precursor of language. Early,
ritualized games like 'peek-a-boo' were analysed in an influential paper
by Bruner (1975) who stressed two important aspects. One of these is the
'scaffolding role' of the mother, who helps the baby to develop a shared
focus of attention; and the other is that, no matter how brief and simple
the play sequence, it is based on 'rules'. In these early ritualized play
sequences the mother–child pair practise turn-taking, a rule which is the
prerequisite of dialogue.

Social play continues to remain attractive throughout childhood. As the
child grows older, the size of groups playing with each other may grow
bigger, and the play itself can become more varied, sustained over longer
periods of time and increasing in complexity. However, no matter what
the age of the children, or the level of their interactive play, the central
components are the same; the players have to communicate, share their
intentions and follow the rules of the play. The creation and sharing of
rules may be seen as the most important learning function of sociodramatic play. Children's 'rules' may be a far cry from the kinds of rules
adults use in formalized game-structures as in chess or football. In children's play the rules may initially be created spontaneously and these
are 'picked up' by the partners. They may or may not be stated explicitly, they may be short lived, suddenly dropped or arbitrarily altered
(Garvey, 1979).

The success of social play requires sensitive awareness to social signals (Blurton-Jones, 1967), the ability to accept or make acceptable contributions to the rules which operate at any moment and to share in each other's imaginings. To sustain co-operatively imaginary sequences of play events, to complement appropriately each other's fantasies is no mean achievement. In social play children appear to make use of and challenge their developing symbolic competencies to the full. Sociodramatic play is seen to be at the heart of the human heritage of culture-creation and culture-use.

We started with the contention that children love learning and children love playing. It is suggested that the two occur together spontaneously. Some important 'learning' relates to the development of flexible thinking, symbolization and the creation of rules. All three are at the heart of human intelligence. However, there is a further point we need to examine in some detail. The very quality of learning, its speed and intensity may be linked with something very basic: the role of *intention in learning*. Put in other words: who is the initiator? the planner? the decision maker? Whose question is it we are trying to answer? Do all children need to initiate at times and to follow at other times? Is the balance right in our schools? Has self-initiated play a contribution to make here? Before we tackle these questions, we need to take a seemingly bizarre detour.

Cats, goggles and children

The detour to be made here includes a brief look at the work of Nobel Prize-winning scientists, Hubel and Wiesel (1962). This research does not relate to children in any direct sense. Their famous experiments deal with the perceptual system of cats. The neurophysiological issues are not the subject matter of this chapter. However, these ingenious experiments inescapably trigger speculation which may have a bearing on the present argument. The issue we wish to pick up is the role of self-directed action in learning. It is tempting to speculate that if scientists can demonstrate that the self-directed action of cats affects their ability to learn, then volition in humans may have even more powerful effects on human learning. A word of caution may be in order here: the jump from cats to humans is a large, imaginative leap and it needs to be treated as such. To speculate is fun, it may be illuminating, but it should not be confused with 'evidence'.

Kittens are born blind. This is why Hubel and Wiesel chose them to investigate the role of stimulation on the development of vision. Some kittens were exposed only to vertical, others only to horizontal lines, as they began to open their eyes. By varying these conditions, Hubel and Wiesel succeeded in demonstrating the effects particular features of the environment produced on the visual cortex of the kittens. It was found, not surprisingly, that the deprived kittens were facing problems when they entered the ordinary, fully lit world. The kittens who received only 'horizontal' visual input, when put into an ordinary room, were unable to see vertical lines. They bumped into the legs of chairs and tables, but could jump on to the seat of a stool. The kittens who received vertical stimulation, on the other hand, did the opposite: they moved between the legs of the furniture with ease, but found it difficult to locate a plate of milk. These problems, however, disappeared remarkably soon, once the kittens resumed 'normal' living.

It was this latter point, the quick readaptation to the normal environment, which intrigued Richard Held and his colleagues (Held and Hein, 1963). They set out to investigate the mechanisms involved in learning to adapt to changing visual input. They had a hunch that the animals' free movements in the real world facilitate the rehabilitation of the visual system. Ingenious experiments were devised in which pairs of scientifically 'matched' kittens were exposed to the same visual stimuli, with one difference – one kitten could move around in a given space freely, whereas the other kitten 'travelled' the same distance on a 'gondola', a device into which the kitten was strapped and carried. Both kittens had the same visual input, the difference was that one kitten was actively moving about, the other was moving passively. The results showed remarkable differences in the kittens' ability to adapt to the real environment. The 'active' kittens could judge height and distance and could avoid collisions with objects straight away; the 'passive' kittens could not. The 'passive' kittens took several days to develop the same level of adaptation. Held came to the conclusion that 'an animal's own movements change what it sees and hears ... it is a key to developing and maintaining spatial orientation in advanced mammals' (Held, 1965, p. 84).

Important implications of these findings relate to the interconnectedness of motor and perceptual systems. For the present discussion the focus is the role of self-directed activity in the adjustments the kittens were achieving.

Follow-up experiments included a series dealing with people. These were based on the everyday experiences people have when they change a prescription for spectacles. Usually it takes a few days to get used to a new pair. Initially they seem to distort the world. Held proceeded to 'distort' the world quite dramatically, by devising goggles containing various kinds of prisms. These goggles could turn the world upside-down or make straight lines look curved. It is known (Kohler, 1962) that people wearing such distorting goggles readjust after a while and see things normally, the 'right way up'. However, when the goggles are removed, subjects experience temporary disorientation, in many ways similar to what the kittens experienced. Held studied the way people learnt to adjust to the goggles, and to readjust to the absence of the goggles.

These experiments also focused on the role of movement, on the differences in subjects who were either active in directing their own movements, or passive, being carried around. Some of the subjects were moved around in a wheelchair or on a trolley, others were walking around as they pleased. The results of these experiments (the series included several variations) were in line with previous findings:

> Again the degree of adaptation achieved by the subjects who had been involved in active movement was far greater than that of the subjects who had been carried in the wheelchair . . . In these circumstances several of the subjects who were able to move voluntarily achieved full adaptation, whereas subjects whose movements were passive achieved virtually no adaptation.
>
> (Held, 1965, p. 88)

Now let us turn to children. The argument proposed here is that if self-directed voluntary action has such a significant effect on learning at the neurophysiological level, it may not be far-fetched to suggest that there must be a powerful connection between self-initiated active involvement and the *quality* of learning at *all* levels of complexity. It is suggested that 'learning' moves into a 'different gear', it is more intense, sharper, quicker and it is probably also retained better when it occurs in conjunction with and not in spite of the person's own intentions. The phrase 'self-directed action' has now been replaced by the word 'intention'. This is to acknowledge that children's learning involves complex processes. In this context it would be a mistake to assume that 'self-directed action' refers simply to physical movement. Intentions are rather more subtle forms of 'self-directed acts'. They may be seen as the active engagements of the mind, actions which direct attention and thought.

It is, of course, a truism that teachers cannot teach unless the children want to learn. Gagne (1969) called attention to the essential role of motivation, and so do most educational theorists. Are we going round in circles, have we made a 'detour', just to make the same point? Yes, and no. It is the same issue, but we have arrived at it from different starting points and draw from it different conclusions. What a particular writer takes to be the most acceptable 'model' of the child determines the starting point. These were discussed earlier. What are the differences in conclusions?

It is easy to pay lip service to the importance of motivation. In practice, however, this is surprisingly often overlooked. The experiments with kittens and goggles were discussed here to underline the *fundamental* importance of personal involvement for the *quality* of learning. Once it is fully understood how powerfully such personal involvement may affect children's abilities to organize their own understanding, the conclusion must be that children's intentions, their self-directed active engagements, have to be given serious consideration in education. In practice, however, often the opposite takes place. Instead of continuing and encouraging children's spontaneous involvements, we ask them to stop, to push aside *their* intentions. We redirect the children, we ask them to follow *our* intentions. We create a break in what the children are already interested in – no wonder we then have to spend a great deal of effort trying to remotivate the children, trying to get them to work up enthusiasm for the preselected 'objectives' we are interested in. It is the contention of the present argument that such teaching strategies are counterproductive. They not only waste the teacher's time, they also mitigate against the development of robust, alert thinking. They prepare the way for the schism which poisons much of school learning. This is how a six-year-old – as reported by the teacher – expressed the meaning of the schism: 'I learn everything I want to know from my mum, I learn everything I don't want to know in school.'

To avoid such a schism, play must be an integral part of the school curriculum. It is in play that much of children's self-initiated, voluntary, active learning is expressed, it is in play that children explore what 'they want to know'.

Sharing intentions in the classroom

Children do not live in a world of their own. They live in 'our world'. Adults, parents and teachers inhabit the same space the children do. There are no horizontal divides, invisible cut-off points between child level and others higher up. We share the same world. Children are not born into 'the world', they are born into 'our world', and it is the social world towards which young children are uniquely drawn. The initial social orientation, which forms the basis of children's interests and learning in the early years, continues when they grow into school age. Shields (1983, p. 19) puts this view succinctly:

> They [the children] learn what sequences of behaviours go with which sphere of activity, how to play the appropriate role in reciprocity with others, how to play the role of daughter or son or older or younger brother or sister, how to play pupil role in relation to teachers . . . we must recognize that what we do is defining a culture for the adult-watching child. We are creating his expected role. We are displaying the expected role of teachers, the expected procedures of nurseries and classrooms, what is done in them and what is not done in them, what can be expected of teaching, what counts as learning, what skills are important, what is valuable and what is trivial.

The most obvious indicator of what is 'valuable and what is trivial' in the classroom is the teacher's attention. What teachers are involved with and what they spend their time with defines what is valued more clearly than the occasional praise, nod or reprimand. There may be considerable gaps between what some schools claim to value and what the children perceive as being valued. This is often the case regarding play. Many schools support the view that play should be given a place in the school day. Accordingly, children are given time to play. The point is: *when* are they playing? In some infant schools the mornings are for work, the afternoons for play, or free-choice activities. In other schools there are no definite times assigned for work or play. Children are expected to complete the 'work' assigned by the teacher and, when they have finished it, they are allowed to play. Individual children may spend different amounts of time playing and working, depending on their level of ability, speed of working etc. In all these situations children play *after* they have finished working. Work is what children do with the teacher, guided and supervised by the teacher; play is what they do on their own, as they please. Work and learning are thus separated from playing and having fun. Work is the serious business. This is what children come to school for, this is what education is about. Play is recreation, the carrot, the reward. If you work well, you will be allowed to play. The views of play implied here are: that play should be allowed for recreation; that play can be used as a reward (or bribe?); that learning and play are separate.

This, in our view, is a misinterpretation and misuse of the educational significance of play. In the situation described, the message for the 'adult-watching child' must be that what constitutes important learning is initiated by the teachers. What the children initiate (which is largely expressed in play) is not so important; it is less valued. Children, then, cannot see themselves as planners, as proposers, as participators in decision-making.

Sometimes the self-directing aspect of learning is given safe haven in the so-called creative or art activities, when children are encouraged or left to 'do as they like'. So far, so good – but the crunch comes when you look at the walls, the displays, the work taken to assembly. More often than not, these prestigious events are reserved exclusively for projects, themes and topics initiated by the adults. Children get the message quickly. Such acts are not value-free. The children's active, self-directing role gradually has to give way to a more passive role of following instructions. Learning to follow instructions is of course hugely important. The point being made here is the question of balance: does one type of pupil role dominate, almost to the exclusion of the other?

In some regimes the intentions of the teacher dominate, they have over-riding importance most of the time. If children can fit their intentions in with those of the teacher, well and good. The teacher very seldom makes an attempt in the opposite direction to try to fit in with the intentions of children.

For the latter to occur, at least some of the time, the classroom climate has to allow for play that is taken *seriously* by the teacher. This may sound like a contradiction in terms, as play is said to be 'non-serious' by definition. Teachers who take play seriously are not dominating children's play, they are paying serious attention to it. There cannot be educational justification for play which occurs at the periphery of the teachers' attention, with unattractive, over-used materials, to be shared by large numbers of children for short bouts of time. This is often called 'just messing around', and it easily deteriorates into chaos, or bored, idle, unproductive filling in of time.

The kind of play we seek educational justification for is the meeting ground where children and teachers *share intentions*. It is suggested that, by catering for, attending to, participating in, contributing to and challenging the play involvement of children, teachers are able to create the context in which each other's intentions can be understood, elaborated and jointly moved forward. This implies, of course, that the teacher has a direction in mind, it is the perspective of the professional adult who knows more than the child does. It is a delicate task and it requires professional skills. The idea of 'moving forward' can easily deteriorate into 'hijacking' the child's intentions, turning them upside-down to smuggle in our own. Many 'play-way' teaching tricks seem to be doing just that. What is suggested here is very different. It is a genuine attempt to share and elaborate intentions jointly rather than trying to impose the teacher's will on the child through the back door. To meet the child half-way is not an abdication of the teaching function. On the contrary, it is an attempt to maximize the effectiveness of teaching. Much research highlights the intuitive understanding of most practitioners: that to teach well the teacher has to start from where the child is.

This 'basic truth' has been discussed in the literature under various labels: as the 'problem of the match' (Hunt, 1963), the 'discrepancy principle' (Kagan, 1972), as 'cognitive disequilibrium' (Piaget, 1969) and as the role of the 'contingent adult' in teaching (Wood, McMahon and Cranstoun, 1980; Wells, 1983), etc. In all these discussions the central issue is the link between the child's and the adult's thinking. Good teachers attempt to make their teaching 'contingent' upon the children's growing understanding. By including play in the mainstream of the curriculum in the primary schools, children and teachers are given the opportunity to work together towards shared goals. Thus the children's early natural curiosity continues to remain an important motivator in the learning encountered at school. Teachers and children become partners in the joint endeavour.

A word of caution: this is not a suggestion that teaching should be based on 'discovery' or 'activity methods'. Nor is it a proposal to make education centre on 'children's interests'. It is a suggestion for *sharing* initiatives. Sharing implies that the teacher is a significant contributor in all these encounters. It was stressed earlier that for children the most interesting aspect of the environment is the social world, particularly the adult world. Even babies seem to be 'going for it' with avid curiosity and attention. Parents make excellent teachers (they teach children their mother tongue) probably because they intimately share everyday experiences with their children and also because they provide a glimpse of how the adult world ticks. Parents and adults know how to operate things: they make things happen; they make things work. Parents also make demands on their children, they have expectations. They also instruct, tell and show how. Teachers, by definition, are to do these things in an organized, efficient manner. Indeed, it would be a very strange teacher who would not demand, instruct, give information and show how things are done. This is expected, not least by the children themselves. Some well-meaning educators in their anxiety to meet children half-way, have gone to the extent of actually withholding information, in fear of imposing ideas on the children. These teachers have got into a habit of replying to children's quests for help with 'work it out for yourself'. When is it reasonable to expect just that, and when is it educational to give the answer, or show the best way of doing something? This is the professional judgement teachers have to make in each instance. It is a mistake to interpret the argument for play as an attempt to minimize teacher input.

To argue for giving a greater share in the curriculum to the children in initiating their own involvements is to argue for a better *balance* between what is proposed by the adult and what is proposed by the child. This will bring home to children that their own initiatives are valued, that they are not trivial. This will also help the teachers to come closer to the children's ways of thinking. Teachers cannot know children as intimately as parents do. It is particularly important for teachers to pay attention to children's play, because it is there that opportunities for mutual sharing of ideas are maximized. To give time for play in school is not to give a 'break' or rest from learning, it is not a concession to immature minds. Rather it is a way of making teaching and learning more productive. Vygotsky (1962) suggested that instruction is most effective when it is addressed to the child's 'zone of proximal development'. How can a teacher know where the child's 'zone of proximal development' is? Perhaps the attempt to find out is not so much a matter of measurements, of mapping out a 'zone' with precision instruments (tests and scores). Rather it is a matter of paying attention to the situations where the 'zone of proximal development' most naturally manifests itself: in the play of children.

Every teacher knows how important it is to come to know the new child entering school. You cannot begin to teach, unless you have formed some ideas about what it is the child is capable of, what it is the child already knows. This is particularly important when the new entrants are barely over four years old. It is obvious that younger children are generally less articulate than the older ones. This means that the teacher, in trying to assess their level of development, may get a very distorted picture if he or she relies primarily on what children say. Often the child's true understanding is far more sophisticated than what may be glimpsed from the answers they give to adult questions.

A far more reliable picture emerges in the play of four-year-olds. Therefore, it is particularly important for play to continue in reception classes. The communication between teacher and child in play settings should not only facilitate the teacher's assessment of the child, it should also help in making the teacher's input relevant to the child in a

familiar play context. Thus, it should enhance new learning, provided that
the teacher is skilful enough to integrate the teaching of new concepts with
children's spontaneous play activities. Much frustration, boredom and
time-wasting may be avoided if teachers focus on the educational significance of play. This brings us to the final point of this chapter.

Conclusions – the economic argument for play

This chapter argues for having play in school. The proposition is not new,
it has been presented in several forms in the past with various emphases
and varied reasoning. Some of these may be summarized as follows:

1. The romantic argument – the concern is for the 'whole child'. If children feel 'happy' while playing, then every effort needs to be made
   to provide them with play opportunities.
2. The behaviourist argument – play is enjoyable, it acts as a reward. The
   educator needs to control it judiciously. After a certain amount of
   learning, children deserve to play.
3. The therapeutic argument – children struggle with fears and anxieties.
   In play they are able to express and overcome these. Therefore play
   should be provided for better mental hygiene.
4. The cognitive argument – children learn to solve problems, to think
   creatively, to communicate, they learn social rules while playing. For
   all these desirable learning outcomes play should be encouraged.

Reduced to brief statements here, these are the arguments most frequently encountered in the literature. We wish to add a further argument
to the above, the economic argument for having play in school. This may
sound rather dry in comparison with the starting hopes to 'define rainbows and hunt for pots of gold' (Burghardt, 1984). No rainbows have
been defined and pots of gold remain hidden. A turn to economic considerations reflects our times.

The economic argument suggests that the management of learning in
the classroom is most efficient when play is included and valued in the
curriculum. Efficiency is enhanced because teachers have to spend less
time trying to motivate children to learn; because teaching is more effective as teachers achieve a better 'fit' between their instruction/explana-
tion and the child's thinking; because the quality of the child's learning
is enhanced when it is in tune with self-directed, voluntary involvement.

For these reasons, to use present-day jargon, the inclusion of play is 'cost-
effective'. It is not so, on the contrary, it is a waste of money and time, if
teachers merely tolerate play at the periphery of their attention. Inclusion
of play in the curriculum does not mean the substitution of instruction by
teacher involvement in children's play. As argued earlier, the efficient management of learning includes both, and requires a better balance between
teacher-initiated and child-initiated pursuits in the classroom.

We do not know precisely what the knowledge is and the skills are that the children of today will most need in the future. Flexibility, confidence and the ability to think for oneself – these are the attributes one hopes will not let them down. If play is conducive to the development of these, we had better have it in school.

Suggested further reading

Paley, V. G. (1992) *You Can't Say, You Can't Play*, Harvard University Press, Cambridge, Mass.

4

The Equal Opportunities Curriculum

Celia Burgess-Macey and Kerry Crichlow[1]

Our starting point for this chapter is the belief that equality should be at the centre of quality early years provision. Children's cultural, linguistic, class and gender backgrounds are not an optional extra for early years practitioners to consider – rather they are central to an understanding of the child's development and achievement, and to the development of a broad, balanced and relevant curriculum.

We will start by reviewing some recent research that in itself reinforces previous evidence. We will go on to consider recent changes to the legislative framework for childcare and education which has had an impact on the provision of services. In particular we will focus on education legislation, the Children Act, statutory monitoring and assessment procedures and the new draft guidelines for desirable outcomes for children learning. We will then look at some issues that practitioners will need to consider, together with some examples of practical strategies.

The view that equalities are central to quality early years provision is not new or radical. A range of international, national and local policy and guidance documents, from both the statutory and voluntary sector, make specific reference to the need to make equality of opportunity a reality for children and their parents and carers. The United Nations Convention on the Rights of the Child Article 29 states quite clearly that all children have a right to have their cultural and linguistic identities recognized and protected and that they should receive support from all care and education institutions and all those concerned with their care and education for the development of their language and community identities:

> The education of the child shall be directed to the development of respect for the child's parents, his or her own cultural identity, cultural language and values . . . and for civilisations different from his or her own . . . the preparation of the child for responsible life in a free society, in the spirit of understanding,

peace, tolerance, equality of the sexes and friendship among all peoples, ethnic and religious groups and persons of indigenous origin.

(United Nations, 1989, p. 75)

The Report of the Committee of Inquiry into the Quality of the Educational Experience offered to 3- and 4-year-olds (DES, 1990a, p. 7) makes the point that 'educators should recognise and respond to the diversity of society, and the need to avoid stereotyping on the basis of race, sex and special needs'. The following extract from the Northumberland County Council Curriculum Guidance for the early years is typical of many. *Maintaining the Balance* sets out key principles for learning and experience which include the following:

> The curriculum must ensure the entitlement of all children to a broad and balanced curriculum so that none are disadvantaged because of their gender, race, social background, learning needs or disability.
>
> (Northumberland County Council, 1993, p. 3)

In its guidance document, *Equal Chances – Eliminating discrimination and ensuring equality in playgroups*, the Pre-School Learning Alliance (formerly Pre-school Playgroups Association) states:

> Children have a right to grow up and learn in an environment free from prejudice and without discrimination. We know that without this freedom their development will be damaged.
>
> (PPA, 1991, p. 5)

The task for practitioners is to translate these well established principles into action, as has always been the case. We have seen many individual and collective initiatives through which practitioners have struggled to do justice to these principles in their practice. In response to an increased interest in and focus on the early years curriculum over the last five years, many Local Authorities have produced clear and detailed guidance which aims to help staff review and improve their provision. The main emphasis of these documents is on the responsibility of the adults who work with young children to develop the whole child, including his or her social and personal development, to build on his or her previous experience, including cultural and linguistic experience through active learning, exploration and play.

> In a diverse society it is particularly important that we look critically at play and social mixing. We need to be aware that there may be an equal opportunities dimension where children are seen to be dominant, withdrawn, dependent or isolated.
>
> (Early Years Guidelines, Hillingdon Education and Social Services, 1994, p. 13)

The documents also stress the need to do all the above in partnership with parents. These messages are in stark contrast to those given in recent government education legislation. Despite the existence of such excellent documentation, in practice there is a tendency for practitioners to take up those aspects of equalities which are easier to implement, such as including resources from diverse cultures in the book and imaginative play area, or involving mothers on a one-off basis in multicultural cooking activities, rather than looking at the more difficult aspects of their adult role such as challenging discriminatory remarks by children, or entering into a genuine dialogue with parents which would allow parents to challenge established and accepted practices. The multi-cultural aspects of curriculum development have sometimes been highlighted at the expense of implementing the anti-racist agenda of challenging attitudes, assumptions and power relationships. Thinking about these wider issues needs to be included at the planning stage and staff need to support each other in identifying how they meet them.

For example, a teacher had planned that the children would make and eat samosas. When a white child refused to take part in the activity because this was `Paki food' the teacher did not know how to respond and simply reprimanded the child 'Don't be rude'. The child then departed for another activity leaving the teacher feeling uncomfortable and Asian children in the group feeling upset, quite possibly wishing that the activity had been to make sandwiches. The teacher who knows his or her children will anticipate this kind of remark and be able to place it in the context of a discussion about the different foods we all eat and the need to value and learn about different ways of approaching the same basic human need. He or she will also be able to calmly reassure the black children about the value that the setting places on their cultural and family experiences. She will need to remind the white child that the words he or she has used, but not the child him or herself, are unacceptable and that they represent values that the adults in the setting reject. He or she will point out that the child has hurt other children's feelings and give him or her the chance to apologise. If this remark is not an isolated incident he or she will need to discuss it with other staff, so that they can make a positive response, and also discuss the school policy and approach to learning together with the child's parent or carer. He or she may need to evaluate his or her own practice and next time he or she plans to introduce food from other cultures he or she may start from the children's interests in what they eat, talk about sameness as well as difference, talk about the problem all people have when they want to take food for a journey, discuss different types of portable foods and different containers for the food to be carried in. The children may make several types of pasty, Cornish pasty, Jamaican pattie, samosas, filled pitta breads, sandwiches, butties, pizzas as well as design containers for them.

At another school, staff observed that a disproportionate number of black boys were being sent to the head teacher. They decided to review their behaviour policy in discussion with the children. One thing they discovered was that behaviour such as 'cutting your eye' and 'kissing your teeth' were considered disrespectful by black parents and children, but were accepted by many white teachers who were unclear how to interpret such behaviour. As a result the behaviour policy was amended to make it clear to all children.

At an infant school, a teacher was able to use her facility to use three Asian languages as part of her communicative strategies in the classroom. This behaviour changed the views of all the children who came to accept that being bilingual was natural and retained this view even after they moved further up the school.

Research shows that it is necessary to reflect on our responses to examples such as these:

> The cumulative effects of teachers' attitudes towards Asian children was to create a feeling of insecurity for these children in the classroom . . . they were extremely unpopular among their white peers . . . Such responses tended to counteract the positive attempts by teachers to address multicultural issues and led to ambivalence from Asian children on curriculum topics or school celebrations focusing on aspects of their tradition or customs. On the one hand they expressed pride in having aspects of these acknowledged in school. Yet on the other they were concerned that this often exacerbated the teasing, ridicule and harassment which they felt they received daily.
>
> (Wright, 1992, p. 12)

Recent research

There is considerable research evidence and data which focuses on the impact of racism on the educational experiences of young black people. However, most of this research relates to secondary age pupils, and for this reason many early years practitioners have felt that this evidence has little relevance for their work with under eights. There has been a reluctance, in part stemming from a false view of childhood as a time of innocence, free from the harsh influences of the adult world and adult views, to recognise that children from birth are social and cultural beings learning how to make sense of their world in the rich context of family community and society. In a racist, sexist and class society, children must begin to interpret from a very young age what it means to be black, white, female, disabled, rich or poor, a refugee and so on.

Cecile Wright's (1992) research was conducted in nursery and primary schools and is significant in its focus on the adult role and response. She showed that adults refused to confront overt racism experienced by children, even when they were aware of it, and often themselves had very negative stereotypes of different groups of black children. Her finding that African Caribbean boys were particularly the targets of criticisms by teachers is reinforced by our own observations in schools. She noted that 'Afro-Caribbean boys were generally associated with aggressive, disobedient and distractible behaviour' (Wright, 1992, p. 12). She found that in some cases boys had acquired their reputation for being extremely disruptive in the nursery and that from staffroom conversations teachers had low and prejudiced expectations of them from the start of school. Rastafarian children were prone to experience particular prejudice. In the current worrying trend towards excluding children from school earlier in their school careers (as early as in their first week in Reception class), it will be important to monitor the disproportionate numbers of black boys within these overall figures. An essential point made by Wright is that black children's emotional, intellectual and social development is impeded by racism, and that this will continue to disadvantage them throughout their school careers.

In her excellent book, *The Early Years: Laying the Foundations for Racial Equality*, Iram Siraj-Blatchford states that 'the most common form of racism young Black children experience is through racist name calling or through negative references by white children or adults to their colour, language or culture' (1994, p. 9). She refers readers to the research evidence which indicates that racist name calling is of particular cause for concern (Kelly and Cohn, 1988; Troyna and Hatcher, 1992). We would endorse Siraj-Blatchford's broad conclusions that it is vitally important that racial inequalities are challenged in the early years, and that to do this practitioners need to have some understanding of the causes and roots of racism.

It needs to be recognized that racism is damaging for white as well as black children, and the issues are as pertinent for all-white schools as they are for multi-ethnic schools (Troyna and Hatcher, 1992). The National Childminding Association has confronted this issue in its anti-racist policy statement which states, 'Racism damages all children, white and Black: it disadvantages white children by giving them a false sense of superiority and a distorted picture of the world they live in'.

In their useful book, *Where it really matters*, Epstein and Sealey describe strategies for developing anti-racist education in predominantly white primary schools. They conclude, 'in order to respond to the needs of all children teachers have to be able to understand racism, how it works and what its effects are' (1990, p. 18).

It is especially important for all adults working in the early years to develop strategies to challenge racism. All the important and intimate cultural practices associated with family and community life are source material for children's play. In play children test out new roles, meanings and behaviours. If children cannot play without fear of ridicule how can they learn in an atmosphere free from fear. In the conclusions of the government report, *Education for All*, the Swann committee argued that

> The fundamental change that is necessary is the recognition that the problem facing the education system is not how to educate the children of ethnic minorities, but how to educate all children.

(DES, 1985b, p. 769)

The legislative context

The Children Act

The Children Act 1991 is a milestone in that it is the first piece of legislation affecting young children which makes specific reference to racial equality. The Act places a duty on local authorities to consider racial group and identity and the linguistic groupings to which children belong in making arrangements for their care. In inspecting day care facilities, local authorities have the power to consider whether the care provided is seriously inadequate with regard to a child's religious persuasion, racial origin and cultural and linguistic background. The fact that this is seen as central to providing quality care gives legislative weight to those organizations, bodies and individuals who have argued this case for many years.

The Education Reform Act 1988

One of the main implications of the Education Reform Act for equal opportunities relates to the decreased power of Local Education Authorities (LEAs). It was LEAs who had promoted policies on multicultural education and equal opportunities. Significantly, one of the most high profile LEAs in this area was the Inner London Education Authority, which was specifically abolished under the Act. Support for equal opportunities work in the early years often came from advisory services, which have been decimated as a result of cumulative budget cuts by central government and the requirement to delegate increasing amounts of central funds to schools. Tighter controls on the ways in which LEAs are allowed to spend central government funding for staff and curriculum development have increasingly excluded both early years and equal opportunities as these are not subjects of the National Curriculum.

Local management of schools (LMS) links a school's budget directly to the number of pupils on roll. One consequence of this is that there is pressure to admit four-year-olds into primary school classes before the statutory age, whether or not they have appropriate staffing ratios and curricula for such young children. There are several equalities aspects to be unpicked here. There is considerable evidence that early admission to formal schooling does not accelerate learning (Barrett, 1986; Willes, 1983; Early Years Curriculum Group, 1995; Sharp, Hutchinson and Whetton, 1994). The need for children to have access to a developmentally appropriate curriculum is supported by recent research in Southwark and Birmingham LEAs which shows that children, especially those who are developing bilingual learners, benefit from spending time in pre-school education settings.

It must be recognized that there are pressures on particular groups of parents to want early admission to school, relating to their own needs for

free, quality full time care for their children. This would disproportion-
ately push working class parents, for example, into opting for early admission to primary school since the lack of affordable childcare, particularly
in cities and urban areas is well documented. There is also mounting evidence across the country that parents have been pressurised into taking
their children out of pre-school care and education settings with which
they were perfectly satisfied, by threats from primary school heads with
early admission policies. Parents fear that, if their child is not admitted
then, there will not be a place for him or her in the school of their choice
later. Although this trend has an impact on all parents, there has been particular pressure on the parents of ethnic minority children, who already
may be aware that their children are likely to be disadvantaged in terms
of achievement in primary school and later. Their own experience of school
in this country, or the cumulative community knowledge which has existed
since Bernard Coard (1971) wrote the seminal text, *How the West Indian
Child is made Sub-Normal in the British School System*, will have taught them
to be vigilant in trying to get the best deal for their child. Early admission
to primary school may therefore seem attractive. In inner city areas such
as the ones in which we have worked, some black and ethnic minority
parents choose to send their children to private schools with traditional
approaches to learning and often higher pupil–teacher ratios than comparable state schools. The reasons for this are complex, often relating to
parents' reflections on their own schooling or a perception that by becoming consumers in the private market they wield more power in placing
demands upon the school. The private sector often trades upon the class
inequalities present in the British education system, where there are distinct and separate curricula for the public and the private sectors. Nowhere
is this more apparent than in the Caribbean itself, whose education infra-
structure closely mirrors the British class system. Needless to say, the curriculum in private schools is far from multicultural.

LMS gives responsibility to governing bodies for managing the entire
school budget and deciding priorities in terms of how they direct those
resources. The Office for Standards in Education's *Framework for the
Inspection of Schools* (OFSTED, 1993), identifies an efficient school as one
which makes the best use of all available resources to achieve high educational outcomes.

In terms of equality of opportunity for young children in primary
schools, the effect of this huge shift of responsibility for deciding on broad
priorities for spending from a local framework to the individual school
can be as simple as recognizing, or refusing to recognize, the particular
resourcing needs of a quality early years curriculum. A recent OFSTED
report on an LEA nursery school commented that the unit costs per pupil
were high, but that the standards achieved by all children in the school,
including the one third with special educational needs, indicated that the
school provided good value for money (OFSTED Inspection of Ethelred

Nursery School, 1995). Without a practical commitment of resources to a quality early years curriculum, there cannot be equality of opportunity for those children who have historically been denied access to their entitlement.

The National Curriculum

The Education Reform Act 1988 describes the National Curriculum as a basic entitlement for children to a broad and balanced curriculum. It is therefore very sad that in the National Curriculum programmes of study, the multicultural dimension is almost entirely lacking. This is even more true now the original orders have been revised. Firstly, the revised curriculum has also done little or nothing to address the needs of bilingual pupils, despite the fact that in the consultation process many LEAs and other educational organizations made recommendations on this issue, and that research evidence from several countries shows the educational value of children's maintaining and increasing their competence as speakers, readers and writers of more that one language. For young children it is particularly indefensible to ignore and diminish their home or community language. In the new English orders (DFE, 1995b) and in the draft Guidance on Desirable Outcomes for Pre-school Education (SCAA, 1995a), those references to promoting awareness of children's additional languages have mainly been removed. The value of a child's competence in its own community language is reduced to a tool for learning to speak English rather than as of value in its own right, and the primacy of standard English is reasserted. 'The richness of dialects and other languages can make an *important contribution to pupils' knowledge and understanding of standard English'* (DFE, 1995b, own emphasis).

Secondly, in the original National Curriculum Council Guidelines (NCC, 1990), certain cross curricular themes and dimensions were included as 'official clarification of the educational aims set out in the Act' (Runnymeade Trust, 1993, p. 5). They included citizenship, health education, multicultural and gender issues and personal and social education. Multicultural education in particular was seen as 'a dimension which permeates the whole curriculum' (NCC, 1990). Unfortunately, this good intention has been undermined in subsequent publications from the School Curriculum and Assessment Authority (SCAA), which replaced the NCC, and the Department for Education (DFE). The change in the emphasis placed on multicultural education between the original and revised curriculum orders is most marked in technology. The original Non-Statutory Guidance stated:

> Design and technology has an important part to play in preparing pupils for life in a multi-cultural society . . . It is equally important that schools where there are few or no ethnic minority pupils ensure that their pupils understand the cultural diversity of modern society . . . There are rich opportunities to

demonstrate that no one culture has a monopoly of achievements in design and technology.

(DES, 1990b, p. B3)

This approach was reflected in the attainment targets which stated that children needed to know 'that in the past and in other cultures people have used design and technology to solve familiar problems in different ways' (AT1) and 'draw information about materials, people, markets and processes and from other times and cultures to help in developing their ideas' (AT2). In the revised new orders *all* references to technology from other cultures have been removed.

Even where the few remaining references to the multicultural dimension of the National Curriculum are made, such as in the programmes of study for art and music, they are vague and undeveloped statements. For example, the single statement on the need to include 'the richness of our diverse cultural heritage' (DFE, 1995c, 1995d) does not reflect the innovative ways in which many teachers and other adults working with young children have challenged the Eurocentric bias of the traditional curriculum. This represents a backward step.

The Inspection Framework

The original and revised Handbook for the Inspection of Schools (OFSTED, 1993) required that arrangements for equality of opportunity be considered when making judgements on 'the extent to which the particular needs of individual pupils and groups of pupils arising from gender, ability, ethnicity and social circumstance, are met' (OFSTED, 1993, p. 56). It specified detailed areas for consideration including school policy statements, admissions policies, pupil groupings, curriculum content, resources, access to the curriculum and pastoral provision. The guidance on the curriculum for under fives says:

> the curriculum for under fives should be broad and balanced with a strong emphasis on children's social, linguistic and physical development and on learning through enquiry, talking and playing ... Where pupils speak English as a second language, inspection should take account of how well the teaching and programme has been adapted to meet their needs.

Inspectors who were aware of the issues involved could use the Framework to comment positively on schools as the following example from Ethelred Nursery demonstrates:

> There is a high level of awareness of the issues involved by all who work in the school and the understanding is shared by parents who express satisfaction with, and support for, the healthy attitudes to race that are exhibited by all the children. The school values the diversity of its community and makes this apparent in a number of ways.
>
> (OFSTED Inspection of Ethelred Nursery School, 1995)

When 71 OFSTED reports were analysed by LEA Advisers for Equal Opportunities it 'sharply revealed variation in approaches to equal opportunities. The key issues were the use of language and the tone either to value the cultural and linguistic diversity of the pupil intake or to problematise it . . . In some reports no mention was made of pupils' cultural heritage' (Minhas, 1994, p. 90).

A new shortened OFSTED Framework is about to be published. Not only have the separate sections on Equality of Opportunity and Special Education Needs been completely removed, but these considerations have mainly to be addressed in Leadership and Management and Efficiency sections, not in relationship to the curriculum offered to the children. Also, Inspectors will not longer be required to report separately on 'Quality of Learning'. This section often included comments on children's motivation, interest and relevance of learning to cultural and community interest.

This is very bad news indeed. It therefore comes as no surprise that the 1995 Discussion Paper on Quality Assurance Regime for Institutions which Redeem Pre-school Education Vouchers (DFEE, 1995) makes no reference to inspecting for equality of opportunity or multicultural issues, and, even where reference to the Children Act Guildelines is made, the sections of the Children Act on those issues are not referred to.

Planning

Fortunately, there are many examples of good practice in schools and early years settings which practitioners will need to draw on to reinfuse the National Curriculum with an equal opportunities perspective. The National Curriculum does not dictate the resources to be used, or the illustrative examples and activities selected to turn learning goals into actual learning for children. Teachers will have to add this in their planning. Many schools have included in their school curriculum policies and schemes of work, and in their long, medium and short term planning processes, the consideration of multicultural and equal opportunities issues. Many excellent practical suggestions exist in local guidelines and in those produced by organizations concerned with early years. The Early Years Curriculum Group has produced a booklet, *The Early Years Curriculum and the National Curriculum* (EYCG, 1989), which is helpful and the Runnymeade Trust book *Equality Assurance in Schools: Quality, Identity, Society* (1993) has made the most comprehensive attempt so far to suggest both key tasks for ensuring equality and setting out the knowledge, understanding, skills and attitudes that children will need for life in a diverse and interdependent world. For each subject area of the school curriculum they have set out indicators of good practice and examples of activities for each key stage.

The Planning Guide for Key Stages 1 and 2 produced by SCAA (1995b) makes no references to equal opportunities considerations in planning and the examples of units of work include none with a multicultural context. The section setting out planning tasks makes reference to the need to 'identify all aspects of the school curriculum' (p. 32), and lists eight points to consider in reaching decisions. None include any equal opportunities issues and although school examples cite policies on 'aspects of personal, social and moral education' (ibid., p. 33), the term cultural has disappeared entirely from the agenda, as has the term diversity.

When challenged about this omission at a presentation to head teachers, an officer from SCAA said that the schools could 'use their flexible time' to include multicultural education. This approach entirely undermines a perspective that sees it as a dimension within all areas of the curriculum which was the guidance previously issued by the NCC on cross curricular themes (NCC, 1990). A similar absence of an equal opportunities perspective is apparent in the SCAA draft Guidance for Providers on pre-school education (SCAA, 1995a). The sections on desirable outcomes include personal and social development (again note the lack of cultural) which includes no outcomes related to self-esteem as a member of a specific cultural group or to respect for the cultures, language and beliefs of others. 'Children respect others' is included, but respect without content is meaningless.

Young children's linguistic achievements are entirely limited to achievement in English, and early literacy to recognition of the English alphabet and to English print system. The 'Guidance for Providers' section is so thin in real content as to be useless and again in the 'Significant Features of Good Practice' there is no mention of equality of opportunity. All the examples of appropriate educational activities are from within mainstream Eurocentric cultural practice. Even where parents' contribution is acknowledged, a somewhat anachronistic and inaccurate example of a father growing oranges on his allotment has been selected. Many real and relevant contributions from parents have been rejected in favour of a romanticized view. With such a dearth of advice and support for multicultural approaches in official texts, early years practitioners will have to look elsewhere.

The way forward

The Early Childhood Education Forum is a national body coordinating the main organizations concerned with children 0–8 years old. They state in their agreed principles 'cultural and physical diversity should be respected and valued: a proactive anti-bias approach should be adopted and stereotypes challenged' (Minutes of Meeting).

To find examples of an anti-bias approach, it will be necessary for practitioners to look for materials produced by the Early Years Trainers Anti-Racist Network and Black Childcare Network as well as the previously mentioned Runnymeade Trust book. There are also useful publications produced by the National Children's Bureau, the Pre-School Learning Alliance and the National Voluntary Council on Children's Play.

We need to develop a multicultural curriculum within approaches to anti-racist education. Adults need to ask themselves certain questions about what they are aiming for. Lilian Katz cites four anti-bias curriculum goals which relate to the early years curriculum:

(1) To nurture each child's construction of a knowledgeable, confident, self-identity and group identity.
(2) To promote each child's comfortable, empathetic interaction with people from diverse backgrounds.
(3) To foster each child's critical thinking about bias.
(4) To cultivate each child's ability to stand up for him/herself and others in the face of bias.

(Katz, 1994, p. 6)

In anti-racist education, it is particularly important to identity the concepts which children need to understand (Epstein and Sealey, 1990). Epstein and Sealey suggest four clusters of concepts – concepts to do with Diversity, Justice, Racism and Bias. Understanding these concepts will be as important for adults as it is for children. They offer a checklist for features of anti-racist teaching, which we have found helpful in the evaluation of school provision (op. cit., p. 58 – examples are from Lambeth settings).

Use multicultural examples and resources in all subjects of the curriculum and areas of learning

Examples
A school for children with severe learning difficulties used tapes of music from a variety of cultures in their sensory room.
An infant school used a traditional African board game (OYO) alongside Solitaire to teach children concepts of number.

Depict people from a range of societies and backgrounds

Example
A primary school for International Women's Day made a book about women they wish to celebrate. These included Rosa Parkes, Claudia Jones, Mrs Porter (Chair of Governors, ex-suffragette) and Pearl Warson (ex-primary inspector who had recently died).

Involve the wider community from outside the school walls

Example
A school doing a project on a carnival invited artists from the Black community and parents into school to help with the workshops on specialist aspects of carnival art.

Offer opportunities for children to detect bias

Example
Children were asked to look at adverts in magazines for toys and decide whether they were for boys or for girls. They then discussed with the adults their own preferences.

Help children to recognise and challenge stereotypes

Example
An infant school class did a project on making their own newspaper. They included reports on matters of local interest and articles in different scripts. They compared this with the range of local newspapers in the area.

Allow children to direct their own learning, follow their own interests, use 'real' information

Example
After a visit to the Commonwealth Institute, children designed their own cloth patterns and some went on to make designs for how they would use the prints in clothing.

Encourage expression of children's opinions, sensitively confront negative attitudes

Example
Children were encouraged to express their opinions about women they admired and on the role played by mothers in their lives.

Encourage co-operation, group work, talk

Example
A nursery class theme in the imaginative play area developed into a baby clinic run by children in role. The presence of a variety of skin creams and oils allowed the children to discuss the appropriate ones used in their families.

Develop social skills, self-awareness

Example
During circle-time in a primary school, children from the nursery upwards discussed issues of racism prompted by incidents in the school.

Develop concepts of justice, fairness, conflict resolution

Example
Children were encouraged to discuss how they could make the playground fairer to boys and girls. They decided to have some days that were 'no football' days and to organise collaborative games.

Expect, facilitate and value high standards of achievement from all children

Example
Display children's work; give specific feedback on their work; give children time to improve their work; support and guidance to help them do so.

Explore global issues and interdependence

Example
Children looking at posters from OXFAM discussed the issue of food and how inequalities in the distribution of food between the world's people might be resolved.

(Epstein and Sealey, 1990, p. 58)

The question of working in partnership with parents is a crucial one to give attention to. It must include staff examining their attitudes to groups of parents or individuals and increasing their knowledge of childrearing practices, attitudes to children's place in the family, appropriate behaviour and so on.

In *Equal Chances* (PPA, 1991), the example of some children's reluctance to engage in messy play is looked at in the light of parents' proper concerns about their children's skin, clothes and hair. They discussed ways the playgroup may address these concerns through providing effective protective clothing or providing alternative, less messy media, e.g. clear starch for finger painting, non-sticky dough, pastel colour paints etc. A nursery reassured parents about their serious attention to dietary practices by displaying prominently the different diets catered for in the nursery and names of children who need them. This also informed temporary staff and all members of the nursery team so that no mistakes could be made.

In *The Best of Both Worlds – Celebrating Mixed Parentage* (EYTARN, 1995), strategies are discussed for giving children positive messages about different aspects of their racial identity. 'Children need to feel good about all/several facets of parentage and identity and be taught it is OK if they identify more with one than another at different points in their lives. Language needs to be positive to foster pride and self-esteem. Racism is an issue for these children and adults' (EYTARN, 1995, p. 10). Staff need to consider how they encourage children of mixed parentage to explore feelings of identity and self-worth, e.g. colour matching, self-portraits etc., and how they can encourage parents and empower them to take part in the process.

A curriculum does not operate in a vacuum and can be undermined by the hidden curriculum of attitudes, ethos and institutional practices which are discriminatory. In their useful chapter, Joseph, Lane and Sharma (1994) describe the processes that adults will need to go through to develop an anti-racism policy. The stages include discussing values statements; outlining a programme of action; developing a policy; producing an explicit policy which is monitored; collecting ethnic data on all aspects where decision-making or assessment are involved; developing strategies to counteract the learning of racist attitudes by young children through the curriculum; and considering a contract of good practice between parents, children and the service. As adults with responsibility for providing quality care, is it vital that we are aware of the legal obligations contained within that role – for example the Race Relations Act 1976. The outcome will necessarily be specific to each provider, responsive to and reflective of the local context within which they work.

Conclusions

Each individual setting will need to work out a strategy for itself, one which aims to ensure equality of opportunity for children and adults.

There is no end point, schools and other settings will be at different points and are unlikely to have done all the above consistently. The process needs to be one of continuous evaluation as a normal part of the way adults review their work with young children. This work will now clearly need to be done without official government backing, but is essential if we want to give children an education which promotes rather than undermines equality of opportunity.

Suggested further reading

Klein, G. (1993) *Education Towards Race Equality*, Cassell, London.
Runnymead Trust (1993) *Equality Assurance in Schools: Quality, Identity, Society*, Trentham, Stoke-on-Trent.
Siraj-Blatchford, I. (1994) *The Early Years: Laying the Foundation for Racial Equality*, Trentham, Stoke-on-Trent.

Note

1. The views expressed in this chapter are the authors' own and do not necessarily represent those of Lambeth Education Department.

5

Parents and Professionals: Partnership in Early Childhood Education

Victoria Hurst

The work of parents and practitioners in collaboration together is an aspect of teaching today which arouses much interest in all who are concerned about education and which can be a most rewarding experience for child, parent and practitioner; it is central to the philosophy of early childhood education which is based on the belief that the learner must be an active participant in learning and that it is the professional duty of the early years practitioner to negotiate fruitful encounters between the learner's existing knowledge and understanding and the established disciplines of knowledge. The learner's personal experience becomes the foundation of learning in this theory (Dewey, 1938), and the child's home life, parents and mother tongue assume a great educational importance, which the Hadow Report of 1931 recognized as being unchanging in spite of the economic, social and administrative developments that affect the education service.

This partnership of parents and professionals is a very challenging area of work, however, where priorities need to be carefully weighed; it is vital to be clear about the nature and strength of the learning relationship between children and parents before making judgements about ways to work together. A broad acceptance of the value of parental involvement conceals a wide range of intentions; in a survey of the school information brochures of 560 English primary schools Alan Weeks (1987) found that 49.5 per cent mentioned home–school co-operation. The objectives of parental involvement however varied considerably – of the 49.8 per cent that had PTAs 185 gave as their first objective financial support, 169 gave social support, and only 78 educational support. Only 56 schools specified all three kinds of objectives.

It is the purpose of this chapter to try to see where parental involvement fits into what is known about how young children learn, and how practitioners may best approach working in partnership with parents. The relationship of parents to schooling will be seen in the broad context of the wider educational setting which affects how parents and practitioners see their own and the others' roles and responsibilities in the educational curriculum offered to the young child in school today.

All of us who are concerned with early childhood education need to look at our practice in the light of understandings about parents and children and to formulate guidelines along which to develop and support children's educational experiences. Practitioners should find it helpful to concentrate upon what is now understood about the relationship between children's performance in all aspects of their school lives and their experiences at home in their families.

Research and its implications – a brief summary

Much of the research relevant to this area is focused on ideas about how children learn, and about the role of the home in emotional, social, physical and cognitive development, and in children's learning of every kind; this extends, through the evolution of the child's self-image, to the influence of the home upon children's attitudes towards themselves, their educational expectations and their anticipated roles as adults, perceived in the context of their parents' experiences, self-esteem and expectations.

The Piagetian model of children's learning

Although some important modifications have been made to the conclusions of Piaget, his principles continue to form the foundation of present day educational theory about the learning of young children. From his research he formed the conclusion that learning develops in a continuum from earliest childhood onwards, in which the person learns by internalizing increasingly complex mental pictures of the world around. These schemata, or, at a later stage, concepts, are constantly modified, elaborated or extended in the light of new experiences and form part of increasingly elaborate mental models of the world and how it works. The search for an equilibrium between the established mental structures and the new learning leads children to develop new understandings of the world that are capable of being increasingly diverse, generalized, and specialized.

An example may illustrate the kind of practically based reflection that underpins young children's thinking, and the way that their spontaneous observations or questions often give clues to the kind of concepts they are building up; a child of four, who dropped and broke an egg when lifting it from a newly bought box, cried in perplexity, 'But why have you cooked this egg?' Further conversation showed that she believed that eggs, like chocolate and butter, were firm until warmed up in cooking, and that hard-boiled eggs were eggs eaten raw.[1]

An existing hypothesis about the world was being brought into contact with contradictory evidence from experience of reality, and would be modified in consequence. Two notions crucial to the understanding of this process are the need for repeated experiences from which conclusions can be drawn, and the crucial role of feedback from the environment (whether human or not) in confirming or disproving the child's ideas.

In both the repetition of experience and the provision of feedback all who spend time with young children contribute heavily to their learning; parents can be seen, for this reason, to have the basic, constant and most influential educational role in the development of their young children. Piaget (1951) draws particular attention to the way in which imitation is central to children's learning, and he gives many examples from his own observations of how from a very young age children imitate, first with physical movement and then with various modes of play and representation, what interests them in the world around. Repetition and consistency in the environment are essential for this process, as are wide opportunities for children's own repetition and representation in various ways of what they have observed. Athey (1990) has drawn attention to the impact on nursery children and their younger non-attending siblings of parents' active involvement in their learning.

What children have gained from their experiences before they come to school will, in this way, be the foundation for all their future learning at school and at home.

Children's language development

Studies made of the development of children's language show how, during the first few weeks, even days, of life, infants learn to share in 'conversational exchanges' of body movements and facial expressions with their mothers (Schaffer, 1974; Trevarthen, 1993). By three years old most children show, by the way they use language in their play and social transactions, that they have accumulated a wealth of social and psychological understandings and insights (Shields, 1978; Dunn, 1987). Whoever undertakes a major caretaking role with a young child becomes the chief resource for all these different kinds of learning, which will be the child's learning tools and resources to be used, adapted and developed as needed, for all subsequent personal development and education. Studies of children's linguistic interactions at home have shown that nursery-age children from a wide variety of backgrounds participate in complex linguistic exchanges with their families, in which the resource of shared experience becomes

---

1. Charlotte, four years six months, personal observation.

the medium for levels of sophistication in communication which are not paralleled in exchanges outside the home – at school, for instance – except where school provision enables children to draw on their home experience (Wells, 1987; Tizard and Hughes, 1984). When this does happen, children learn fast and retain the understanding. The impact of this work has initially been felt to reflect most strongly on teachers' estimations of the appropriateness of their interactions with children in the classroom, and it is of course right that these should be questioned and re-examined: the value of this research, however, is not just that it enables teachers to see how far they may be underestimating children's linguistic capacity but, more positively, that it enables teachers and parents alike to see what a powerful resource for language children's homes are. It is worth emphasizing that both studies found a higher level of interaction at home than at school whatever the social class and educational background of the home might be. In reality, this means that practitioners will be less able to extend children's thinking without the active and continuous support of parents.

These two major areas of research described so far provide a theoretical picture of children's development in which the role of the home is as the formative resource for fundamental learning and communication; by comparison with this, school, where children spend far fewer hours and to which they come with the characteristic lines of their affective, cognitive and linguistic development already determined, cannot expect to exercise a comparably formative influence. What schools can expect, however, is that there will be many opportunities to develop a partnership that is supportive of parents' efforts to give their children a good start in life. Helping parents to find their way in the educational complexities of schooling is part of the drive towards better educational chances for all children.

The influence of attitude on educational performance

The problem of inequalities in educational achievement among children of similar measured endowment has led to an awareness of the influence of parental expectation and experience on children's performance. While there is no cause for concern about the wide variations in the cognitive and linguistic environments offered to children by their homes, there is a critical area of influence to be seen in the effect of community expectations and morale, which are most usually linked to feelings about the family's economic and social situation and prospects. The concern shown by the Newsom Report in 1963 (CACE, 1963) about the effect of home background on school success has been followed up and developed in work which connects educational outcomes with issues of social deprivation, inner city problems, racial discrimination and the difficulties experienced by particular groups of people such as inadequately supported parents of young children, the low paid and the unemployed. Where parents, for whatever reason, feel that they are excluded from the main groupings of society and from its usual channels of organization, communication and reward, it is unlikely that their children will see their education as having a personal relevance. This can be reinforced if parents do not feel they know enough about how to help children with their education. Hughes, Wikeley and Nash (1994) found that this was the only substantial complaint reported by the parents of 150 children going through Key Stage I. A survey by the then Department of Education and Science during the introduction of the National Curriculum found that parents in the lowest socio-economic groups had by far the least knowledge about the new structure for their children's education (Public Attitude Surveys, 1989).

The effects on communication skills, self-image and role expectations brought about by children's exposure to the depressed expectations of individual parents and of their local communities represent not just a cultural divide but also an educational impasse which has been seen as requiring the education service to assume a community development role rather than providing compensatory programmes (Poulton and James, 1975). It should be noted that this view of parental involvement is very different from seeing it as a way to enable parents to learn from teachers and that it carries the corollary that the deployment of professional expertise and knowledge can, if not sensitively handled, further weaken the self-respect and confidence of parents. This is a very serious issue; if children's needs are to be met by their parents, the parents themselves must be self-confident (Pugh, De'ath and Smith, 1994).

The education service

So far this chapter has included findings from child development research which indicates how important it is for practitioners to link up provision for children with what they have done and are doing in their homes, and to learn to speak the child's home language, in both cases by making contact with parents an inbuilt part of their approach. It has also been seen that parental morale and self-confidence have a direct effect on children's educational achievement and that schools need to be aware of their own potential for influencing parents' and therefore children's self-esteem and educational expectations.

The education service itself has undergone a series of developments in its view of its role in relation to the community in general and parents in particular; much change has come about as a result of external political pressure for the 'rights of the consumer' in relation to any public service, and in particular to the education service (Education Reform Act 1988). However, since the 1960s there has been increased emphasis by practitioners conscious of children's needs on the need to negotiate for a mutually supportive relationship with parents, and to incorporate new ideas about their rights to information and to participation in decisions affecting their children's future. At the same time, the role of the community in monitoring the provision and delivery of other services, through, for instance, community health councils, has also changed greatly, and under the influence of educational pressure-groups and reformers the role of the community has been extended through the governing of schools. In addition, parents now have an agreed right to information about available educational provision in their local authority and about the philosophy and practices of individual schools, and an agreed right to participation in decision-making through representation on boards of government of schools (Education Act 1980). The value of their parental expertise and insight is acknowledged in the provision made by the Education Act 1981 for their participation in the process of making a 'statement' about a child who may be in need of special educational provision. This may be contrasted with the historical inheritance of a different kind of close relationship between home and school – one in which parents were seen as having duties, not rights, as an early nineteenth-century example shows:

Rules for the guidance of parents

1. They must send their children regularly to school at the proper hours, clean, washed, and combed, viz. nine in the morning, and two in the afternoon.
2. That on Sundays they are to send their children to the school-room at such hours as shall be directed by the master, before they go to church.
3. They must never detain them from school except from sickness, or by leave of the visitors. In the former case they must inform the master of the circumstances.
4. No parents are permitted to take their children out of the school without their appearing before the committee.

'Standing Rules and Regulations formed by the Society for promoting the Education of the Poor, in the County of Devon and City of Exeter, in the Principles of the Established Church, and According to Dr Bell's Plan', reproduced in First Annual Report of the National Society, p. 36.

(Silver and Silver, 1974)

The change in emphasis is very marked; much depends on the interpretation but nowadays local authorities hope that parents will share in the school's work with their child and feel themselves to be participating members of the team; the rewards of education, future and present, are invoked as an incentive instead of the heavy moral sanctions of the past. On the other hand, the role of education is still often defined as being to effect change in parents and the point of informing and involving parents must be, according to this view, to enlist their support and enable them to co-operate more effectively (as in the suggestions of the Plowden Committee), while the aim of involving the community in the school may be seen as not dissimilar. Where the research reviewed above introduces a new approach is in pointing to the educational advantages for children of practitioners and parents engaging in an equal partnership, in which both are seen as learning from each other's expertise.

In a Renfrewshire study (Donachy, 1979) of programmes to promote parent–child interaction, it was noted that 50 per cent of parents in areas judged to be disadvantaged subsequently sought pre-school opportunities for their children where before they had formed part of the 'reluctant residue' who did not take advantage of provision available locally for their children. The critical factor in these programmes was identified by the researcher as being the extent to which parents were encouraged to develop self-esteem as teachers in relation to their own children; Barbara Tizard (1987) has suggested that the recent discontinuity of results from home–school reading programmes should lead us to look carefully at what seems to make some programmes more successful than others and in particular to be aware of the home-visiting element in the successful Haringey programme. The underlying implication that what goes on at home with parents is of central importance characterizes both the Renfrewshire and the Haringey projects, whether the work took place at home or at school, and may well be shown in the future to be the indispensable factor in a wide range of educational programmes; it is certainly the way forward which must be explored in the attempt to help children from all kinds of backgrounds to derive the maximum benefit from their educational opportunities. A new approach provides the rationale and a format for parents' monitoring of their children's developing literacy skills and much practical advice on extending them (ALBSU, 1995).

Children in the school-based Renfrewshire programme were compared with others receiving the ordinary educational provision with no intervention between tests; not only were the results encouraging but the only difference found between high and low gains in the experimental group was the much greater involvement of fathers as well as mothers in the former group (McCail, 1981). Genuine involvement of each parent as their own child's educator is the challenge that faces all early childhood education practitioners today.

Parents and teachers – getting together in practical terms

For the classroom practitioner there exists a wide range of issues about partnership with parents, from the two-way communication of information between parents and practitioners to the teaching of reading and maths, and from the parents' experience of the school's relevance to their daily lives to the practitioners' experience of the parents' relevance to the professional task. All these issues relate to one another through their effect on the way parents and practitioners feel about their partnership, and it is important for this reason to try to keep in mind the broad outlines of the justifications for partnership which were discussed in the first section. To recapitulate; we need to involve parents in their children's education in school because, without this connection between home and school, schooling can become cut off from the child's deepest and most influential experiences, and practitioners can find the door to the child's motivation for learning closing in their faces. Again, early learning and language are rooted in home experiences and the practitioner must try to get this vast body of influences on to the school's side, or else face the possibility of having to start relating to the child, particularly the very young child, at a level of communication and cognitive activity much lower than that which the child confidently employs at home (Tizard and Hughes, 1984). Lastly, parents' own experience forms the context of expectation in which children perceive themselves, their world, and their future, and this makes it most important that parents should feel school to be somewhere they have a right to be, which has relevance to their experiences and personal hopes for their children, and where what they say matters.

How do parents see their relationship with the school?

Individual teachers should be aware of the extent to which the parent body is consulted about what happens in the school as a whole, and how well the local authority's provision reflects parents' estimation of need, particularly in relation to the provision of pre-school places or after-hours and holiday care, for this is the setting in which parents will be experiencing what each individual practitioner attempts to do. Many practitioners must find that parents who feel that their needs are not taken into consideration respond much better to school when they begin to feel that it has some relevance to what they want for their children and that their contributions are welcomed on serious issues as well as in minor ways. Those who are concerned about how this problem of alienation might be overcome might like to consider, among other examples, the work on partnership with parents currently in progress in the Commune of Modena in northern Italy, which aims to provide services to meet the needs of families with young children. Nursery schools from the age of three and nurseries for younger children where there is demand are a part of local policy, and partnership with parents extends into the curriculum as well. In 1979 the author was present at a meeting where the six teachers of the Scuola Materna Simonazzi discussed their plans for the term with a group of twenty parents and a local authority co-ordinator of relations between school and community. The plans had already been talked over informally with the parents of each year-group and, when agreed on by this meeting, would be presented by a working party of parents to the entire parental group. The kinds of theme presented were connected with the children's experience; the three-year-olds, for instance, were going to investigate their homes and the environment – a documentary film made at the time shows this to include visiting the houses of school-mates and teachers. In this example, an appropriate

curriculum has been developed 'as a part of the programme of a continued relationship between the kindergarten on the one hand and the parents and city on the other hand' (Commune di Modena, 1979).

What is a realistic starting point?

A child's first experience of educational provision, and the subsequent
experiences of transition from one form of provision to another, form crucial steps towards fuller participation in public modes of education, and
require as much support as possible, in order to avoid the anxiety and
bewilderment which can easily beset both parents and children at this
time. In particular, we need to be aware that continuity of experience
between home and pre-school provision and between pre-school and
school will provide children with reassuring elements of certainty and
the opportunity to continue with their personal interests and concerns
while they are adjusting to their new environment. In addition to the
emotional security they will gain, the educational arguments for cognitive and linguistic continuity are extremely strong. Joyce Watt has
researched how practitioners in nursery and primary schools can increase
the continuity of children's experience during these educational transi-
tions; she believes that an important part of the solution must lie in

> increasing and expanding the role of parents at both stages. I take it for granted
> that the involvement of parents is part of the fabric of quality education at
> every stage ... Nevertheless the point has to be emphasized again that it is
> parents who provide for the long-term continuity and, in practical terms, they
> probably have a particularly critical role to play as their children start primary
> school. Ironically it is at this point that many who have been involved at the
> nursery stage may cease, for whatever reason, to play an active role. Not all
> parents can or will want to be involved in the same way: they need to find
> roles which they see as significant to themselves as individuals and to the ben-
> efit of their children. Many schools still have a long way to go in finding sig-
> nificant roles for parents or in seeing them as major resources for their children
> in the transition into school. Parents, like teachers, need encouragement, they
> need support, they often need to learn new skills, new attitudes, but, in the
> context of the present discussion they may also need sheer information, not
> just about the school and how it operates, but about the choices open to them
> as parents on when or where their children may start school and the possible
> implications of those choices.
>
> (Watt, 1987, p. 14)

Having considered the general setting in which the parents' expectations
will have been formed, the practitioner may look to see what can best be
done in the classroom. It is most important to start from where the
parents are in their relationship with the classroom, rather than from
what might seem to be the best practice or what is already being done
elsewhere. If the overall aim of this work is to build up close and mutually supportive working relationships between parents and practitioners,

then it is the effect of what is done within the context that is critical, not how it relates to any other persons or places or practices. The impact of an invitation to spend time in the classroom may vary enormously from one group to another and from one parent to another. Both the cultural and the personal starting points of parents may make this an over-whelming or unhelpful experience. Parents will usually prefer the oppor-tunity to talk on a one-to-one basis from all the other options, since this is how they can obtain up-to-date information and share their own insights about their child's progress.

In general, by far the most helpful thing to do to prepare the way for closer working relationships is to set up viable and effective channels of communication between home and school, remembering that the com-munication will need to be two-way and that there must be built-in opportunities for individual parents to make contact with their child's teacher both informally and formally.

The first contact with parents is likely to be an initial visit, in which the prospective parent and child are brought to the classroom to make the acquaintance of the teacher and children. The meeting is one at which some extremely important information is exchanged, through what is said and the way that it is said, and through what is not said. Throughout a child's time at school the social relationship between parent and teacher will carry a considerable weight, embodying the practical and emotional aspects of their partnership for the child's education. As individuals, both parent and practitioner are vulnerable, each being exposed to the possi-bility of criticism of how they fulfil their role from people who have a different approach to the situation, and who are not necessarily sensitive to the problems and perplexities the other encounters. The converse is luckily also true – that there is nothing more encouraging to parent or practitioner than to feel that the other, expert in a different sense, appre-ciates and values what they are trying to do. Setting up a good working relationship in whatever way is possible is the main task of these early meetings, where there is an opportunity to give the new parent and child an insight into how the class functions and what the practitioner's meth-ods and intentions are, and to give the practitioner a view of the child and parent together in the classroom. If it is possible for the practitioner to visit the child and parent at home in advance, this can be very valu-able in making it clear to the parent that what goes on at home is of importance to school and in giving the practitioner a shared base of ex-perience with the child, however brief the visit. Children often refer to previous home visits in their early approaches to practitioners at school, seeming to find reassurance and delight in the practitioner having been their guest on their home territory much as they are now on territory where the practitioner feels at home. Naturally there will be times and situations when home visits are not possible or not desirable and, as with all other ways of working together with parents, practitioners and parents need to scrutinize proposals to be sure that they are likely to have the desired effect of improving the working relationship.

Settling in – the basis of the future relationship

Young children, whether at infant or nursery stage, need time to establish their confidence in a new situation, and the way in which parent and practitioner work together to settle a new child in class can have a strong influence on the child's future happiness at school, and a formative influence on the parent–practitioner relationship. Difficulties of many kinds can arise; parents have often had school experiences themselves which make it harder for them to help their children, and practitioners may then find that they are having to deal with the feelings and previous learning of both child and parent at once. This can lead to the view that separation is best done like an eighteenth-century amputation – as fast as possible: the trouble with this method is that it can easily lead to lasting feelings of damage on all sides, and breaks the links between school and home which are potentially such a rich resource for learning. With the whole of the child's education to come, and in the knowledge of the formative role of the family's attitude to school, it is surely well worth while planning for a settling-in programme which takes account of the need for child, parent and practitioner to develop their relationship gradually over the first few days and weeks. Children whose mother tongue is not English may need special consideration in various ways: for instance, practitioners should assess the advantages of building up for use when the parent is not present a linguistic survival kit of a few strategic words and phrases in the child's home tongue, while headteachers and governors must take account of the staffing requirements of the children's and parents' needs for time with practitioners.

At this early stage it is important to try to establish an understanding that the welfare of the child will require the insights of both parent and practitioner, and that each needs to accept the other's expertise over the process of the child's settling in. Some parents may not see the need to give the child time to become acquainted with new adults, new children and the new setting, and there may have to be explanations of the school's policy and the experience this is based on; some schools may need to be more flexible about admission and settling-in arrangements so that parents' needs and other commitments can be accommodated; all schools must evaluate their staffing and resourcing policies for early years classes in the light of parents' and practitioners' views of the settling-in process; some parents may have had distressing separation experiences themselves and therefore find it hard to leave their child: practitioners themselves may have had experiences which make it hard for them to understand the needs of a particular child and parent, and explanations will be needed here of the home point of view. Adapting to school is a major experience for child and parent, and there should be on all sides an awareness of the necessity of growing slowly into their new stage. There is no aspect of early childhood education which illustrates more clearly how creative and responsible a task it is than this 'floating off' of a child into the new world of school. On the success of this endeavour rests the success of the child's future experiences of education – mistakes can be made at any stage, but if the foundations are well laid in this way schooling will be associated with the continuous learning which has been going on at home for the whole of the child's life. The actual details of how settling in is managed will naturally vary from school to school and child to child; a process of negotiation must take place to see how the needs of the child can best be met in the particular context.

Under-age children in infant classes

The distress and difficulty caused to children, parents and practitioners by early admission to infant classrooms is now becoming widely recognized. Very few infant schools have been able to demonstrate the ability to meet the needs of under-age children, and those that have done so have found that they are in effect re-inventing nursery education standards. Headteachers and governing bodies, and local education authorities as well, must accept that the responsibility for very young children's emotional welfare is a heavy one and that children who have not reached their fifth birthday must not be admitted unless they and their parents can be guaranteed appropriate ratios of trained staff to children, teachers who have been trained for the education of children aged between three and eight years of age, a curriculum for the nursery age-group and the accommodation and resources to provide it.

The alternative to this commitment is to risk the children's welfare and betray the parents' trust in the school. In Wales, where substantial numbers of three- as well as four-year-olds have been admitted prematurely, parents have begun to count the cost at home while teachers have identified what it means to them to try to provide for children in these circumstances, and how little educational benefit such provision can offer:

> Parents state that their initial beliefs that early admission would give their children a headstart have been replaced by a realisation that their children were tired, had difficulties in sitting, listening and concentrating for long periods. Many parents said their children found difficulties in the playground and on buses taking them from home to school. There were many examples of distress and anxiety.
>
> Many teachers expressed feelings of immense frustration, despair and isolation when they failed to balance the conflicting curricular and emotional needs and demands of the wide age range of children in their classes, often from 3–7 years.
>
> Many teachers are struggling to deliver a broad, balanced curriculum. Concerns centre around the formal curriculum experienced by many under 5s

or the low level tasks given to occupy young children, such as copying, colouring and filling in worksheets. Such experiences are counter-productive in developing active, independent thinkers and learners.

(Davies, 1995, p. 2)

What future for three- and four-year-olds ?

The coming of the National Curriculum, and pressure for easily measurable financial accountability, mean that we must make special efforts to protect children under five from these formal and constraining influences which are, for instance, causing schools to introduce literacy in inappropriate ways (Drummond, 1995). All provision, whether maintained, voluntary or private, must be scrutinized for its capacity to provide for learning through playful experience, within warm, relaxed and enjoyable relationships, and in settings where children's needs to explore, talk and play freely with well-qualified adults in planned indoor and outdoor learning environments are acknowledged and met. Parents are in the key position here because they see the day-to-day impact on individual children and can point out how, for instance, attempts to make children perform like older pupils can backfire and alienate them. Again, the parent of a three- or four-year-old is the one best equipped to argue against separating these age-groups, since he or she knows what the three-year-old gains from the older children's examples and how the four-year-old grows through helping younger children. This information is important for the development of appropriate national and local policies.

Exchanging information

The working relationship which has been established during the very early stages at school will be continued and developed through the daily contacts and communications between home and school, a large part of which consists in the exchange of information. Much of the flow of information from the school and practitioner may be in the form of written material or oral messages taken home by the children, but even so this is likely to need to be discussed individually with many parents, who will wish to be sure that they have understood what it means for them and their child. In the same way, there will be information from home about the child which the practitioner will need to know. There are implications in this for the organization of the classroom which should be seen as important, because the creation of opportunities for the exchange of information during the school day meets vital needs. Practitioners who place a high priority on being available for parental contact at the beginning and end of sessions should compare different ways of organizing the day at these points and may find that an alteration of routine will create a more relaxed atmosphere in which parents may approach them as they arrive with their child. One teacher found that developing a more flexible start to the day had advantages for all – children, parents and teacher:

> I made available specific activities as well as allowing children access to the full range of areas and equipment in the classroom from the beginning of the day.
>
> As the children entered the class I encouraged them to become involved with an activity of their choice (after the first session little encouragement was needed).
>
> This more flexible start to the day allowed me to be available to those parents and children who really needed my attention. I had time for individual needs and other children were not reduced to being mere spectators.
>
> (Gillespie, 1986, personal communication)

Parents and education in the classroom

As well as being seen to have time for parental contact practitioners need to make it clear that they welcome parents' support for their children's learning, whether in the classroom or at home. Recent research has pointed to the benign and long-term effects of parental involvement in children's education, and suggests that one of the key qualities of successful provision for young children is the degree to which the children's parents are actually able to share in their children's school learning and to follow it up at home. Initial concern at the apparent lack of long-term effect of, for instance, pre-school provision in American and British programmes is now being replaced by the realization that the effects of high quality provision on children's and parents' morale, effectiveness and educational aspirations may lead to very significant benefits indeed (Woodhead, 1985). Both the high quality American Headstart programmes and the project conducted by Athey and Bruce at the Froebel Institute (Athey, 1990) have found significant lasting improvements as a result of work aimed at parents and children together; the Headstart follow-up found a striking decrease in the incidence of drop-out and allocation to remedial classes, and an increase in 'achievement orientation' in the children, while the mothers' vocational aspirations for them tended to be higher than they were for themselves, while the children in the Froebel project showed and maintained an IQ gain of around 20 per cent compared with their siblings who had not participated (Athey, 1980, 1990). Work with both home- and school-based programmes to improve interactions between child and parent has indicated how vital it is that professional help should be focused upon increasing the parent's self-esteem as the child's constant educator (Donachy, 1979).

The noticeable gains in reading ages of children involved in the early home reading schemes have led to their rapid increase (see, for example,

Marian Whitehead (Chapter 6) and the work listed in Hannon *et al.*, 1985) and to the introduction of a similar approach to the teaching of mathematics, although this is at a less developed stage (Bayliss, 1986). None of these projects has the intention of changing parents into schoolteachers or of reducing the educational role of professional teachers, but rather that of increasing the effectiveness of education by drawing on the great potential of the parent as educator at home.

The appropriateness of educational policies is also improved through the participation of parents in their children's education, for serious questions are raised for providers and policy-makers in the education service. The opening paragraphs of this chapter identified the many different intentions there can be for parental involvement; IMPACT (Maths with Parents and Children and Teachers) challenges the deficit models of children and parents which can undermine the educational progress of children while seemingly supporting it:

> I have been increasingly disturbed by the move on the part of many schools to introduce profiles of what are deemed to be a child's achievements to date on entry into school, known as 'base-line assessment'. . .If some children in a school, or even all the children in a particular area, are said to be 'under-achieving', the idea that this can be addressed by involving their parents surely takes us back to a deficit model of parenting.
>
> (Merttens, 1992)

A more positive view is that 'records are about getting to know the child, and what the child needs' (Bartholomew and Bruce, 1993, p. 100). In this the parents' insights can and should play an influential part in determining what are seen as achievements.

Parents and the language of the home

The parents' language, whether it is a variant or dialect of native English or another language, is the first language in which the child learns to communicate and to represent experience and thought. 'Language in its origins is fundamentally intertwined with the rest of mental life' (Donaldson, 1992, p. 106). The ways in which practitioners signal to parents that their way of speaking is accepted as an important means of communication are also ways which enrich the classroom experience of children and assist the practitioner's efforts to enlist children's commitment to their schooling. The home language, whatever it may be, needs to be attached to the educational process for the child to make the most gains from it simply because this is the child's mother tongue; equally, the gains in awareness of the wide range of effective human styles of communication can do nothing but good to all the children in the class both from the point of view of establishing the wide range of different languages and from the point of view of developing cognitive and social flexibility in the transfer of understanding and procedures in different settings, which represents important conceptual gains in 'disembedding' children's thinking from their personal experiences and backgrounds (Donaldson, Grieve and Pratt, 1983).

Practitioners can make use of a wide range of ways of benefiting from parents' help in the classroom, in particular when parents can, by talking to, playing with, reading to and helping children, extend their experience of the world and of ways of communicating. This is not to say that the practitioner is no longer important – far from it – but that the practitioner can now call on this strategic support for a wide range of educational activities in the classroom. How parents help when they come to the classroom is a matter for decision in the light of what benefits are looked for from their presence; washing paint-pots in isolation may be of practical help to staff, but playing in the home-corner, cooking food that is enjoyed at home, telling a favourite story or singing songs will bring a home focus to educational experience which will be of much greater value.

It is important not to underestimate the effort parents put into contributing to their children's classrooms. A young mother had to go and wash the baking trays before starting cooking in her child's group; she had been up all night with her baby. What messages might she be getting about the value staff were putting on her efforts?

Sharing languages

A wide range of linguistic backgrounds can be a valuable resource for schools but it does also require efforts to ensure that communication is really effective. Communications from the school should be available in as many different mother tongues as are necessary and the practitioner should be able to call on the help of bilingual staff where translation is needed; parents who have fluency and understanding of English can still benefit both in fuller communication and in morale from the willingness of practitioners to use the child's home language for communication in this way. The very large number of world languages present in schools in some parts of Britain can lead to difficulties in getting help with translation, but determination and imagination in the use of bilingual parents' help may overcome some problems. There is much advantage also for children in this as well, as indicated above, and this co-operation can be extended to as much involvement of the child's mother tongue and home culture in the classroom through the parent's story-telling, singing, cooking and so on as seems appropriate in the given circumstances.

Sharing the aims, contrasting the roles

The recent increase in awareness of the fundamental nature of the parental role in education leads on to questions about the role of the professional, and whether in fact, if parents are so powerful an educational force, there is any need for a professional at all, particularly in the pre-school years. In fact, however, it is, as we have seen, the combination of the two roles which is so particularly important for children's educational achievement, and the closer that home–school contact is the more it is possible to perceive the essential differences in the roles. Teresa Smith, who has outlined (1980) a critical approach to parental involvement, has recently (1987) pointed to the way that partiality is a necessary function of parenthood while impartiality is just as necessary to being a teacher, a view confirmed by Katz (1980).

At the same time, practitioners need to learn from parents about the educational qualities of the home relationship which can be built upon in school: the most significant of these is that quality of intensity and excitement in the one-to-one relationship which practitioners benefit from when it can be provided for in the well-organized classroom through close links with the home. Parents also have much to gain from school in learning about their child's activities there, how their ideas of their child correspond with the practitioner's, and how they may support school work with their own efforts at home (Smith, 1987).

Conclusions

The involvement of parents in the education of their school-age children is probably the greatest single opportunity for educational advance open to us today. There is no doubt that partnership with parents demands of practitioners a new approach to their role and new insights, skills and sensitivity in their work; it demands a much increased capacity to exercise their professionalism with flexibility and sensitivity, but in return it offers a much surer foundation for educational achievement. However, a survey of initial teacher training in 1985 found that a third of primary teachers have little or no preparation to work with parents, and have to develop the necessary skills and understanding by trial and error in the classroom (Atkin and Bastiani, 1985). Furthermore, data now emerging (Blenkin and Yue, 1994) shows that many teachers of children under eight have not been appropriately trained for that age-group; they will need opportunities to learn about working with parents through professional development.

In view of the importance of the task, and of the level of professionalism required to carry it out, working with parents must assume a high priority in teacher education as it must in classroom practice; teachers and nursery nurses must be supported with initial and in-service training, and with classroom help from extra staff and resources where needed.

Human thought deals with how things are, or at least with how they seem to us to be, but it does this in ways that typically entail some sense of how they are not – or not yet. It deals with actuality and with possibility; but some recognition of possibility is already entailed even in the discovery of actuality whenever this is achieved by the characteristically human means of asking questions.

(Donaldson, 1992, p. 9)

These questions show us how children advance their knowledge and understanding of the world and they show us, too, why it is that children must have a personal, playful and imaginative experience of education. It is only the collaboration of parents and practitioners that can ensure this for them. In this collaboration it is the process of listening to parents and of consulting them about what their own agenda might be that is the essential ingredient for success. We must therefore give attention to this process itself and improve our capacity to 'listen, to modify perceptions, and to present a different point of view' (Jones *et al.*, 1992, p. 74). What these writers have called a 'Willing Partnership' will not come into being without recognition of the importance of the process of communication in 'breaking down assumptions about boundaries and roles' (ibid., p. 75) and in enabling changes to take place.

Suggested further reading

Smith, T. (1980) *Parents and Preschool*, Grant McIntyre, London.

6

Narrative, Stories and the World of Literature

Marian Whitehead

Children, only animals live entirely in the Here and Now. Only nature knows neither memory nor history. But man – let me offer you a definition – is the story-telling animal.
Wherever he goes he wants to leave behind not a chaotic wake, not an empty space, but the comforting marker-buoys and trail-signs of stories.

(Graham Swift, 1983, p. 53)

These claims are not uncommon in those circles where people talk about life, literature and the human condition. They enjoy great vogue among educationists and the world of early childhood education is particularly involved in storytelling. As with many apparently recent developments, the interest was always there but it has come to the fore in current discussions and publications.

In the first edition of this book I discussed a 'new wave' of claims for the centrality of narrative and story in the early years of education. Since then that wave has become a powerful ground-swell which shows no sign of ebbing, despite the education legislation imposed during the last eight years. But the thoughtful teacher still needs to assess the background assumptions and implications of any claims, even those so palpably good as 'stories with everything'. This chapter attempts to move beyond the 'hurrah for stories and poems' position to a consideration of why this claim is significant and how we might relate it to the process of educating young children. In order to do this I shall review the ground-swell of claims for stories and then look in more detail at the nature of narrative and story. A section on literature will consider the worlds of story and poetry and provide a context for the concluding discussion of learning through literature.

The ground-swell of claims

Many of the recent claims for narrative have been made by academics and practitioners who are distinguished in the field of early childhood studies and have been signalling the special nature of narrative for some years. Among this group we find Jerome Bruner, Gordon Wells, Barbara Tizard, Martin Hughes, Margaret Donaldson, Shirley Brice Heath, Marilyn Cochran-Smith and Frank Smith. All these researchers have been concerned in some way with the nature of language, communication, culture and learning in early childhood. This cluster of interests has led each researcher to identify the central role of narrative and its manifestations in conversation, storymaking, play and literature. Before considering in greater detail the nature of narrative and story it would be useful to indicate the kinds of claims being made.

Jerome Bruner (1984) noted that stories and dramatic play are crucial in helping children move from the 'here and now' uses of language to the many possibilities and interpretations which underpin written language. Early language develops in a setting of human social and cultural concerns, it functions to get things done and to create social situations. These powerful features of language, function and situation, are always present in the dramatic stories and the personal anecdotes of daily life. Bruner (1986) went on to develop these claims into a theory of two modes of thought; the paradigmatic which is logical and scientific, and the narrative which is bound up with our psychic hold on reality and creates those 'possible worlds' which are central features of human intelligence and behaviour. This analysis is fully explored in *Acts of Meaning* (1990) where narrative is placed at the heart of the cultural meaning-making which shapes our lives; in other words, it is what makes us tick. For the young child, oral story and anecdote constitute the primary way of entering the 'possible worlds' of abstract thought and language, the language of fiction and print.

At the end of his work on the Bristol Language Development Research Programme, Gordon Wells (1981, 1985a) concluded that books and stories helped children ignore the immediate context and allowed words to create imaginary worlds (1985b, 1985c; Wells and Nicholls, 1985). Anecdotes and stories shared with adults would appear to be the earliest way of contemplating and understanding abstract ideas. Stories functioning as bridges to abstraction and hypothesizing were evident in one child as young as twenty-five months in the material collected by Wells (1981).

Indications that very young children are able to handle abstract and complex ideas through the medium of story and anecdote are present in the work of Margaret Donaldson (1978). She shares with Bruner and Wells the conviction that difficulties in learning arise when early schooling demands that language and thinking be divorced from actual situations and everyday human concerns. However, stories and the talk and musings they stimulate are one area in which young children already use words to reflect upon ideas and the possibilities of experience.

An anthology of children's thinking and storytelling can be found in research by Tizard and Hughes (1984). The group of four-year-old girls studied were actively engaged in the construction of stories which attempted to link the already known to the new and puzzling, thus integrating past, present and future experiences. This thinking and 'languaging' shared with a caring adult was the dominant feature of the girls' home-based waking hours and led Tizard and Hughes to conclude that children are persistent logical thinkers, actively involved in intellectual search.

This sense of children thinking at full stretch and with surprising insight and skill suggests that a powerful story-like mode of human thinking develops early. However, it may be neglected and pushed out by too early a demand for formal, abstract categories of organization. Frank Smith (1983) sees this potential conflict as a profound issue in education. We may be trapped by the metaphors we use to conceptualize our thinking. Thus how we think about the activities of the brain, how we think about thinking, does affect what we value and foster in school. Smith suggests that we might choose between two metaphors, creating worlds or shunting information. All the research would seem to suggest that young children are powerfully involved from the start with creating worlds. Shunting information may be a useful sub-skill to acquire, a means to an end, but it is not a primary activity. So perhaps it should not be a primary objective in the early years of schooling, despite the current National Curriculum emphasis on subject information and end of key-stage testing to check that information has been shunted to children.

The work of Heath (1983), Cochran-Smith (1984) and Paley (1981, 1990) in the USA indicates that different cultures have central but different ways of using narrative and story for making sense of everyday life and introducing children to the ways of thinking of the community. Difficulties may arise when the meaning-making ways of the home culture are not identical with those of the schooling system which the children enter. Paley (1981, 1990), however, succeeds in creating an evolving early years curriculum based on her children's stories and role play in the kindergarten. The result is a relevant and culturally rich curriculum which enhances children's linguistic, social and moral development.

The implications of such cross-cultural studies of young children in their communities seem clear and unavoidable. Shared talking, storytelling, picture book discussions and dramatic play are crucial in any curriculum which aims to introduce children to new worlds while preserving strong and undamaged their own powerful ways of making sense of experience.

Narrative and stories

Why are we huddling about the campfire? Why do we tell tales, or tales about tales – why do we bear witness, true or false? We may ask Aneirin, or Primo Levi, we may ask Scheherezade, or Virginia Woolf. Is it because we are so organized as to take actions that prevent our dissolution into the surroundings?

(Ursula K. Le Guin, 1981, p. 194)

The ground-swell of interest in narrative and stories emerges from a well established approach to literature and the reading process. Claims that human beings have always told stories tend to obscure the one remarkable characteristic which underlies all stories: narrative. Narrative is the organizer and shaper of all stories. Those told orally in gossip, anecdote, reminiscences, jokes, proverbs and rhymes. And those written down as memoirs, myths, folk and fairy tales, novels, ballads and lyrics. Or those presented visually as pictures, cartoons, films and drama. At its simplest, narrative sequences events temporally in order to tell about them. The minimal narrative can be reduced to someone telling someone else that something happened (B. H. Smith, 1980, 1981).

'Tolfink carved these runes in this stone' (Le Guin, 1981, p. 194). This minimal tale is carved on a pillar in Carlisle Cathedral and highlights the mark-making nature of the narrative impulse. It is the drive behind the simplest graffiti – 'Kilroy was here'. The need to record our passing is the primal minimal story, but so minimal a story runs the risk of being dismissed with a bored 'so what?'. More than the recording of existence and events is needed to transform a simple narrative into an interesting story. The breakthrough comes with the impulse not just to record the passage of events, but to saturate the sequence with feelings, attitudes and motives.

Once we narrate not just the life in time but the life by values (Forster, 1962) we are storytellers. This coming together of sequenced happenings with value judgements and implied attitudes characterizes the kind of narrative and story-making activity which much of the educational research discussed earlier focuses on. Narrative and storying are the dominant ways of organizing raw experiences into a system of symbols and images which make sense. The previous section referred to young children using stories as a sense-making device and major claims for the significance of narrative in human thinking, memory and intelligent behaviour support this hypothesis (Meek, Warlow and Barton, 1977). Hardy (1977) suggests that narrative is a primary act of mind and the organizing mode of human memory. R. L. Gregory (1977) describes our constant story-making as a kind of 'brain fiction' which states and considers alternative possible realities. Gregory applies this view to the formulation of a definition of intelligence: the ability to generate appropriate and novel solutions to problems. It would appear that the hypotheses of the scientist are merely possible and novel stories. We are all, like the scientist, creators of imaginative worlds or stories which enable us to try out alternatives, predict possibilities and make sense of experience.

Narrative and stories as means of organizing and telling about past events and predicting possible outcomes for the future are as important to whole societies as they are to individuals. Cultures preserve and practise their history stories, their war stories and their catastrophe stories as if their survival depended on them – perhaps it does. We have only to think about such examples as Gulf War stories, or the commemorations of Auschwitz and VE day, to sense the urgency of 'telling it' so that the stories are preserved and worked on, in order to make sense of some kind. This is national myth-making at work but the myths also permeate and modify the personal sense-making stories of individuals.

When young children incorporate chunks of the stories they have been told into their own story-making activities they are working with powerful cultural blueprints (Hughes, 1976). What is important here for teachers is some sensitivity to the fact that the shape of the narrative as well as the cultural assumptions may vary. An enthusiasm for sharing stories with children and encouraging their anecdotes may be counterproductive if we assume that the only acceptable narrative is the linear essay-like pattern of Western literate traditions. This has a clear beginning, a middle and an end and includes sets of 'logically' ordered propositions. However, the only requirement for minimal narrativity is 'X telling Y about Z'. While satisfying this demand narratives will also be influenced by culture and stages in individual development. In early childhood and in private musings for the self (because X and Y can be one and the same person), a flower-like shape is often created. The central proposition or idea is circled with petal-like musings which originate in the central idea and extend it. It is a typical early processing stage for new experiences. A delightful extended example can be found in the Tizard and Hughes data (1984, p. 119) – four-year-old Rosy attempts in many conversational turns to come to terms with the social and economic assumptions behind paying the window-cleaner for his services. In the following example from the Bristol data (Wells, 1981, p. 107), Mark, twenty-five months old, creates the petals of his narrative by musing on the central theme: the absence of the man who had earlier been working in the garden.

Mark: Where man gone?
Mother: In the house.
Mark: Uh?
Mother: Into his house.
Mark: No. No. Gone to shop Mummy.
Mother: Gone where?
Mark: Gone shop.
Mother: To the shop?
Mark: Yeh.
Mother: What's he going to buy?
Mark: Er – biscuits.

Mother: Biscuits mm.
Mark: Uh?
Mother: Mm. What else?
Mark: Er – meat.

The examples quoted are of urban British schoolchildren with their mothers and already the adult is shaping the anecdote towards the familiar story pattern ('Gone where?', 'What else?') and the assumptions of the culture (you have to earn money; you buy food in shops). But in cultures which are strongly influenced by traditional oral patterns of song, rhyme and repetition, a more poetic and incantatory kind of narrative may be common. The following example from Heath (1983, p. 170) is described as a rondo, for obvious reasons. Lem, aged two-and-a-half years, is playing near the porch when he hears a bell in the distance:

Way
Far
Now
It a church bell
Ringin'
Dey singin'
Ringin'
You hear it?
I hear it
Far
Now

The song-like form was emphasised by Lem's bodily swaying back and forth. The invitation to participate, 'You hear it?', should be linked with Lem's earlier initiation into the shared gospel singing and sermons of his black American community's church.

Making meaning or sense out of raw experience is a personal endeavour but cultures preserve and pass on organized systems or sets of symbols which simplify the task. These symbol systems are stories. They are cultural blueprints for understanding experience (Hughes, 1976).

Before considering some aspects of the stories and poetry of the world of literature it might be useful to summarize this story so far. Continuing research on narrative and stories in early childhood development and education suggests that they are ways of making sense of raw experience. Narrative is a way of marking out our existence and giving it a pattern in time and a value. Whole societies and cultures also give meaning to their corporate existence by telling stories and retrospectively shaping events. The stories of the culture influence and shape the narratives of individuals. Particular educational significance attaches to the ways in which narrative and stories may be bridges to abstract thought, hypothesizing and literacy. But the bridges carry two-way traffic; literature and literacy are sustained, enriched and developed by the power of oral narratives, proverbs, memories, rhymes and songs.

The world of literature

We do not find ourselves in books, but we do expect to be able to make our way in them as experienced storytellers of our own lives.

(Jane Miller, 1986, p. 7)

The following introductory comments are intended to highlight the complexity of the world, or worlds, of literature. Without acknowledging some areas of difficulty and ignorance we might assume too readily that we do know exactly what literature is, what it does and how it does it.

Literature may strictly refer to all that is written down but in the context of this discussion it is taken to mean stories and poetry, mainly works of imaginative fiction. Many of the stories and poems encountered by children in the early years of education will have had their origins in the oral culture and pre-literate history of the people. This makes for a constant and invigorating interchange of traditional forms and contemporary material. Another interesting area of interchange is suggested by the summary at the end of the previous section. Narrative and storying are a complex fusion of personal experience with cultural influences. In the light of modern studies of the reader, the author and the book (Iser, 1974, 1978; Barthes, 1974), we cannot claim to know exactly all the ways in which a work of imaginative literature is read or received. The analysis of children's responses to stories read to them is even more difficult. Finally, in this century, we cannot even claim that experience of literature and 'high' culture makes us good.

Justifying the teaching of literature

All these reservations have not prevented considerable claims being made for the educational benefits of literature. The traditional English teacher's claim picks out three main strands: skills, cultural heritage and personal development. This approach is strongly influenced by late nineteenth century views of the great and the good in English literature and is slanted towards selective and restricted secondary education. The skills claim is that contact with literature develops and extends the individual's skills in writing and reading. The heritage claim sees the body of 'received' literature as a part of the cultural inheritance to be handed on intact to the next generation. The claim for personal development suggests that the content of literary works may make us good by refining our own responses and feelings and extending our experience of the human condition. If these justifications sound familiar it is because although they have been modified, adapted and the priorities somewhat altered, they have been taken into the primary phase of education, as well as into the original planning for English in the National Curriculum (DES 1988a, 1988b).

In this new tradition, personal development linked to knowledge of the world of inner psychic reality has become a major interest of the English teacher and the primary specialist. The skills justification has become very particularly associated with learning to read and write. The cultural heritage claim has expanded to include far more of the traditional oral forms of folk and fairy tales, myths and legends, ballads and nursery rhymes. This powerful package of justifications has now undergone further subtle modifications as early childhood specialists influence the teaching of literature more widely.

The next chapter indicates the close links which have been forged between literature and literacy in the early years curriculum, and outlines ways in which the teaching of literature can take the young child into literacy. In the context of this book the very phrase 'teaching of literature' feels uncomfortable and 'sharing literature with young children' is a more accurate reflection of early childhood approaches.

We are now more aware than ever that literature somehow helps and delights the young child. The fascination of the spell includes such important elements as the satisfaction of subconscious desires and needs, the confirmation of everyday experience and the extension of experiences (see White, 1954; Butler, 1979; Tucker, 1981; Styles, Bearne and Watson, 1992). These elements, however, are valid for education at any age or stage and support the contention of this book that features which are central to a concept of education must remain central whatever the age of the learner.

Entertainment and education

Many cultures and societies have regarded narrative, story and literature as major sources of entertainment and education and the two functions have traditionally gone together. Formal schooling in the recent past may have separated them but traditional literature indicates that the communal sharing of stories and poems was powerful entertainment. Pleasure is therefore the first and all-pervasive theme in the world of literature, even if the school-based teaching of reading has undermined this truth (DES, 1975, 1982b). The danger in picking out just a few of the sources of pleasure in literature is that this detracts from the most important feature. The pleasure is all-pervasive, it accounts for the satisfactions of all of the themes to be discussed. But in an attempt to take a fresh look at literature in early childhood education some broad themes have been identified because of their centrality to the concerns of early childhood, as well as to literature.

Sounds and rhythm

The pleasures of literature are located in the earliest aspects of language. Stories and poetry are rooted in the repeated sounds and tunes of vocal language and the bodily rhythms of breathing, rocking and gesture.

Sound and movement together are characteristic of the body-naming and counting rhymes we play with our babies:

This little pig went to market.

They are present in the nursery rhymes which lend themselves so well to actions:

This is the way the ladies ride.

As the rhymes move out to the street and the playground, rhythmic gestures and rhyming sounds are still retained:

One, two, three
Mother caught a flea
Put it in the tea-pot
And made a cup of tea.

And they are often preserved and extended by professional writers:

Each, peach, pear, plum,
I spy Tom Thumb.

(Ahlberg and Ahlberg, 1977)

For the small child pleasure must also arise from success in predicting the next rhyming line:

Pease pudding hot
Pease pudding cold
Pease pudding in the pot
Nine days old.

Or predicting the next development in the repeating pattern of the narrative:

And then she went to the porridge of the little, small, wee bear and tasted that; and that was neither too hot, nor too cold, but just right; and she ate it all up.

It is now increasingly obvious, and well-documented, that children's success in literacy is partly related to their pre-school awareness of rhyme and poetically repetitive sounds in language (Bryant and Bradley, 1985; Goswami and Bryant, 1990). The crucial factor in many three-year-olds' early phonological experiences is their knowledge of nursery rhymes such as Humpty Dumpty and Hickory Dickory Dock. The English-speaking children studied in the research were also tested on their ability to detect rhyme and alliteration in single words, as well as on their ability to produce rhyming and alliterative words themselves.

Alliteration, called 'onset' by the researchers, and rhyme can take the young child a long way down the road to reading success and to even earlier success in writing and spelling. However, this is not old-style phonics and 'learning sounds', it is an exciting endorsement of the significance of the poetic, playful and subversive elements in language which are celebrated in this chapter.

But there is more than pleasing sound and movement in the body of traditional literature, there are culturally significant messages too.

Learning

Pleasure and success are potent teachers and have been used in teaching the young for centuries[1]. Oral and literate cultures have always passed on important lessons about the ways of the world in stories and poems. This is particularly noticeable in the literature we still share with young children because much of this material originated in a pre-literate but fully adult culture. Many of the so-called 'nursery' rhymes sung to soothe or amuse a restless infant contain snatches of love songs, tavern songs, hymns, political lampoons – anything that came to mind! The average nursery rhyme collection still reflects the assumptions and expectations of an earlier culture. There is a strong emphasis on respectful and conventional manners, as in all the 'how do you do's' and curtseys of 'One Misty, Moisty, Morning' and 'As I was going up Pippin Hill'. There are also awful warnings of what happens to such disobedient and foolish rebels as 'Don't Care', 'Tom, Tom, the Piper's Son' and 'Little Polly Flinders'. Courtship, marriage and child-rearing are constant preoccupations and there are hints of an erotic earthiness which has been bowdlerized for nursery consumption:

> Sukey, you shall be my wife
> And I will tell you why:
> I have got a little pig
> And you have got a sty.

The innumerable references to casual violence, eating and being eaten, may sustain darker psychoanalytic interpretations but they simply delight the young child's taste for slapstick situations and outrageous humour.

The use of entertaining stories as guides to the ways of a culture is as old as myth and legend. In these stories explanations are offered for the origins of the universe and of human life. Discussions about the nature of good and evil are conducted in terms of gods, heroes, monsters, the natural world and other parallel worlds. Stories of the world religions are found in this genre and are evidence of the power of learning allied with entertainment. Although some myths and legends from around the world may be successfully introduced to young children (Cook, 1976; Rosen, 1991), the early years of education are often better served by folk and fairy tales. The human concerns of these stories and their variations on the theme of growing up and gaining independence constitute the archetypal story of everyone's childhood. Whatever the cultural origins of the stories they all tell the young that courage, resourcefulness and not a little cunning are necessary on the journey from dependence to maturity. There are also darker themes and lessons in the fairy stories because they are the cleaned up or 'bourgeoisified' tales of the adult pre-literate culture: 'Even now, after their long sojourn in the nursery we can still recognize the traces of such fully grown-up concerns as cruelty and tyranny, betrayal and forgiveness, loss and recovery' (Whitehead, 1980, p. 48). Children do experience some of these problems and the sensitive handling of them through the distancing and mellowing conventions of this tradition has a place in the early years.

The education allied with entertainment aspect of literature need not be limited to learning the ways of a particular culture. Stories and poems also take us into new worlds and extend our experiences immeasurably. This 'open sesame' quality reveals the life-styles and beliefs of other cultures in words and rhymes which are totally understandable, for instance *Bringing the Rain to Kapiti Plain* (Aardema, 1981). Literature can also summon up the historical past while staying close to our present lived experience, and this can all happen in a picture book for young children, *Babylon* (Walsh, 1982). And of course stories can suggest the most extraordinary future possibilities, as in *Up and Up* (Hughes, 1979)!

Literature is not limited to passing on the messages of the culture, it frequently challenges the taken-for-granted assumptions of a society. In this connection, the traditional forms can still be used by contemporary writers and artists to explore changing perceptions of gender roles: *The Paper Bag Princess* (Munsch, 1980), *Clever Gretchen and Other Forgotten Folk Tales* (Lurie, 1980) represent an important trend which has continued. Contemporary books for young children are contributing new models of stronger girls and gentler boys. The new heroines are imaginative and determined (*Amazing Grace*, Hoffman and Binch, 1991); or practical and confident when outwitting a stupid wolf stuck in a fairy tale time-warp (*Last Stories of Polly and the Wolf*, Storr, 1990). They may also display true courage in overcoming fear and rescuing a brother from the 'death' of an undeveloped emotional life (*The Tunnel*, Browne, 1989). A mother also changes her exclusively nurturing role and employs shock tactics to re-educate her stereotypical sons and spouse (*Piggybook*, Browne, 1986).

Gentler boys range from Jasper, thinly disguised as a kitten, cultivating his garden (*Jasper's Beanstalk*, Butterworth and Inkpen, 1992), to the rather exploited but willing hero of *Carry Go Bring Come* (Samuels and Northway, 1988). And it is a loving and resourceful older brother who solves a baby sister's eating problems in *Eat up, Gemma* (Hayes and Ormerod, 1988).

These examples of the rich diversity of human behaviour, along with the imaginative questioning of the gender stereotypes which limit the possibilities of life for female and male children, are a kind of literary play. Safely protected by the story or book form, children are able to try on a different role and ask, 'What if. . . ?'

Play

Literature may be understood as a way of playing and several characteristics are common to the two activities. They are both major ways of attempting to make sense of the world.

In this process, stories and poems are play resources which children may use along with other found objects, materials, toys and their own bodies and movements. Play is safe because it is not for real, and literature constitutes a safe playground in that the most disturbing events can be contemplated and mastered. Play and literature allow for lots of 'trying it out', repetition and re-presentation being the crucial features. We might link this with the desire small children have to hear the same stories, look at the same picture books and recite the same verses, over and over again. One element in this is the mesmerizing quality of repeated phrases, unusual words and the patterned nature of language. *The Fat Cat* (Kent, 1972) has a familiar folk-tale pattern which exploits all these features, but such unlikely poems as *The Daffodils* and *Ode on a Grecian Urn* have been known to work the same magic (White, 1954, p. 142). One element in this passion for repetition must be the satisfaction gained from expectations fulfilled.

Literature is a sort of language role-play which can prepare us for what might happen when, for instance, a tiger comes to tea (Kerr, 1968), or there is an unusual bear in the bath (Newman and Foreman, 1993). The possibilities of repeating and re-presenting do not stop at the level of language patterns. Feelings, images and ideas are explored and tried out in a safe way, with the heat off. Mention has already been made of the opportunities which stories and poems give for approaching jealousy and rudeness, anger and anxiety. The great success of *Where the Wild Things Are* (Sendak, 1967) is that it allows for play not just with the feelings but also with the images of anger, powerlessness and anxiety. And all this rage is expressed and finally controlled within the love and forgiveness symbol of food – a supper that is still hot! Literature also provides opportunities for play with gentler emotions, minor mishaps and quiet daily achievements, as in the words and images of Shirley Hughes, Pat Hutchins, Petronella Breinburg, Ezra Jack Keats and Jan Ormerod.

Children's responses and questions indicate that they are very interested in playful exploration of all the possibilities they meet in literature. Poems and stories are in themselves storehouses of ideas, sets of possibilities and interpretations. They open up endless vistas of speculations and suggestions, as every teacher of young children soon learns. What if a baby only ate avocado pears and grew enormously strong, as in *Avocado Baby* (Burningham, 1982)? After all, children are constantly told 'eat up all your food and you'll grow big and strong'. What if the classroom gerbil was a kangaroo – *Maybe it's a Tiger* (Hersom, 1981)? What if all the world were paper and all the seas were ink?

This nonsensical pushing out of the boundaries of the normal may have a serious purpose. It can explore the range of the natural, human and cultural experiences which might befall us and this sort of knowledge is important for the young and inexperienced. This aspect of literature is also quietly subversive, a sort of safety valve for the child:

> I know someone who can
> take a mouthful of custard and blow it
> down their nose.
>
> (Rosen, 1983)

and for the adult:

> When I am an old woman I shall wear purple
> With a red hat which doesn't go, and doesn't suit me,
> And I shall spend my pension on brandy and summer gloves.
>
> (Joseph, 1977, p. 22)

But, as the poem hints, subversion is more than just a safety valve, it is a very deep kind of play (Geertz, 1976) which risks all to push out the boundaries of convention and belief, or challenge the structures of power in a culture. Many societies have contained these challenges within the allowed licence of 'carnival', but it is now quite usual to describe the subversive and playful aspects of literature in terms of carnival (Bakhtin, 1968). Literature constantly resists social control and offers children, and adults, parody, role-reversal, rudeness and 'time off' from conformity.

Safe from the need to do something about it in the world of practical affairs, we are more fully able to explore the implications, ideas and values of the literary world. It is this freedom from external demands and the resulting depth of exploration of all the possibilities of the material that suggest that response to literature is like playing.

Forms and feelings

Literature is playful, subversive and pleasurable but it is also a way of giving form to feelings which are inexplicit and inarticulate. Young children experience powerful feelings which do need some form of validation and expression. Without wishing to reduce literature to therapy or a counselling service, we can still acknowledge a psychoanalytic dimension to views of literature (Winnicott, 1971; Bettelheim, 1975; Tucker, 1981). Writers and illustrators of children's books claim that powerful feelings are given pictorial shapes and names in their books: '*Wild Things* really is the anxiety and pleasure and immense problem of being a small child' (Sendak, 1977, p. 243).

The shape of the narrative and the characterization of the protagonists makes a pattern. What may be experienced in daily life as just overwhelming feelings becomes named and pictured in literature as greed or fear or jealousy. A surprising number of story and picture books for the young explore complex and difficult issues in a totally accessible way.

Images and narrative sequence allow for the controlled contemplation of potentially disastrous feelings and situations. Anthony Browne's picture books deal with loneliness, depression, neglect and jealousy: *Hansel and Gretel* (1981), *Gorilla* (1983), *The Visitors Who Came to Stay* (McAfee and Browne, 1984). Jealousy and the fear of losing love are at the centre of *John Brown, Rose and the Midnight Cat* (Wagner, 1977). This rather threatening theme is distanced by the traditional device of an animal persona. It's just a big, cuddly, shaggy, dog that is jealous of a stray cat – as the full-page pictures show! Such distancing devices as animal disguises and non-blood relatives (step-parents and step-siblings) are part of the traditional folk tale genre. The metaphors and symbols for human feelings which these traditional tales provide continue to reverberate in the culture. Witches and giants, resourceful little pigs and trolls, Anansi the spider-man, all are ways of telling about guilt and fear, courage and resourcefulness.

The power of the story, in prose or poetry, is that it not only names the conflict but proposes a plan of action and a resolution. The pattern of the narrative may be highly traditional with a journey formula, magical transformations and starkly polar characterizations of good/bad, rich/poor, clever/stupid. A modern pattern might involve the magic of dream, wish fulfilment (*Aldo*, Burningham, 1991) or even daydream sequences as in *Come Away from the Water, Shirley* (Burningham, 1977). The magic odyssey might pass through inner city streets – *Nini at Carnival* (Lloyd, 1978). But the endings always have new achievements or explanations and a satisfactory sense of completion. Such clear resolutions are rare in the everyday world but they may influence our hopes and expectations of personal happiness and success.

Images

When considering literature for young children we should give careful attention to the pictorial images. Much of the narrative sequence and characterization in stories is carried in the pictures. The best-loved books often depend on the child's awareness of what the pictures are showing about the story. *Rosie's Walk* (Hutchins, 1968) is a favourite example, with the real plot and build up of tension dependent on good 'reading' of the illustrations. A picture book of *101 Things to Do with a Baby* (Ormerod, 1984) has a stronger story suggested within the simple catalogue of innocent activities. This multi-layered quality of all satisfying literature is apparent in the best of the picture books and accounts for their lasting appeal. The complexity of layers of meaning contained in pictures as well as text makes them books to grow into and grow up with.

Picture books themselves have 'grown up' and come out of the nursery cupboard in recent years. There is a wide acknowledgement of their complexity and multilayered nature, and scholars describe them as richly 'over the top', subversive and indeterminate (Lewis, 1990). The latter characteristic refers to the 'gaps' in the texts and the pictures: we are not told or shown everything and must draw our own narrative conclusions about Granpa's empty chair (Burningham, 1984), for example. Subversion is now used in picture books to turn the traditional folk tale themes upside down, as in *The Three Little Wolves and the Big Bad Pig* (Trivizas and Oxenbury, 1993), and even to challenge the very conventions for constructing books (*The Stinky Cheese Man*, Scieszka and Smith, 1992; *Black and White*, Macaulay, 1990).

This richness, variety and open-endedness in the modern picture book has made it an important genre for literary study in both the primary and secondary phases of education, as recent analyses demonstrate (Michaels and Walsh, 1990; Baddeley and Eddershaw, 1994; Marriott, 1995).

Books and their images carry great prestige in a highly literate culture and to see ourselves in these stories and these images gives us a reflected status and value. All our children need to see themselves reflected and reaffirmed in the stories and the books we share with them. In the earlier discussion of justifications for the teaching of literature it was suggested that literature can be a major way of confirming and valuing individual and community experiences. The implications for the images in books are particularly significant because the pictures are so salient and important to the young emergent reader of literature. Children must see their race, gender and social experiences reflected, as well as finding new worlds, new experiences and the wilder side of fantasy.

Thinking in pictures is a crucial feature of human cognition although we tend to underestimate the role it plays in our waking and dreaming hours. Cognitive psychology would suggest that representing experiences and objects in the mind as images is an early and potent human development. The emergence of this form of thinking indicates the beginnings of symbolic thought. In literature the power of words to trigger images in the mind is one of the major sources of our pleasure. Poetry has a significant role to play here although we should not underestimate the picture-making power of such phrases as 'a gingerbread house', or 'trip-trap, trip-trap, over the wooden bridge', and 'Rapunzel, Rapunzel, let down your gold hair'.

In sharing poems and rhymes with young children we are developing an awareness of words as specific and concrete in their ability to describe and pay homage to the 'thingness' of things. The mental pictures of 'a golden pear', 'a pea-green boat' or 'me and Harrybo's go-kart' (Rosen, 1983), may stay and glow in our imaginations.

Metaphor may arise from our ability to picture things and perceive similarities between apparently disparate objects, or events. Metaphor, as the ability to describe one thing in terms of another, is the great gift of language in its literary or poetic forms. Certainly the vivid pictorial comparisons of metaphor permeate the most prosaic uses of language and the whole life of a culture. We continue anachronistically to look under 'the bonnet' of a car, 'make tracks' and 'push the boat out'! But we do well to remember that the metaphors and images which strongly colour our perceptions of the world and of our experiences are rooted in only one of many ways of seeing (Berger, 1972) and only one of many ways with words (Heath, 1983). The stories of a culture are the heart of that culture and they are as full of dire warnings as of joyful celebrations.

Stories do not help us to live better; they help us to understand living better. What we choose to do about that understanding is another story (Benton and Fox, 1985, p. 15).

Learning through narrative and literature

The success of children's literature as a field study – her own success – has an unpleasant side to it. At times she feels as if she were employed in enclosing what was once open heath or common. First she helped to build a barbed-wire fence about the field; then she helped to pull apart the wildflowers that grow there in order to examine them scientifically.

(Alison Lurie, 1985, p. 236)

Teachers do not own literature, it cannot be enclosed, and dissection only kills the flowers, but, used with love and respect, literature can support and extend children's learning. I am suggesting a partnership approach in which children, parents and teachers share the literary resources of their communities, past and present. In considering learning through literature we might think of young children as researchers, of parents as teachers, of teachers as readers and of classrooms as literary workshops.

Children as researchers

The weight of research evidence and commonsense observations overwhelmingly suggest a complex view of young children as learners. We can no longer allow such antiquated metaphors as 'blank slates' and 'empty vessels' to influence our approach to educating children – of any age. The young learner is actively engaged in making sense of encounters with persons, objects, images, events and ideas. The process is one of finding out by observing, forming hypotheses, testing out the hypotheses and considering the feedback. In this sense children are researchers. Chapter 7 also focuses on the development of the hypotheses which individual learners bring to the task of becoming readers and writers. Much of the research considered in the first section of this chapter contains examples of children actively involved in the learning-as-research process. The world of literature is encountered and understood by young children through this same process. Stories and poems are not received passively, they are subjected to intensive experimentation and scrutiny.

This is indicated by children's questions, re-enactments and reformulations of the stories and poems they hear and see. They will question the messages and import of the images in a picture book:

Why he making a funny face?
Is that man –
Is that man shouting for them to go away?

(Wells, 1985b, p. 138)

They will query the propositions of the narrative, particularly the values and attitudes:

Father (reads): There was once a wicked queen who had a magic mirror.
Child (3:9): She's nice ain't she? (*refers to picture of queen*).

(Payton, 1984, p. 56)

In this instance the traditional tale has triggered the interesting idea that outward appearances may be deceptive, particularly in the sphere of human behaviour and morality.

Children also seize on any new and unusual extensions of word meanings:

Flowers, bed, beds in flowers. . . ? (flower-beds)

(Payton, 1984, p. 55)

These kinds of responses indicate that, given time, security and the sheer pleasure of sharing books, children of pre-school age already behave like readers. They actively interrogate the text in a process of reconstructing its meanings:

Mother: It's a swatter. He's going to hit the wasp with it.
D (3:0): How d'you hit wasps watters?

(Wells, 1985b, p. 138)

Language plays the central role in learning through encounters with literature. It is the tool for discovering and reconstructing the meanings of stories and poems, as the examples show. But literature is made of language, it consists of sounds and words in particular arrangements and patterns. Young children indicate strong preferences for repeated sound patterns in stories: 'and they went rumpeta, rumpeta, rumpeta, all down the road' (*The Elephant and the Bad Baby*, Vipont, 1969); and repeated questions: 'Will you be my mummy?' (Ahlberg and Ahlberg, 1989); and the repetition of exotic names: 'and Skolinkenlot and Skohottentot' (*The Fat Cat*, Kent, 1972).

This taste for language spills over into a delight in commercial jingles, strange words and lyrical singing rhymes:

Rosy apple, lemon and a pear
A bunch of roses she shall wear.

A passion for tasting and savouring language is the source of poetry and implies that teachers of poetry have a nurturing role to play, rather than handing out neatly dissected flowers.

It would appear, then, that children bring to the learning process powerful strategies for exploring new experiences and a taste for the poetic quality of language. But the earlier discussion indicated that they also have a marked sensitivity to narrative form and are themselves emergent storytellers. Children learn through literature and from literature because they are disposed to order their own memories and experiences in story-like ways. They bring to their first encounters with stories and books language expectations derived from their early socialization and language learning. This implies some cultural variety, but basic expectations of interesting events, recognizably human motives and feelings, and satisfactory outcomes, will be brought to literary experiences by most children. Experiences with books and readings will introduce a range of conventional patterns but we need to remember that they are made sense of in terms of everyday human anecdote and story. 'Once upon a time' is but an addition to the repertoire of openings which began with eye-contact and progressed through patting adults to gain attention, to demanding 'Guess what?'. They are all ways of getting into contact with a listener and making a contribution to the ongoing story-making of human society.

The child-researcher does not just bring intellectual and linguistic skills and expectations to the process of learning through literature. The individual child's inner world of images, experiences and fantasy is also involved in a complex interaction with the world of the author or storyteller. Literature is not just language at its most complex and varied (DES, 1975) but also at its most subjective. We can only guess at the outcomes of the meetings between the inner world of the child and the narratives given by the culture.

We should tread softly but never underestimate the power and understanding of the young child in active engagement with the work of literature. The story of Cushla (Butler, 1979) reminds us that the most severely damaged young life can develop and master the environment through the media of 'a cuddle and a bottle and a book' (p. 102).

Parents as teachers

Parents, or other caring adults in a parental role, play a crucial part in enabling the young child to develop strategies for learning. In this sense the parent is a significant first teacher. As well as being significant in developing the child's early language through pre-linguistic communicative activities and shared mutual conversations, the adult introduces the child to the narrative conventions of the culture.

The evidence on early reading also indicates that parental involvement is a crucial element in the child's success in learning to read. Many of the examples in this chapter are of pre-school age children sharing books at home with their families. The adults appear to be providing all the appropriate educational requirements: a safe environment, interesting material, warm encouragement and useful, that is sensible, feedback. The activities of parents and other adult care-givers also emphasize the great value of reading aloud to young children – and the not so young (Trelease, 1982)! To read aloud is to restore the human voice and meaning-bearing rhythms of intonation to the print on the page. The activity is closely related to ordinary dramatic telling of tales, jokes, gossip, memories and anecdotes. The power of oral telling is obvious when we still resort to asking a friend to 'listen to this', as we struggle with a difficult set of instructions or share our pleasure in a particularly good passage in a novel or a newspaper.

Sharing and pleasure are probably the most valuable lessons we can learn from parents. Parents teach us the importance of building up a shared world of experiences and assumptions with the young learner. Much of parental success with young readers must come from the use of shared family history and anecdote to contextualize and explain the world of the book. Events and motives are interpreted through a constant checking back to similar incidents and experiences in the life of the child.

Luckily parents never can forget that the child on their lap or at their feet is quite unique. This great advantage which they have over the professional teacher does constitute a permanent enhancement of everything the child says and does. The motivation for the child of having the full attention of this totally committed and caring parent-teacher must be powerful indeed. Moreover, reading stories, singing songs and telling tales is not restricted to one time of day or one appropriate place. The parent's role as care-giver allows narrating to be shared in the most intimate and natural ways. The puns, jokes, stories and musings flow spontaneously in kitchens, bathrooms and in bed. They are part of the playing and pretending which fill the young child's day. Parents as teachers are successful to the extent that they can ignore set times and proper places for learning, and avoid fear of failure and tests of success.

Teachers as readers

Delight in literature is more likely to be caught than taught, and in the early years of education young children need to be with adults who turn to literature for their own pleasure. The teachers who are successful in sharing literature with young children are probably still avid readers whose lives are enriched just as much by the books the children enjoy as by their own private reading. However, children's literature is a large and expanding field and some tentative suggestions might help to keep teachers exploring the available material. Old favourites, to be constantly returned to, are one of the great satisfactions of literature, but there is a temptation to stay with the familiar stock of classroom books. Teachers' ongoing professional development must involve being adventurous and committed readers.

Teachers as readers might consider an informal programme of reading around certain themes as a way of extending their familiarity with traditional literature and newer publications. The themes to be suggested here are no more than examples of ways of getting into children's literature and they apply to poetry as well as to story. However, poetry should not be glossed over at this point, or just resorted to in order to 'service' classroom displays and projects, or even to provide phonological exercises (Whitehead, 1993).

Sensitivity to poetic language develops with familiarity and teachers need to read both traditional and modern collections. Teachers' own reading should strengthen their awareness of poetry as play with language, as in nursery, street and playground rhymes, songs and lyrics and nonsense verse. Nonsense verse moves from playing with language to playing with ideas:

All-Purpose Poem for State Occasions

The nation rejoices or mourns
As this happy or sombre day dawns
Our eyes will be wet
As we sit round the set
Neglecting our flowerbeds and lawns.

(Wendy Cope, 1986, p. 14)

Poetry can also be approached as a way of celebrating and paying homage:

Snow-cone nice
Snow-cone sweet
Snow-cone is crush ice
and good for the heat.

(*Snow-Cone*, John Agard, 1983)

Or a way to mourn:

Ample make this bed;
Make this bed with awe
In it wait till judgement break
Excellent and fair.

(Emily Dickinson, 1959, p. 73)

And traditional poetry has always told a good story:

What has happened to Lulu, mother?
What has happened to Lu?
There's nothing in her bed but an old rag-doll
And by its side a shoe.

(Charles Causley, 1970, p. 15)

Our own reading of children's literature might pursue such themes as childhood and schooling, picture books, other cultures, or the works of one author or illustrator. A consideration of childhood and schooling reminds us of our own childhood but it is important to range beyond both the immediate age of our pupils and the social and cultural settings we know. *Slake's Limbo* (Holman, 1974), *The Nature of the Beast* (Howker, 1985), *The Idle Bear* (Ingpen, 1986), *Goodnight Mr. Tom* (Magorian, 1981), *Handles* (Mark, 1983) and *Dear Nobody* (Doherty, 1992) are worthwhile adult 'reads' in their own right. Similarly, poetry collections, such as *Please Mrs Butler* (Ahlberg, 1983), *Two's Company* (Kaye, 1992) and *A Caribbean Dozen* (Agard and Nichols, 1994) appeal to people – children and adults.

In recent years the picture book has become an important art form and a medium for discussing fully adult issues (*The Butter Battle Book*, Seuss, 1984; *War Game*, Foreman, 1993). The use of images to tell a tale, with or without words, has attracted distinguished artists and launched many young children into reading. A picture book can transform the routine sequence of getting up in the morning into a story (*Sunshine*, Ormerod, 1981), or suggest the wildest flights of fantasy. The medium is particularly successful in handling the humour of chaos (*Mr Gumpy's Outing*, John Burningham, 1970) and touching lightly on stress and anxiety (*Geraldine's Blanket*, Holly Keller, 1984). In the picture books the worlds of wishful thinking (*The Snowman*, Raymond Briggs, 1978), surrealist humour (*Meal One*, Ivor Cutler, 1971) and delicious terror (*Mr and Mrs Pig's Evening Out*, Mary Rayner, 1976) find full expression.

Strangeness and variety are not just found in fantasy literature. Human communities are also diverse and fascinating and some reading of the literature of other cultures should inform the teacher's own perceptions. This can range from the traditional tales which carry the meanings and beliefs of the culture (*The People Could Fly*, Virginia Hamilton, 1985) to the contemporary experience stories of many ethnic and cultural groups (*Sunshine Island, Moonshine Baby*, Clare Cherrington, 1984; *Nowhere to Play*, Buchi Emecheta, 1980).

Classrooms as literary workshops

The idea that classrooms for the early years of schooling should be literary workshops arises from all that has been suggested in this chapter. It is an approach which sees children's experiences of literature developing alongside their experiences and explorations of the world of persons and materials. A classroom workshop provides space, appropriate resources, advice and sound examples for the young learner.

Adequate provision for literature involves rather more than a collection of story and poetry books. Careful thought needs to be given to the arrangement of the physical environment and to an atmosphere conducive to silent reading, informal sharing of books and large group storytelling sessions. A teacher's passion for books is reflected in the priority given to organizing carpeted, cushioned and screened quiet areas. We all know the value of a special chair, an attractive plant or flower arrangement and the thematic grouping of some books and artefacts. But it takes determination and love to keep such areas fresh and inviting. The crucial test is, am I irresistibly drawn to this part of the room?

The collection of books should be carefully arranged, with attractive covers or illustrations showing. A row of spines is neither informative nor appealing to the youngest children and the struggle to remove a tightly wedged book from a wire rack or an overcrowded bookshelf is not an incentive to discover literature and certainly not part of the author's invitation to the reader. The question of the actual number of books available for young children should be considered. An ill-assorted and overwhelming collection of books on shelves and in boxes is probably not an inducement to become a reader and storyteller. In the early years it is wiser to have a small but frequently changing collection, although popular demand will of course be considered so that special favourites are rarely 'rested'. It is also important to ensure that the children have immediate access to the books of pictures, stories, rhymes, songs and poems which the teacher is currently reading to them. A special shelf or table set aside for these books enables the children to find them easily and have the chance to retell the picture sequence, story or poem for themselves. This access to known texts is a crucial factor in early reading success.

Certain thematic displays, activities or curriculum areas are enhanced by the inclusion of related books. The non-fiction or information books are usually associated with this sort of provision but *Jim and the Beanstalk* (Raymond Briggs, 1970) has been equally at home in the mathematics area or on the natural science table. Similarly, a table of interesting 'found' collections (pebbles, bottle-tops, old keys) can develop around the story of a small child fascinated by 'holes' (*Dig Away Two-Hole Tim*, Agard, 1981).

Literature is in essence cross-curricular and no respecter of subject boundaries, but it can enhance those discrete subjects which are increasingly taught in the early years classroom. Story and verse can be vehicles for the areas of educational experience which we offer young children (Garvie, 1990; Marriott, 1995).

Obviously literature is at the centre of emotional, social, moral and religious curricula because it is concerned with relationships, feelings and moral questions. But it need not stop there. The geographical and historical study of the human condition can be initiated by exposure to such books as *The Mousehole Cat* (Barber and Bayley, 1990), *Where's Julius* (Burningham, 1986) and *Mufaro's Beautiful Daughters* (Steptoe, 1987). Several of the Ahlbergs' picture books recreate a working class 1940s childhood in all its particularity (*Peepo!*, 1981; *Bye Bye Baby*, 1989). A sense of place and of identity underpin children's development of self-esteem, as well as their geographical and historical knowledge, and adult writers reflect this significant factor in their own engagements with identifiable locations. Foreman celebrates the Cornish town of St. Ives in many of his picture books (*The Sand Horse*, 1989; *Jack's Fantastic Voyage*, 1992), and these texts are as steeped in the sense of that place as the St. Ives books of Jill Payton Walsh (*Goldengrove*, 1972; *Unleaving*, 1976), or Virginia Woolf's *To The Lighthouse* (1943).

As befits the concerns of our own time, many contemporary picture books have powerful messages about conservation (*Tigress*, Cowcher, 1991); some provide excellent insights into scientific method (*Dr Xargle's Book of Earthlets*, Willis and Ross 1988), problem solving (*The Giant Jam Sandwich*, Lord and Burroway, 1972) and the uses of levers and pulleys (*The Lighthouse Keeper's Lunch*, Armitage and Armitage, 1977). The art curriculum can only be strengthened by the quality of picture books. At the very least, Anthony Browne's innovative and surrealistic work and the witty drawings of Posy Simmonds and Quentin Blake provide respite from the current obsession with getting young children to paint like Van Gogh and Monet. The mathematical themes of sequence, pattern, order, time and measurement can be supported and extended by picture books: for example, *Rosie's Walk* (Hutchins, 1968), *Sunshine* (Ormerod, 1981), *Meg and Mog* (Nicoll and Pienkowski, 1972) and *Bedtime for Bear* (Stoddard and Munsinger, 1985). And stimulating books about counting and number are always popular with children and adults: *Ten, Nine, Eight* (Bang, 1983) and *When Sheep Cannot Sleep* (Kitamura, 1986).

I have assumed that the teacher of young children is an avid reader of children's literature and adult literature. And I have assumed the availability of a classroom book collection which reflects ethnic diversity and contains modern publications and a good range of traditional materials. But these are very demanding assumptions and the early childhood educator is also responsible for the whole curriculum. Given these demands it is probably essential that the school or the individual teacher reads at least one of the specialized book guides produced for educators and librarians.[2]

As well as providing published material for the children the teacher can also be a creator of narratives, an author. This can start from the simple idea that we all have a wealth of autobiographical anecdotes which can be shaped into stories. A teacher-made collection of little books can grow out of oral storytelling sessions in which the teacher recalls childhood incidents which may link with and extend the children's experiences. Little songs, rhymes and poems can enhance the tales of 'once, when I was very small . . .'. My own greatest successes in this vein were the old music hall songs my grandfather taught me, such as 'Any old iron' and 'Boiled beef and carrots'. These traditional resources, superbly illustrated, can be found in *Cockney Ding-Dong* (Charles Keeping, 1975).

If the classroom in the early years of education is to be a literary workshop, what more can go on apart from maintaining positive attitudes and good provision for literature? As far as narrative and story are concerned it is useful to think of three main aspects: developing and extending the children's own storying skills; increasing the children's experiences of listening to stories and book language; and expanding the children's experiences with books and supporting early reading strategies. Many reception classes now contain four-year-olds, and it is crucial for their language and literacy development that we upgrade the quality and the quantity of oral language, as well as story and poetry, which they experience. This upgrading of oracy will also be the most powerful way in which we can support the many young bilinguals in early years classes.

Developing and extending the children's own storying skills involves respecting the part played by narrative in making sense of experiences, as well as understanding its significance as a foundation for book language and literacy. Young children's oral anecdotes, tentative musings, and shared talking through of experiences and activities should be both encouraged and actively planned for in all curriculum strategies. Decisions about classroom organization, work in the outdoor space and visits in the outside community need to be informed by a respect for children and adults telling stories to preserve and present identities and give a meaningful pattern to their lives.

The children bring the sense-making stories of their families and the communities they live in into the school. How these narratives are received and developed affects not just attitudes to schooling and literacy in the early years, it probably colours life-long attitudes. The oral storying of the children is also the raw material of books made for the classroom collection but reflecting the unique experiences of the group and of individuals. The words can be dictated to a teacher-scribe or captured on audio tape for later writing up or typing by the teacher. The children can be the illustrators of their own books and sometimes a picture or a set of pictures will also suggest captions and a story. We all know about making books with children but it is a powerful resource which is still under-used. There are many other adults, including parents, classroom assistants and members of the local community, who can be shown how to make books with children (Smith, 1994). Students in college are now taught to use photography in the school, the classroom and the community as a way of stimulating and extending book-making with young children. Another resource is the published picture book without words for which children can be encouraged to create a narrative text.

Increasing the children's experiences of listening to stories and book language is a fairly obvious and quite central responsibility of the teacher of literature and literacy. We learn to be story makers and readers by internalizing the stories of others. The pleasure of literature and the access it gives to other worlds and other lives can be gained by the young child only through listening. This puts a great emphasis on the quality of the books and stories chosen by the adult, the adult's knowledge of literature and the storytelling skills of the adult. Even if careful thought is given to the choice of stories, the effect can be marred by poor telling. Thought must be given to the central propositions in the story; the conveying of the patterns of expectations, climax and tension by using pauses, pitch and volume; and suggesting characterization by voice changes. Listening to professional actors and storytellers, live and on the broadcast media, is one way of sharpening our skills as tellers of tales. But a tale well told in a pub or supermarket check-out queue can be a model of how to go about creating the oldest spellbinding known to human beings. This is a reminder that we should be able and prepared to tell tales without a book on many occasions.

When we choose to read to individuals or groups of children from a book we are introducing them to the distinctive patterns of book language and setting up helpful expectations of text. All the good provision of books in the early years classroom is both an introduction to the world of literature and an early reading activity. As we share books with young children we teach them to use context, knowledge of the world, pictures and familiar language patterns in order to re-create the author's story. As we talk the pictures and the text alive, we put the human voice back into the book. Books are created by people, as children who make books with their teachers and parents soon learn. But the good literature workshop is a place where young children can also be silent and alone with books, browsing through them and bringing their own feelings and experiences to bear on the author's narrative. A book may contain many possible narratives or layers of meaning, and private involvement is also part of the literary experience.

Poetry in the early years of education, and at any other level, is primarily for pleasure. Delight in particular words in particular order can be fostered and shared. Teachers and children together can be collectors of words, rhymes, songs and poems. The classroom can be the location for a word hoard or collection which is gathered by children and teacher. The poems can be in published collections and in class-made books or anthologies. Poems can be written out on individual cards for the special delight of searching through the box for 'that one about the snail'. Poetic language works for young children when its rhythms are felt in the body and its words tasted on the tongue. So, lots of verbal telling aloud is crucial to the sharing of poetry. The desire to 'say it again' gradually deposits whole verses and felicitous lines and phrases in the memory. Apart from this collecting, sharing and telling, I would not advocate teaching poetry by dissection and compulsory 'creative writing' in the early years of education.

Conclusions

Should the last words in a new version of a chapter on narrative and literature go to IT and other media? Perhaps 'yes' and perhaps 'no'. Yes, it is clear that young children are computer and TV/video literate at an early age, often outstripping their carers and teachers when it comes to reading visual narratives, images and icons. But, no, the book is still central to literature and literacy, and should be defended. It is portable, requiring neither electricity nor batteries, and it goes with us into our most private and secret places. The book is also the ultimate achievement in user-friendliness: we can flick back and forth, skip pages and even sniff it, bite it and stand our cups on it! Although computer texts can be scanned too, they are not simultaneously and entirely present as objects while we skip through the 'pages'.

This is not a Luddite defence of books against machines. Let us use literature on software and on audio and video tapes. But let us also nurture the unique engagement of the child's mind with oral tellings, images and texts in books.

Suggested further reading

Marriott, S. (1995) *Read On. Using Fiction in the Primary School*, Paul Chapman, London.
Styles, M., Bearne, E. and Watson, V. (eds.) (1992) *After Alice. Exploring children's literature*, Cassell, London.
Whitehead, M. R. (1990) *Language and Literacy in the Early Years*, Paul Chapman, London.

Notes

1. *A Nursery Companion* (Opie and Opie, 1980) contains a wealth of examples of making learning pleasurable in early nineteenth-century nurseries and schoolrooms.
2. For example, Books for Keeps, 6 Brightfield Road, Lee, London SE12 8QF, or Signal, The Thimble Press, Lockwood, Station Road, South Woodchester, Stroud, Glos. GL5 5EQ.

7

Early Literacy

Clare Kelly

What is literacy?

You may be reading this book from cover to cover or picking out extracts or chapters that are relevant to your purposes for selecting it in the first place. As you read you will probably be picturing images of children and schools you know, you may even be remembering your own childhood as you question statements that do not match your own experience and anticipate others that do. Perhaps you will pause to reflect on or re-read a passage because it re-affirms your own opinion or offers new insights causing you to re-evaluate what you already know.

You may recommend the book to a friend or colleague and if you are a student you may use the ideas, implications and new connections you have made, to set down your own views. As you begin to type or write you will need to give some thought to how you are going to organize the myriad of different impressions, reflections and strands that seem important, in a way that will make sense to your audience. You may well find that, in the act of organizing your thoughts and grasping for the right word or phrase, you begin to be more aware of what you really think and are even surprised by the new insights and connections that emerge on the paper or screen in front of you.

Of course all of this literate behaviour, and a great deal more besides, is taken for granted. We know that literacy is not just about being able to decode written language or encode it using the conventions of a particular system. Being literate is about knowing that a piece of educational research, a novel, a car maintenance manual and a bus ticket are read in different ways. It is about making choices; knowing what to read but also what not to read. It is about being critical and reflective, using our imagination to explore possibilities and implications and knowing how enjoyable and satisfying that can be. Literacy can lead to greater self-awareness because it enables us to learn through vicarious experience, to

extend and re-structure our thinking, but also to understand and participate in public ways of expressing that thinking.

So literacy confers power upon the individual and with that power
comes control. It is the political nature of literacy that gives it such a central place in the education system and causes parents to invest it with
such importance and sometimes anxiety when their children first start
school. We know that experience of failure can have serious repercus-
sions in both the personal and public domain.

Despite intense public interest in literacy, its true meaning is often misunderstood. Many of the arguments advanced in the reading debate of
the early 1990s disregarded the dynamic nature of literacy. Frequent references to 'back to basics' ignored the necessity of ensuring that our children feel confident and at ease with the advanced technologies that
characterise the latter part of the twentieth century and that they are
equipped to take advantage of the possibilities they offer.

This chapter will examine the experiences of literacy and the strategies
for learning that children bring to school, and explore ways in which we
can build on them to support children's development as confident and
independent readers and writers.

At this point it might be helpful to spend a couple of minutes thinking about your own literacy history. You may not remember learning to
read or write, but there will probably be significant people, texts and particular experiences that spring to mind. When I ask teachers I work with
to carry out this exercise, I am still surprised at the large majority who
see their early reading experiences at school as a distraction if not an
irrelevance to participation in family literacy events. Playing schools with
an older brother or sister, reciting rhymes and playing word games seem
to have been powerful ways of gaining control over written language, as
well as the exciting business of storytelling and storyreading in the company of a treasured parent, grandparent or older sibling.

These reminiscences from successful readers and writers are a reminder
that literacy is a social activity and they also reveal a great deal about
the range of experiences that young children could be offered in the nursery or classroom.

The significance of children's early experiences

When children come to school their knowledge and experience of literacy will be different because it will reflect the social and cultural traditions of their family and community. However there are certain common
experiences that will support their developing literacy. These are:

1. being born into a literate society;
2. learning to talk;
3. hearing stories and narrative.

Being born into a literate society

Children begin the journey to literacy from the moment they can focus on print in the environment. Regardless of whether they have access to books in their home, children become aware of written language as they participate in daily living. Some children will have had print interpreted for them, for others the knowledge will be implicit. At home they may watch television, see junk mail, food labels and packaging, newspapers and magazines, perhaps in more than one language. They will notice print on advertising hoardings, shops, buses, coins, price tickets or their favourite sweets. Anybody who has accompanied children on a print walk around the school will know that there is writing to be found on paving stones, drainpipes, children's clothes, sinks and radiators. The meaning of signs and labels are determined by their physical settings and provide children with a powerful demonstration of the nature and purposes of written language.

Learning to talk

Research evidence has shown that young children are active meaning makers engaged in hypothesizing about the world (Bruner and Haste, 1987; Wells, 1987; Wood, 1988). Studies have shown that they come to make sense of language by using the same strategies (Halliday, 1975; Bruner, 1983). By being highly selective in abstracting what seems significant, formulating their own theories about how language works and relying on helpful feedback to revise or confirm their hypotheses, children are able to make successive approximations to the adult form.

Halliday has shown how children come to understand and use language in ways that have meaning for them. Language becomes a medium for achieving their objectives rather than the main focus of their attention and therefore learning is unconscious. Halliday also stressed the vital role of experienced language users who respond sensitively to children's attempts to make meaning while focusing on their intentions.

Psycholinguists such as Goodman (1967) and Smith (1988) have shown that children's experience of learning to talk is fundamental to their development as readers and writers, since they have demonstrated that the human brain can tolerate ambiguity in a quest for meaning. Studies of young children have shown that they apply similar strategies when learning to make sense of written language as they did when learning to talk. Bissex (1980), Ferreiro and Teberosky (1982), Harste, Woodward and Burke, (1984), Payton (1984) and Minns (1990) have shown how children learn from opportunities to see written language demonstrated in real contexts.

Hearing stories and narrative

All children will have experience of story long before they come to school. Some may have access to an adult who will tell them stories, others will hear and may participate in everyday narratives about, for example, what happened at the supermarket or in the playground. Children will also gain experience of hearing and seeing stories from television and films, from books read aloud and from watching and joining in imaginative play. Carol Fox (1993) has shown how access to narrative structure enables children to gain a sensitivity to its distinctive forms and grammar, such as use of past tense, as well as an introduction to more complex aspects of language.

Story exerts a powerful influence on children to make sense of reading and writing. Bruner (1986) has suggested that it is the possibility that texts provide for penetrating 'possible worlds' that initially attracts children to reading. They learn that stories can take on a more permanent form when represented in writing and that by striving to gain control of written language they can re-create deeply satisfying experiences for themselves.

Stories also encourage children to use their imagination to move away from the constraints of reality into a world that allows them to explore possibilities including that of fictionalizing themselves. Wells (1987), Tizard and Hughes (1984) and Fox (1993) have shown that story and anecdote are one of the first ways that children can take on abstract ideas. Wells' research showed that children's experience of books and stories at home correlated strongly with their later success as readers. This, he argued, was directly related to their experience of learning to create alternative worlds from words alone, which demanded higher levels of thought. Such abstract thought was necessary if children were to understand the symbolic nature of written language.

Literacy as a social and cultural practice

Although there will be commonalities in young children's experience, each child will also bring to school a very particular and personal understanding of what reading and writing are for. Literacy is embedded in the social practices for which it is used and therefore children's experience of literacy is inseparable from the life of their family and community. Brice Heath (1983), Schieffelin and Cochran-Smith (1984) and Minns (1990) have documented the ways in which children learn about literacy from participating in family life. Children become attuned to these literate behaviours from a very early age and, with a powerful drive to be like others, will imitate what they have noticed.

Naima Browne (1993) documented her daughter Rehana's understanding of reading from birth to sixteen months. At fourteen months she imitated the reading behaviour of those around her by studying till receipts, inspecting price labels on clothes and referring to telephone numbers in a diary prior to 'dialling', sometimes stopping halfway through to check the number again. At just thirteen months she was already forming impressions about how gender might mediate reading behaviour. Rehana would only hand a newspaper to her grandfather and a book to her mother and grandmother, because she had previously observed that these were their chosen reading materials.

Early Years practitioners know that children come to school with a range of literacy experiences that give them a sense of the place of literacy in their lives. Some may have shared storybooks from infancy and know how to take meaning from them; others may be learning about the messages in sacred books such as the Qu´rān or Bible. Some children will have sat close to family members as they filled out forms in the post office or looked in the newspaper to find out the time of a television programme. For others, moving between two or more languages and scripts will be a normal feature of home life.

From home to school

The transition from home can be smooth for those children who share the cultural values of the school. Others may have to make fundamental shifts to accommodate new forms of 'school literacy'. Brice Heath (1983), Tizard and Hughes (1984) and Taylor and Dorsey-Gaines (1986) have shown the ways in which schools have failed to take account of this cultural mismatch. Young children's subsequent confusion is then interpreted as being an indication of their inadequacies, rather than a reminder of schools' responsibilities to recognize different ways of talking and knowing. As Hilary Minns (1990) suggests, schools do not hold a monopoly on reading and writing. If we ignore young children's previous experiences and competences and underestimate their potential, we will almost certainly be diminishing them as learners. Many Early Years practitioners are resistant to the mounting pressures that accompany increasingly prescriptive planning schedules, National Curriculum directives and rigid assessment requirements, precisely because they make it difficult to regard provision and practice from the child's point of view.

Children's out-of-school experience can be recognized and extended by using captions, packaging, advertisements, songs and jingles, as well as books to support their reading development. They will also need opportunities and invitations to use written language for the purposes they are familiar with in play settings accompanied by relevant printed resources. In this way children's out of school experiences can be extended to include the more distinctive forms of school literacy, so that all children can build on what they already know.

The difficulty for the busy teacher is how to find out about the diversity of children's experiences. *The Primary Language Record* (1988) later extended to *The Primary Learning Record* (1990) was developed with teachers by staff at the Centre for Language in Primary Education. It offers a framework for charting children's development as readers and writers, talkers and listeners and involves teachers, parents and children in building a cumulative picture of the child as a learner. An important part of the Record is to document progress and development by making observations of children over time in familiar contexts. Observing children writing a list or a letter, browsing in the book corner, reading food packages in the 'shop', or writing a prescription in the 'doctor's surgery' will yield information about their view of literacy and how it develops over time. Such observations will also enable teachers to plan experiences that will support that development.

The *Primary Language Record* also incorporates a conference with parents, when they are invited to share their knowledge of the child at home and at school. Teachers who have used the PLR found that despite their own acknowledgement of the importance of family literacy, they had seriously underestimated both the range of literacy practices that were available to young children and the extent of the support that was offered to them, particularly from grandparents and older siblings. Listening to parents and families has been an important way of finding out about the child's distinctive view of literacy and has also led to better informed partnerships with parents who have themselves become more conscious of their own skills as literacy teachers (King, 1989).

If we recognize that becoming literate is bound up with children's identity as members of a particular social group it is easy to see the sensitivity required in helping the child to move forward into new areas of literacy. Becoming a reader and writer, like all forms of learning, is inextricably linked with the personal and affective domain and the individuality of the child. This emphasis is supported by Bussis *et al.* (1985) whose detailed descriptions of forty young readers reveal a diversity of experience and a range of routes into reading. The researchersfound that children had individual learning styles that affected the way they approached the text, the books they chose, the situations they preferred to read in and their choice of reading partners.

By planning an environment that is responsive to children's search for meaning, we can continue to provide the conditions that characterized children's pre-school learning. Thus we need to give children access to a range of models of written language, help them to ask the right questions and provide them with sensitive feedback when they do. Above all we need to help them feel safe about taking risks in relating what they already know to what is unfamiliar and thus to take their own learning forward. Just as Cecilia Payton (aged 3:7) does in the following extract where she is sharing a book with her father:

F. *(reads)* . . . burnt to a cinder.

C. A nice little doll, cinder?

F. Cinder? Cinderella?

C. Cinder doll

F. Sindy doll, no it's not a Sindy doll. A cinder is a little piece of burnt up wood or something.

(Payton, 1984, p. 54)

Jane Torrey's (1969) description of a five-year-old self-taught reader emphasizes how he has constructed the rules for making sense of written language.

> He appears to have asked just the right questions in his own mind about the relation between language and print and thus to have been able to bridge the gap between his own language and the printed form.

(Torrey, 1969, p. 552)

Enabling children to be self-directed learners is not always easy even for the most committed Early Years practitioners. For many Reception teachers, the constraints of lack of time and large classes, which often include four-year-olds, make it very difficult to offer children the individual attention they need. Furthermore, a revised National Curriculum that fails to acknowledge the extent of children's pre-school learning and offers a narrow skills-based model of literacy learning at the early stages, puts pressure on teachers to organize children's learning in ways that give them less autonomy.

The link between reading and writing

Reading and writing are mutually supportive activities although each makes very different demands upon the child. It used to be regarded as necessary for chidren to learn to read before they could be taught to write. We now know that activites such as reading from the computer screen, sharing books, experimenting with writing and seeing others write, offer children information about how meaning is communicated through written language for an audience. Such activities also demonstrate the conventions of print, such as style and organizational structure, as well as offering an opportunity to examine how words are constructed, including the relationship between sounds and symbols.

One of the first ways that young children come to learn about the permanency and consistency of written language is by seeing their names and those of their friends and family represented. Names are saturated with meaning because they relate to real people in the real world. Children soon become aware of the value placed by others on their written name and of its significance for their own identity. Almost by seeing themselves in print, young children are able to develop a new awareness of what written language is and what it can be used for (Minns, 1990). Early Years practitioners know that names can constitute an important part of environmental print in the Nursery or Reception class and are the source of many games which support children in testing theories of how written symbols work. Children become familiar with the letters in their names which often feature prominently in their early explorations of the writing system.

Bookmaking is another way in which the relationship between reading and writing is reinforced. Creating a book through shared writing offers young children insights into the writing process and provides them with personalized reading material. Children can draw upon their own language, experiences and interests to create their texts. Others may be straight retellings of well loved stories, or adaptations which employ well known structures and refrains, reworked to include familiar people and situations. By being in the dual roles of author and audience, children can find out more about how written language conveys meaning as well as how books work.

Texts also provide models for young children's own experiments with writing. In Figure 7.1, Haroun, aged 5:4, used his knowledge of Titch (Hutchins, 1972) as a support to create his own text.

Seven months later, Haroun drew upon his developing knowledge of story genre and book language when composing an adventure story (see Figure 7.2).

We have acknowledged that children learn about the nature and functions of written language from reading and writing. However, the underlying processes involved in encoding meaning as a writer are different to

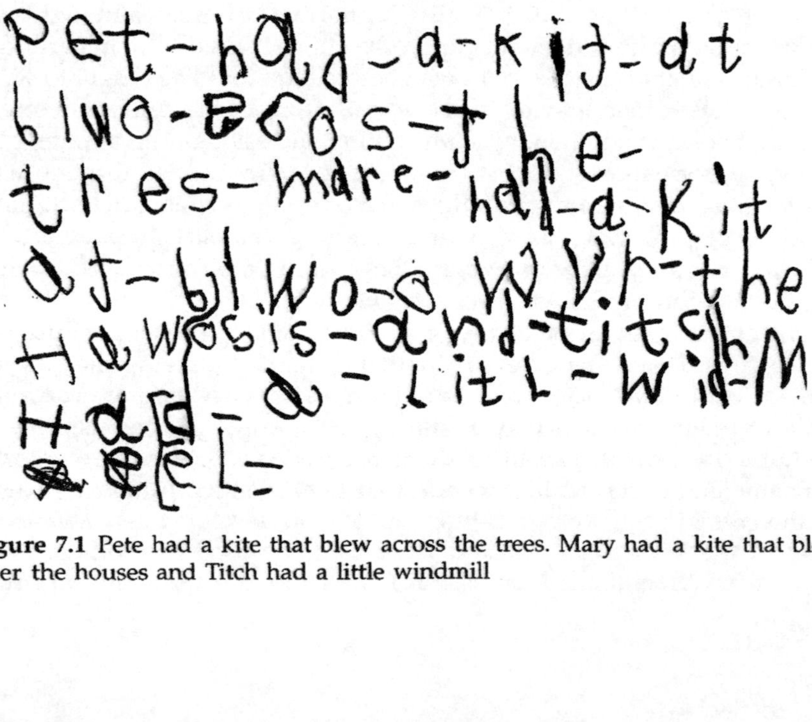

Figure 7.1 Pete had a kite that blew across the trees. Mary had a kite that blew over the houses and Titch had a little windmill

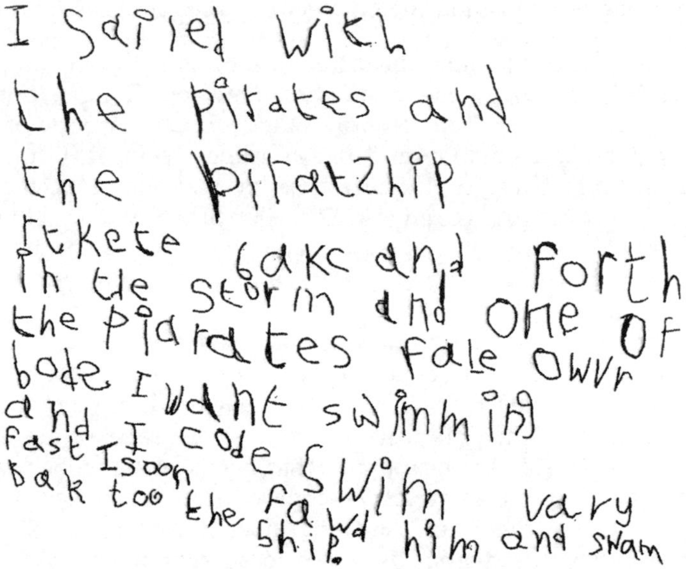

I sailed with the pirates and the pirate ship rocked back and forth in the storm and the pirates fell over and I went swimming fast I could swim soon bak too the ship swim him and swam vary

Figure 7.2 I sailed with the pirates and the pirate ship rocked back and forth in the storm and one of the pirates fell overboard. I went swimming and I could swim very fast. I soon found him and swam back to the ship

those involved in decoding meaning as a reader and for that reason the following sections will examine each aspect separately.

Developing as a writer

To be literate demands an understanding that objects, events and relationships in the real world can be symbolically represented. We have already seen how stories can enable children to develop abstract thought processes, but many other examples of good Early Years practice will encourage this development. Dramatic play, gesture, movement and artistic representation are important ways of learning about symbolizing the world (Vygotsky, 1978; Britton, 1982). Vygotsky has powerfully argued that drawing assumes particular importance as children come to realize that they can draw speech as well as objects.

Writing development has its basis in oral language. Children will come to know that written as well as oral language makes sense. In time however, they will need to understand the differences between spoken and written language if they are to grasp the power and purposes of writing. The formal and impersonal aspects of writing make certain demands on the writer and it is these that can create particular challenges for the child.

Composition and transcription

It is important to keep in mind the different aspects of the writing process. Smith (1982b) has made the distinction between Composition – the expression of ideas, and Transcription – the secretarial aspects of writing such as spelling, punctuation and handwriting. Young children's compositional skills race ahead of their transcriptional ones and teachers act as scribes or encourage children to write independently to free them from the pressures of 'getting it right' and enable them to concentrate on their message. This also offers teachers valuable insights into what a child knows and can do and still has to learn.

If the emphasis is placed on transcriptional elements, teachers may lose an understanding of when children come to ascribe meaning to their drawings and later their writing. We know that children seem to want to be like those around them. Writing to convey a message, rather than just to imitate others, is a significant step that needs to be recognized. The point when children are aware of the communicative function of writing is usually revealed when they ask 'What does it say?'.

If disproportionate attention is given to presentation skills, children will come to see writing as nothing more than a complicated motor skill. Shared writing offers children opportunites to participate in the writing process by composing a text collaboratively and to discuss the conventions of written language. By asking children to routinely write under a picture, copy adult writing or continually write in a book which is only shown to the teacher and then put away, the unique qualities of written language are not being demonstrated. Neither are children being encouraged to be independent learners. There must be many confused children like Ruairidh, a rising five-year-old, in a classroom where tracing and copying were normal practice. He remarked to his mother "I think my teacher's crazy, she keeps expecting me to write things that she's already written!' (MacLean, 1987).

We need to offer children opportunities to explore writing for purposes that make sense to them so that they can find answers to what Marian Whitehead (1990, p. 152) describes as the crucial questions of 'What is it for?' and What's in it for me?'. Like Ruairidh, children's experiences of writing outside school will be for real reasons and specific audiences. Writing needs to be seen as a distinct way of expressing what children have to say, and finding a range of real audiences and purposes is a source of much ingenuity for the teacher. Knowing that their work will be read, responded to, displayed or published in some way will also give children who are ready real reasons for accurate spelling and neat handwriting. As children become more experienced and the range of their writing increases, they will discover that writing can also be used for purposes such as organizing, learning and thinking, that are less dependent on an audience.

As young children are engaged in writing for their own purposes they will also be exploring the features and conventions of their language system. There is a considerable body of research that reveals young children's developing understanding of the writing system (Clay, 1975; Ferriero and Teberosky, 1982; Temple *et al.*, 1988; Goodman, 1990). These researchers, each with their own perspective, have demonstrated the underlying logic of the rule systems that children develop.

Children develop ways of coping with the complexities of the spelling system by looking for regularities and patterns. Studies have shown the systematic way in which children can make logical deductions about the coding system and how their understanding changes with increased opportunities to use and talk about the characteristics of written language (Bissex, 1980; Read, 1986; Peters and Smith, 1993). We know that given access to a range of models of written language and opportunities to explore it for themselves and discuss it with others, children can move through stages in their understanding of conventional spelling (Gentry, 1982; Whitehead, 1990; Czerniewska, 1992; Browne, 1993).

Children's earliest attempts at writing will reveal both the extent and the limit of their knowledge. At the early stages children may be incorporating symbols they recognize such as numerals, letters from their name, and invented letter-like shapes. As they develop an increasingly more refined understanding of the relationship of written symbols to spoken language they will find ways of representing what they hear by, for example, the use of initial sounds or groups of consonants. Encouraging children to gather personal words, and drawing their attention to shape and common letter patterns, encourages them to begin to develop visual strategies for spelling with the result that they are able to draw on a number of different cues to help them spell conventionally.

Parents' own experiences of learning to write at school will almost certainly be different and they may feel confused when their child proudly brings home a piece of writing that they are unable to decipher. If children are to know that their writing is consistently valued, and feel secure in exploring the writing system independently, it is important to explain the view of writing development that informs practice in the nursery or classroom and to show parents examples of what progress looks like.

Developing as a reader

Developments in research into reading and consequent changes in our understanding of how children make sense of written language, have been instrumental in changing practice in many nurseries and schools. The work of Goodman (1967) and Smith (1988) has shown how successful readers orchestrate different kinds of knowledge and draw on a range of cues to make meaning from the text. Margaret Meek (1988) has argued how texts subtly teach children about the diversity of written language, as well as offering them support in making connections between their knowledge of spoken and written forms.

There is an ongoing debate about the teaching and learning of reading which is linked to models of human learning and the relevance to inexperienced readers of insights into how skilled readers operate. This professional discourse was reduced to superficial argument when it was simplified and misrepresented during the emotive public outcry about reading standards and accountability in the early part of the decade. Nevertheless, there is real disagreement between those who believe that reading can be simplified for children if it is broken down into constituent hierarchical skills, and those who argue that using adult logic to simplify a very complex process, and presenting children with manageable parts to be mastered separately, will actually make reading more difficult for them. They conceive of reading as a single stage involving a complex integration of skills, all of which are present from the start.

Those who favour the latter approach suggest that reading is an active transactional process between the reader and the text. Readers create their own meanings beyond the 'surface level' of general agreement so that the significance of particular texts will vary for each reader (Meek, 1988; Chambers, 1993; Martin and Leather, 1994). If children are to become real readers rather than just decoders of print, it is important to make reading meaningful, so that they know from the start that it is something that can be enjoyable and personally satisfying. Otherwise, the impetus and satisfaction can come from moving through books with gradients of difficulty and the message is that reading is a competition or a race, rather than a deeply satisfying experience and a way of finding your way in the world.

Children will not necessarily discover for themselves that there are layers of meaning beyond the words by being read to. From their earliest encounters, young children need to be encouraged to make their own meanings by talking through a story, revisiting it on their own and re-enacting it through dramatic play and other forms of representation. In the following example, George (aged 3:7) who is sharing *Harriet and the Roller Coaster* (Carlson, 1982) with his father, is encouraged to interpret the meaning of the text and the pictures:

F. (*reading*) '*I'm going to ride on the roller coaster'*
    George told Harriet. It's so big, you can't
    see the top. I know. My sister told me
G. Big sister
F. Oh yes you're right. *My big sister told me*
    (*reading*) '*It goes so fast that if you don't*
    hold on you'll fall . . .'
G. What's that ladder?
F. That's not a ladder, it's the end of the roller coaster.
    It looks like a ladder doesn't it.
    (*reading*) '*I bet you're too scared to ride the roller coaster. You'd*

probably start crying.'
G. Why?
F. Because she's scared of the roller coaster
G. Sh..she's she's ill and she might be sick. Why is she ill?
F. Because she's scared of the roller coaster. Would you be scared?
G. No I wouldn't.
F. *(reading) That night Harriet didn't sleep very well.*
G. Why?
F. Because she's frightened.
G. I wouldn't . . . . She's scared.
   She might . . . might cry.
   She's scared of the roller coaster.
F. Yes, that's why she can't sleep.

Such speculations, interrogations and connections become internalized in mature readers. Martin and Leather (1994) have shown the depth and subtlety of very young children's responses to text when they are given appropriate support. Meek (1994) suggests that there are many inexperienced readers of all ages who never come to realize that reading can have deep personal meanings. Teachers know that some children come to school with an expectation that books and stories carry meaningful messages, while others will need more experience of one-to-one interaction with an adult before they can begin to appreciate the possibilities of reading, whether a story, a poem or an information book.

By introducing children to powerful texts, by reading to them and with them, we are also supporting their growing understanding of what reading can be about and what readers do. Every book that children become familiar with will increase their knowledge and their expectation of how writers write and readers read (Meek, 1988). The young child who encounters the accumulative story of *Mr Gumpy's Outing* (Burningham, 1970), the rhythm and patterned language of *We're Going On A Bear Hunt* (Rosen and Oxenbury, 1989), the distinctive layout of *My First Book of Time* (Llewellyn, 1992) or the multilayered meanings in the illustrations of *Bear Hunt* (Browne, 1979) will take that knowledge with them to whatever they read next.

From such encounters children will learn about different kinds of narrative structures and genres and the distinctive 'voice' of each text as well as grasp its meaning. These 'big shapes' of reading provide a helpful framework for reading the words on the page (Barrs and Thomas, 1991). Children are also supported by having the opportunity to return to favourite texts. Holdaway (1979) and Meek (1988) have shown that reading to young children regularly enables them to build up a bank of favourite stories, which they often memorize and take pleasure in reciting. Memorizing whole chunks of text, whether a catchy jingle for *Coca Cola* or a rhythmic and repetitive rhyme such as *Each Peach, Pear, Plum* (Ahlberg and Ahlberg, 1977) frees children to match what is in their head to the written symbols on the page or television screen. At this point they are able to examine the text more analytically and begin to concentrate on the 'small shapes' of reading: the words and letters and how they relate to the meaning of the whole text.

Becoming an independent reader

In time and with appropriate support, young children learn to use what they know about the big and small shapes; the patterns of written language and their understanding of making meaning, to read the text independently. This can only come about in an environment that is responsive to children's search for meaning and order and where they feel confident enough to take risks. Studies of young children becoming readers show that some of the key elements in this environment seem to be: access to a range of texts; demonstrations by skilled readers; and opportunities to practise reading.

Access to a range of texts

The texts that children meet in school will give them strong messages about what books have to offer, and what reading is for. Children need to be offered texts from a range of sources, including the computer screen, television and the environment. The debate about 'real books or reading schemes' has been sadly misinterpreted. It is not about a set of resources, but rather a fundamental way of viewing children's development as readers. If we consider that children learn about written language in the way that they make sense of all their experience, then we need to offer texts that will enable them to read for their own intentions and purposes and in doing so find out about how written language works.

Young children will need to be introduced to texts that are powerful and meaningful and can be developed beyond the surface features of the print, so they will want to return to them. High quality illustrations can both support and clarify the text as well as expand it and build on young children's visual literacy which is already highly sophisticated from familiarity with video, film and television.

Texts that incorporate rhyme and recurrent tunes and contain language that is rhythmic, natural and memorable, will make it easier for children to predict and anticipate the text. Goswami and Bryant (1990) have drawn attention to the importance of offering young children opportunities for engaging in songs, rhymes, and alliteration. They found that chanting, singing and playing with language gave children a sensitivity to rhyme which provided a basis for the development of phonological awareness and was strongly related to later success in reading.

Many of the 'new generation' of reading schemes have incorporated insights from research into reading into their materials, but many texts still appear stilted, bland and humourless in comparison with literature written to engage children rather than instruct them. There are many examples of reading scheme books which reflect a view of learning to read as making progress through a series of sequenced stages. Some teachers feel that children should have experience of both quality literature and reading schemes, but any discussion of balance needs to acknowledge the differences in the model of learning to read that each represents.

Demonstrations by skilled readers

Reading aloud to children does not just provide a pleasant and relaxing end to a busy day, but is a vital part of any literacy curriculum because it demonstrates what skilled readers do. It enables children to find out about the distinctive tunes of written language, particularly for those children who are bilingual and are taking on English through reading. We have already noted how children memorize texts that have strong rhythmical patterns, and teachers and parents are often surprised to hear their own intonation being reproduced in children's independent recitations or reading (Barrs, 1992). Reading aloud also introduces children to a range of genres, which alerts them to the possibilities of different kinds of texts. Young children can very soon develop preferences for favourite authors and illustrators and learn to recognize their distinctive styles. Watching demonstrations of reading by adults also enables children to find out how books work – the way they are held, the direction of the print, and which aspects are significant (the dedication) and which can be ignored (the publisher's details).

With experience, children will benefit from demonstrations of how skilled readers draw on a range of cues, including their experience of language, and their knowledge of grapho-phonics, to make meaning. When children are already beginning to notice features of print, their attention can be drawn to, for example, initial letters, common word endings and words within words, in the context of the whole text. Goodman (1993) challenges proponents of explicit, systematic phonics programmes. He argues that knowledge of phonics is not a prerequisite for reading since it is only likely to be helpful when the reader already knows what the word is likely to be. He believes that by isolating words, letters and sounds from their context, children are encouraged to pay equal attention to individual elements and ignore the way in which changes in intonation, pitch and stress have a major effect on phonic relationships. Goodman suggests that phonics is only valuable when used in conjunction with other important sources of information and only in the context of making sense of print. Collecting words, making alphabets, looking at rhyming words, discussing features of written language during shared reading and writing, are ways of drawing children's attention to graphophonic elements in real contexts.

Opportunities to practise reading

Shared reading with an experienced reader offers young children shared enjoyment and opportunities to engage collaboratively in bringing meaning to a text and experiencing how it feels to behave like a reader. It demonstrates that reading is an active process, and children can be shown, by a few deliberate mistakes, how readers anticipate, predict and self-correct. Publishers are increasingly becoming aware of the value that Early Years practitioners place on reading with Big Books (Holdaway, 1979) which are now more widely available.

Practising reading in different contexts, with adults, with other children or alone, will increase children's confidence so that they can begin to move from known texts to those that are less familiar. Early Years professionals know the importance of continuity between reading experiences at home and school and working with parents and families to support their children's reading (Jackson and Hannon, 1981; Tizard, Schofield and Hewison, 1982).

Paired reading offers particular opportunities for children to explore and discuss texts at their own pace and for teachers to observe and develop the strategies that young readers are using as they become more independent. Goodman and Goodman (1978) have shown how children's miscues reveal evidence of the sources of information that they are drawing on in their quest for meaning. The skill for the teachers and parents in reading in a one-to-one interaction is in knowing how much support to offer children and when to let them take over. Those children who feel confident in their own ability to learn for themselves, and are striving for independence, will know how much support they require.

Conclusions

This chapter has discussed the nature of literacy and its roots in the social and cultural practices of families and communities. It has attempted to show how insights from educational research into how children make sense of written language have informed practice in Early Years settings. Children have been described as active participants in their own learning, who are already experienced in using language for their own purposes when they come to school. With opportunites to see and explore texts and to work in collaboration with skilled readers and writers, young children come to use written language in situations that have meaning for them. Children's errors provide valuable information that will move their learning forward if they feel sufficiently confident to take the risks that are necessary. Teachers who observe children closely and who have an understanding of children's literacy development can respond to what children are trying to do in order to support their growing independence as readers and writers.

Many Early Years teachers feel increasingly frustrated by the imposition of explicit systematic instruction on children, in the form of reading and writing programmes. Such methods ignore children's individuality and prevent them from using their problem solving astuteness, with the result that they can very soon come to accept that school learning is a passive activity. The implications for the learning of young children who come to hold such a view are well documented by Tizard and Hughes (1984) and Barrett (1989).

Many of the calls for more direct instruction have arisen as a result of a revised National Curriculum for English which implies a skills based model of literacy learning that ignores or distorts educational research of the type discussed in this chapter. The increasing use of psychometric tests, both nationally through SATs and as more local education authorities implement their own procedures for testing reading, have had implications for the very youngest children. In some parts of the country, children's 'readiness' for reading is being assessed by reductionist baseline assessment procedures.

Many Early Years teachers feel that they are under pressure to teach in ways that do not accord with what they know about children's learning. Some teachers in nurseries who have felt the backwash of the National Curriculum, as well as those at KS1 who are required to work within it, have taken heart that if the programmes of study are seen as a minimum requirement, there will still be opportunities for continuing to teach in a way that supports children's learning rather than controls it. Clearly there is a need to continue to develop innovatory practice and debate its theoretical basis, despite constraints from such a narrow curriculum. Early Years professionals need to become stronger in asserting their own professionalism if they are going to have the confidence to continue working in ways that they know are successful in supporting young children in becoming fully literate.

Suggested further reading

Barrs, M. and Thomas, A. (1991) *The Reading Book*, CLPE, London.
Browne, A. (1993) *Helping Children to Write*, Paul Chapman, London.
Meek, M. (1994) *Learning to Read (2nd edition)*, Bodley Head, London.
Wells, G. (1985) *Language, Learning and Education*, NFER/Nelson, Windsor.

8

The Young Child's Early Representation and Drawing

John Matthews

This chapter is about the origin and development of visual expression and representation in early childhood and how its growth can best be encouraged and supported. I will describe the formation of a family of expressive and representational modes of which drawing is one member. With these modes the child is able to express emotions and to represent objects, events and states of mind. We will be looking at actions performed by the child on a range of visual media including drawing, painting, construction and dance. Whilst special attention will be focused on how children give meaning to drawing, the intention is to look at drawing within the development of representation as a whole. I will argue that children's use and organization of visual media forms an essential part of their cognitive and affective development. There is an important relationship between the growth of the child's visual representation and the growth of other representational modes, for example, language acquisition and mathematical understandings.

To understand the full significance of the child's forms of expression and representation will require us to scrutinize certain assumptions and paradigms of education, and the roles and goals of 'art' education in particular.

To many people there is little, if any, meaning in the drawings shown in Figures 8.1 and 8.2. Figure 8.1 was made by a boy at 2 years 2 months; Figure 8.2 by the same boy 8 months later. Typically, drawings like this are classified under the generic but derogatory heading of 'scribbling'. Many writers have skipped over this 'scribbling stage' to concentrate on the period when children produce more recognizable images. Even those who acknowledge scribbling as important have little to say about it, other than in terms of the child's emotion or motor control. Some have thought that 'scribbling' is important only in that it fortuitously supplies a pool

Figure 8.1 *Configurative Representation*: drawing by Ben age 2 years 2 months. A zig-zag line represents the shape of 'Granny's hat'

of accidental shapes which at some later date the child learns to purposely reproduce. Others have felt that its value lay in the child finding a vocabulary for later designs and pictures (for example, Kellogg, 1969). At best it has been considered the clumsy beginning of a long apprenticeship to 'accurate' representation; at worst, a false trail which the child abandons in favour of drawing recognizable 'pictures'.

I am going to argue that these notions are misconceptions. I am not, however, going to claim that the drawings in Figures 8.1 and 8.2 are the beginning of visual representation. It will surprise many people to learn that the genesis of expression and representation occurs long before this. Drawings like this actually signal the end of a long phase in which the child has already learnt the main principles of visual expression and representation; and the beginning of a new phase in which these principles are elaborated.

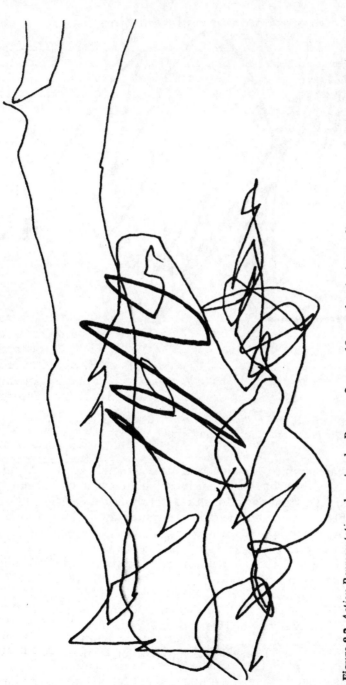

Figure 8.2 *Action Representation*: drawing by Ben age 2 years 10 months. A zig-zag line represents the movement of 'smoke, water and boats'

Expression and representation

Children develop a family of expressive and representational modes from patterns of action formed in infancy. This process depends on an inter-action between a self-initiated, self-generated programme of expressive and exploratory strategies and what is available in the environment. It is neither solely self-driven nor completely reliant on imitation of cultural exemplars or instruction.

A moment's reflection should suggest to us that this process of devel-opment requires a special kind of support from the educational environ-ment. I will describe this more fully later on, but suffice it to say at this point that, though representational thought is probably initiated and pro-pelled by programmes in the Central Nervous System (CNS), neverthe-less it atrophies and dies unless certain kinds of experiences are available within the interpersonal environment. Moreover, some kinds of miscon-ceived instruction do severe damage to the process.

How the meaning of drawing has been hidden

Drawing plays a central role in early representation. Unfortunately, some definitions of both art and development have masked the meaning of children's drawing. One of the paradigms which has directed research and education has been the notion that drawing is solely about record-ing the optical-array as seen from a single station-point; that is, drawing is thought to be solely about the depiction of volumetric solids and scenes as if observed from a fixed position in space.

This paradigm of the 'frozen' visual array (Gibson, 1979) has had a long tradition. A recent manifestation is in some influential experimen-tal psychology in which children's development in drawing is measured in terms of how well they map *projective* relationships on to the drawing surface. In practice this often means that psychologists focus on how a child shows one object in front of another, relative to the child's view-point.

Not surprisingly, very young children (along with most older children, most adults and the artists of many non-Western cultures) measure up very poorly to this paradigm. *In the terms adopted by these psychologists,* very young children are not skilled in mapping three-dimensional layout on to two dimensions. Hence, their development has been couched in terms of deficits. Typically, development is described in terms of the 'stages' through which children pass until they are able to overcome the supposed obstacles in their perception and production, and learn to draw pictures which contain this type of view-specific information.

Inevitably, this general model has influenced education and curriculum planning. Curricula are devised with the intention of 'correcting' these supposed deficits which prevent children from reaching the goal of 'accurate' representation. For reasons which will later become clear, this approach is destructive to development. Actually, the misconception about art education is part of a larger misunderstanding about the relationship between development and education, as this book is designed to show.

How to damage children's visual representation

The National Curriculum for Art in England and Wales, to a large extent, continues this misunderstanding. The designers of this National Curriculum, in response to criticism, tried to acknowledge the multidimensional nature of visual representation, but in doing so merely bolted a lot of different, conflicting ideas about art together under a thin disguise of dubious developmental 'stages'. In the document which sets this out there is no understanding of the coherence and purpose of children's representational modes (Matthews, 1993, 1994a). The designers of the Art curriculum cannot be entirely blamed for this. They were not allowed to tamper fundamentally with the curriculum's overall design which was never intended to address the issue of the relationship between development and education (Blenkin and Kelly, 1994) – far from it.

I had originally blamed this limited approach to drawing on a diluted version of a western ethnocentric model dating from the Renaissance. Certainly, in Britain and elsewhere, there is a pervading influence of a limited approach to observational drawing. But there are other paradigms too. The development of children's own imagery is often sabotaged by drilling them in prescribed routines to produce kitsch and cutesy images. These cottage-industries within nurseries and primary schools reduce children to slaves on a production line, turning out stereotyped trivia of the most banal kind. This method, in which the teacher instructs in a rigid series of stages towards a pre-envisaged end point, will destroy children's articulation of representational and expressive modes just as effectively as the still-life paradigm. The National Curriculum will not relieve this situation. Though new objectives dressed in sophisticated art terms replace yogurt-pot Christmas angels, these are equally arbitrary. When they happen to match children's development, they do so not by design but fortuitously, by coincidence, as most hit-or-miss education has always done. What the different models or exemplars have in common is that they either derive from naive realism or else from a naive understanding of picturing and depiction.

The meaning of young children's drawing

Representation: location, shape and movement

The drawings which very young children produce do not fit into any of the major categories of depiction used by adults. Research shows that the recording of the shape of an object is only one of a set of interests and concerns the child shows in his or her drawings and other representations. Research by Wolf and Fucigna (1983), Athey (1990) and Matthews (1983, 1994a) has shown that children between two and four years of age use visual media not only to convey the *shape* of objects, but also to represent their movement through space and time. For example, the zig-zag shape in Figure 8.1 represents the shape of 'Granny's hat', whereas the zig-zags in Figure 8.2 represent the movements of smoke, the sea and a boat. The former kind of representation I term a *configurative representation*; the latter an *action representation* (Matthews, 1983, 1994a, 1994b).

Many observations testify that children use actions performed on visual media to consider the characteristic properties of things; where things are, where things come from and where things go; the persistence of their identity or their transformation. These concerns in early drawing – location, region, movement to-and-from, transformation and persistence of identity – are paralleled by language acquisition. The structure of language, and probably the structure of all representational modes, may be built on these basic conceptual categories hard-wired in the Central Nervous System (Jackendoff, 1994).

Expression

In addition to realizing the representational potential for actions and marks, very young children also detect and exploit the expressive characteristics inherent in media (Smith, 1983). This is not restricted to 'art' media *per se*. The child discerns and uses the expressive potential of a range of objects, events and materials, including the actions of his or her own body. Recent research in Singapore and the Far East suggests that this development is not tied to transmission of any particular culture (Matthews, 1994b). This is an important point and one to which I will return.

In contrast to conventional wisdom, or that from some schools of psychology, we find that very young children have a powerful agenda for representation and expression. It cannot be described in terms of deficits and it clearly requires a quite different kind of provision than is offered by many curricula, including the National Curriculum for England and Wales. Young children do not scribble; they represent shape and movement, and they also begin to use media to express emotion. How does this development start?

To understand the significance of representation and expression we need to look at its beginnings in infancy.

The beginnings of representation and expression

From babyhood the child generates a family of actions which form the basis of representational modes. The infant makes certain types of body movement, particularly of arm and hand, which are designed to test objects and surfaces and to establish the infant's relationship with these. From a few months of age, the infant uses scratching movements of the fingers to pick at and inspect interesting visual targets. Even earlier, during the first days and weeks of life, three important actions of the hand and arm emerge. These are: *horizontal arc* – a lateral fanning gesture of the arm, mainly issuing from the shoulder; *vertical arc* – in which the arm and hand descend in a sudden stabbing movement; and *push-pull* – an arm and hand action, to and from the self, usually used in conjunction with a hand-held object. The infant uses this trio of actions with both enthusiasm and systematicity in order to obtain a variety of effects. The actions are modified and adapted according to the kind of situation. For example: a horizontal arc can be developed to gather or scatter objects on a flat surface; the push-pull can move wheeled toys back and forth; a vertical arc can be impacted on water to obtain a splash, or on a table-top for the sound. As we will see, the actions are further modified when used in conjunction with drawing and painting media. With increasing differentiation, the child learns to form other movements from this basic repertoire – for example, a rotational movement (Matthews, 1983, 1994a).

As well as being linked with the acquisition of manipulative skills and the conception of objects, these actions also have an expressive and communicative aspect to them. Petitto (1987) noticed that parents cannot help but interpret them and respond to them. The actions support and underscore language acquisition. In relationship with a caregiver, these early actions gather layers of emotional tone and colour and acquire significatory aspects. They become an expressive and representational vocabulary.

Early mark-making

When the actions are applied to mark-making materials the effects are especially powerful. The horizontal arc leaves smeared arcs; a push–pull a longitudinal line to and from the self with acute angles at each end of the movement; a vertical arc produces dots or blobs on a horizontal surface, or sometimes longitudinal lines when adapted for a vertically inclined surface (Matthews, 1983, 1990, 1994a).

Tool use, in the form of traditional media like brushes and pencils, or electronic media, extends these possibilities. In the case of traditional marking tools, the infants bring to these their knowledge of graspable objects and discover the 'trace-making effect' (Michotte, 1963, p. 289). In the case of computers, there are other understandings to be made, and we will consider these later.

Mark-making has a special significance in the infant's life. In no other situation is a trace made of body action. Drawing offers sensori-cognitive feedback of a particularly intense order, which aids the child in monitoring his or her own movements. Normally invisible trajectories of the body and limbs become visible; records are left of their passage; the ephemeral, transient abstracts of spatio-temporal events. This has great import, for in drawing there occurs an 'interaction between production and perception' (Willats, 1984, p. 111). Children make actions but also see the consequence of those actions in terms of *shape*.

An interest in the action trace of pigment on a surface is shared by some other mammals too (see, for example, Bush and Silver (1994) for beautiful photographs of cats painting!). However, as important as the sensori-motoric aspect of these actions is, for the human infant there is a still deeper level of significance to them. They start to perceive the spatial relations specified in visual terms alone. This causes them to modify their actions (and therefore the shapes) in accordance with dawning structural possibilities. Right from the outset of marking, and in contrast to any number of accounts of children's drawing, both old and new, the child uses the medium of drawing and painting to express emotion and to represent ideas about the world. What can these ideas be? Where did they come from? Actually, they are forming when he or she is a newborn baby.

Babies have ideas about events, objects and people

Contrary to ideas in the earlier part of the twentieth century, research shows that the neonate is not a blank slate but enters our world with certain expectations about objects, events and people. Studies have suggested that neonates are interested in the location and configuration of discriminable units and objects and also in their flight-paths (Bower, 1974, 1982; Spelke, 1985, 1990). Spelke has produced evidence which suggests that the neonate initially places more reliance on the character of a partly hidden object's flight-path than on its colour and form, as a means of identifying its unity and integrity. How one interprets these findings remains controversial. However, if babies are interested in the form, location and movement of objects, we might expect them as young children to display these interests in their early representations. Studies by Wolf and Fucigna (1983) and Matthews (1983) show that this is indeed the case.

Intellectual companionship between caregiver and child

Babies also enter the world with expectations about people and have capacities to engage in communication with them. Whilst initially self-driven, the full development of representational understanding does not occur in a social vacuum. It depends on a relationship in which the caregiver is also intellectual companion to the child. Within a psychological 'bubble' (Stern, 1977) enclosing both infant and caregiver, exquisitely orchestrated interchanges occur. The patterns of action of infant and caregiver, involving speech, facial expression and body movement, are precisely coupled to each other. Infant and caregiver are able to partici-pate in shared acts of cognizance (Trevarthen, 1987) because each part-ner is sensitive to universal indices of intention and motivation in the rhythmic periodicities of the other's actions (Trevarthen, 1975). Within this interpersonal capsule, action and object are given meaning. As Trevarthen says, skills in handling, viewing and using objects are not the *cause* of the ability to form a relationship with another but rather a *con-sequence* of it (Trevarthen, 1975). At its best, this level of interaction serves as an exemplar for later relationships between child and teacher.

Patterns of action

The 'interactional synchrony' (Condon, 1975, p. 87) between infant and carer forms the basis of later symbolization. Building upon the move-ments of early infancy, the child forms organized patterns of action which we see in the nursery. Yet, these important representational actions often go unnoticed as such. At first sight, such commonplace activities as singing, jumping, running, talking, shouting, mark-making, constructing with blocks, may seem trivial, random looking. Moreover, it might seem that there is no relation between them, aside perhaps from the fact that the same child may seem intensely engaged in each of them in succes-sion, or even in some of them simultaneously.

Yet across this range of apparently quite dissimilar actions, children investigate an array of semiotic possibilities and discern underlying reg-ularities or structures. The child's discovery and use of these structures signals the beginning of understandings which are logico-mathematical, spatial, musical, linguistic and configurative. Embedded initially in the organization of the child's actions, they are nevertheless the beginnings of symbol and sign use. These patterns of action become interiorized to form internal descriptions of reality.

Drawing

One of these patterns of action is drawing. After finding that the marker leaves a trace, children systematically seek out the rules which regulate the use of a medium. This can happen from 1 year of age or even earlier.

Recorded observations (Matthews, 1990, 1994a, 1994b) show that nat-ural actions of the body are extended and 'amplified' by tool use (Bruner, 1964). Horizontal arcs smeared in milk with the outstretched arm and hand, or vertical arcs slapped into water with the bare palm, or push-pulls with toy cars or breakfast bowl at 13 months, may, a month later, be applied with a brush. Marking tools are held in a variety of grips; arc-ing and fanning through space or on surfaces (horizontal arc); stabbing down against targets (vertical arc); or describing jagged longitudinal lines (push–pull).

My observations show that in an unrestricted situation, without seeing art materials before, children discover for themselves, without instruction, the 'affordances' (Gibson, 1979) of mark-making materials. Whilst many societies design special surfaces for drawing and writing (rectangular pieces of paper, or electronic visual display units, for example), in an unrestricted situation the child will adopt other salient targets – his or her own body, a wall, a window, the dog. But even in these unusually free situations, the child seems to gravitate intuitively towards the most sensitive mark-receiving surface his or her culture provides. This seems to be guided by a desire for maximum contrast or effect. Thus, the child tries to stop skidding off the paper because, perhaps, the surface of a table does not afford the sharp contrasts offered by marker against paper.

Whereas the character of the very earliest mark-making may have been a reflection of the natural movements of the skeletal and muscular frame, very soon external orientation cues (Freeman, 1980), including the edges of paper sheets, are spontaneously adopted as guides for line production.

This above is noteworthy, for even a blank sheet of paper is a product of a geometrical system about which the child initially knows nothing. The child's task of orientating him/herself, both physically and psychologically, to the medium and its complex and sophisticated art praxis, is as significant as the child's physical use of the tools themselves. Therefore, it is worth considering how children encounter visual media. Should you simply introduce the child to a medium as if as an apprentice to a ready-made adult discipline, with established conventions and canons? I do not think so, and not only because such a conception is anachronistic given the range of contemporary art. What is important to us is not the content of the discipline in itself but its relationship to what is going on in the child. The learner-centred approach advocated here allows both the teacher and child to continually reconceptualize visual media. My feeling is that, as far as possible, the child should be permitted to bring his or her own understandings to these media domains.

The child gives meaning to drawing

From about 18 months to 3 years, children perceive a relationship between the actions they make and the shapes these produce. They find that different actions result in different shapes. The original trio of mark-making gestures are more finely differentiated and combined. The child pays closer attention to the local orientation cues mentioned above; horizontal arcs yield lateral lines when guided by the lateral sides of the paper; push–pulls become longitudinal lines when aligned with the sides of the sheet. The marks themselves become targets for further drawing. Horizontal arcs and push–pulls flow into each other and combine to make contrasting linear vectors and junctions. This signals the discovery of an important structural principle – the *right-angular junction*, which we will see developing later (see Figure 8.7).

Structural principles

Other shapes and forms of mark-receiving surface may elicit variations of these drawing actions, but what is equally striking is the persistence of certain shapes, regardless of the type or shape of drawing surface. These are the Deep Structures of visual representation. One example is when the horizontal arc and the push–pull are 'opened up', as it were, by a more circular movement of the wrist and arm, to form a continuous rotational shape (see Figures 8.3 and 8.5).

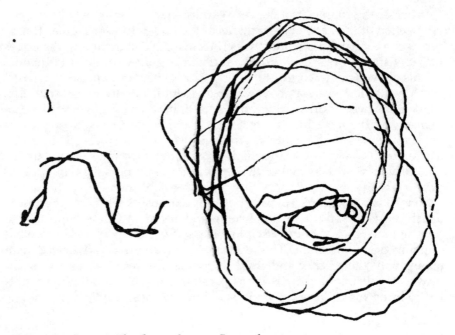

Figure 8.3 Drawing by Joe at 2 years 5 months

Continuous rotation

This *continuous rotation* is sometimes use by the child to indicate the presence of a volume or shape in space (configurative representation); sometimes to represent the dynamic movement of an entity (action representation). In these latter cases, the child may accompany a whirling trajectory with words which describe the event, for example, 'The Big Wheel is going round and round'.

Closed-shape

The continuous rotation sometimes leads to a single *closed-shape* (see Figure 8.4). The closed-shape is a very important find for the child. It has an important feature – a boundary which differentiates space in a powerful and salient way. A difference is marked between inside and outside. A figure and ground relationship is created. We will see representational use of the closed-shape later.

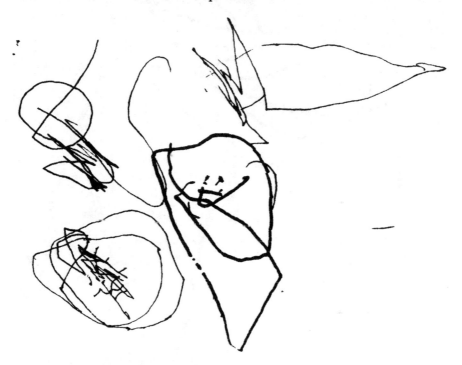

Figure 8.4 Drawing by Hannah at 2 years 5 months
Figures 8.3 and **8.4** *Rotational* drawing sometimes results in *closed-shapes* with which *inside* and *outside* relationships can be encoded

Other combinations of shape lead to the discovery of other structural principles. Dots or blobs, the result of the vertical arc, are placed *inside* and *outside* closed-shapes (see Figures 8.3, 8.4 and 8.5). Lines are attached to each other (see Figure 8.7) and to closed shapes (see Figure 8.5). This latter combination is an important one and we will return to it shortly. Marks and shapes are *grouped* together in different ways; arranged in *linear sequence,* or scattered over the drawing surface. Often, drawing or painting are part of complex spatio-temporal games; the organization of marks and shapes the residue of patterned impacts and tracemaking events which have internal structure, cadences and periodicities.

Children may remark on the shapes and their properties, using terms

Figure 8.5 *Core and radial.* Drawing by Hannah at 3 years 4 months. Inside-outside; attachment

such as 'round', for closed-shapes; 'in', to describe enclosed nuclei; 'on', to describe a line which runs across another; and occasionally 'attached' or 'joined', when talking about lines which touch. They build up spatial understandings which are topological in character.

Structure, emotion and representation

Structure

Children explore visual media in three main ways, which are intertwined together. They investigate structure for its own sake. They find actions, marks, shapes sufficiently interesting in themselves to impel further investigation. Children exhibit, to use Bickerton's term (1981) for language acquisition, 'infrastructural motivation'.

Emotion

Secondly, they invest marking actions with emotion. In the hands of a two- or three-year-old, the medium of painting is a vehicle responsive to fluctuations in mood, of the child or of those around.

Representation

The third aspect is that, right from the outset of mark-making, children perceive a relationship between the dynamic and configurative aspects of their actions and shapes and objects and events in the world. They come to realize that actions and shapes can represent objects and events.

Deep structures

This is possible because the child has available an internal programme of search. This programme is guided by a set of invariant or deep structures which form the guiding principles underlying children's perception, use and organization of media of every kind. These deep structures act like structural principles, templates or attractor systems. They are like a universal visual-kinaesthetic grammar in the sense that they form the basis of what the child may or may not select from the environment (Matthews, 1994b).

Between about 2 and 4 years of age, children find that, within various forms and movements, the same deep structures, or invariant shapes and relations, remain essentially unchanged despite transposition from one medium or context to another (Gibson, 1979).

Form, position, location and movement

Some deep structures are derived from the form of objects and spatial layout; others are concerned with position and location; others are types of movement in space and time (see also Athey, 1990). The child will encode certain spatial relations onto the drawing surface, including: *covering; on-top-of; underneath; going through; going around; enclosure; and inside-outside.* The ability to discern deep structures enables the child to 'transport', to use Wolf's term (1983), both figurative and dynamic aspects of the experience in the world from one medium to another. Both *straight line* and angular *zig-zag* courses are made in running games and also find their way on to the drawing surface. In both 4D spacetime and the 2D environment of the drawing surface, stopping, starting and direction change are important features.

The child will explore *series of points* or *displacements in space* in 3D space with hopping games and also in drawings in which dots and shapes are arranged in lines or other groups or patterns. The rhythmical walking of a hand-held toy figure, clomp-clomped along a surface in a series of little arching hops, finds its equivalent in the dance of a marker across a page, making a series of dots. The child might also investigate and represent the *beginnings and ends* of lines; in 3D space, with objects piled at each end of a linear route; in drawing, by demarcating the ends of lines with squiggles or dots (see Figure 8.6).

Figure 8.6 Drawing by Hannah at 2 years 1 month. *Beginnings and ends* of lines are demarcated

Within a range of events the child might discern the same *ascending and descending* trajectories. Ascending and descending games are re-echoed across domains and media; in jumping games, and when hand-held toys are 'flown' in graceful trajectories through the air. From about 1 year 8 months to 2 years 3 months, Hannah starts to synchronize a descending vocalization with descending objects, which she purposely drops. For, example, she allows a tape-measure to uncoil from her hand to the ground whilst singing 'Ooooooooooooo' along a descending musical scale. In drawings from 2 years of age, she associates descending vocalizations with 'descending' lines – that is, lines which move longitudinally along the paper towards her. In this way, ascent and descent are mapped on to the drawing surface. 'A man flying – a man running away', says Joel (2 years 5 months), as he draws a line which describes a graceful arc, and

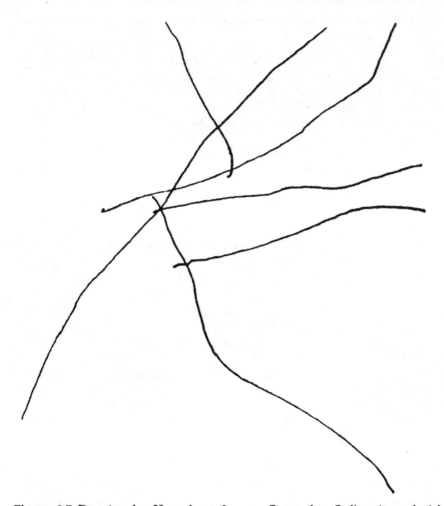

Figure 8.7 Drawing by Hannah at 3 years 7 months. *Co-linearity and right-angular attachment*

'an aeroplane crashing' in a painting by Ben (2 years 4 months), in which a line is traced from the edge of the paper furthest from him to the edge nearest to him. The children are starting to encode *higher and lower* relations on to the drawing surface.

Inside–outside

As objects or even persons can be placed inside three-dimensional containers of many kinds, so dots and other shapes can be placed inside or outside two-dimensional closed shapes (see Figures 8.3, 8.4 and 8.5).

Rotation

The rotational passage of a hand-held toy car may be carried over into a rotational drawing. These rotational movements may be echoed and re-echoed in twirling, spinning games in the playground. The child investigating these movements will be interested in stories and songs about rotation – like 'Ring o' Roses', for example. They will attend to all that rotates – helicopters, washing machines, the Big Wheel at the fair. (There are important teaching implications here which I will discuss later.) A rotational movement, both in 4D space and time, and on the drawing surface, may be enjoyed for its own sake, or it may be used to represent the movement of another object – the whirling helicopter, for example. Symbolic play is implicated here, in which, as Mari Guha says in Chapter 3, the child learns to separate words from objects and actions from meaning (Vygotsky, 1966).

The ability to use an action of the body or another object to stand for something other than itself is echoed and re-echoed the more closely we look at these events. The child's actions may be made in synchrony with emphatic vocalizations which underscore and emphasise certain structural features; reiterating or analoguing peaks and valleys in rhythmic and melodic structure over time. In such cases the child detects and exploits characteristics which are shared across different sensory modalities. Sometimes speech and action are made in precise one-to-one correspondence. This is the beginning not only of counting (Gelman and Gallistel, 1983) but also of an aesthetic awareness. We see this emerging from about 2 years of age, yet, according to any number of studies, aesthetic awareness is not supposed to occur till much later in childhood.

Combinations of action

As further differentiation and combination are learnt, so further specifications are made about the type of action or the type of shape represented. One example is the *zig-zag*, which is a combination of push–pull and lateral; and a variation of this is the *travelling-loop* which crosses back over itself as it travels laterally. As I noted above, these can also specify forms within the visible world – sharp, spiky objects like 'Granny's hat' (see Figure 8.1) or events like the movements of smoke, water and boats (see Figure 8.2).

Symbols, signs and emergent writing

There are further possibilities too. In Figure 8.8, the travelling zig-zag has been used to consider two very different semiotic systems within the same drawing. Using a zig-zagging line, Ben (3 years 3 months) shows 'fire' going through a spacecraft (represented by two parallel lines) and out and down to the lower right. The isolated element at the lower left is also a zig-zag line but it represents a quite different phenomenon – the rhythmic, lateral oscillations in pretend handwriting. Ben is 'writing' about what is going on in the drawing. The upper-case 'B' (for 'Ben') is also shown, composed of another structural discovery, the U shape-on-baseline. These latter forms are aspects of emergent writing, which we will consider later.

Figure 8.8 Drawing by Ben at 3 years 3 months. *Co-linearity* and *travelling zig-zags* combined to show fire *going through* a spacecraft. The travelling zig-zag at lower left is 'writing' describing the events in the drawing. Immediately above is another type of emergent writing – an upper-case 'B' (for 'Ben'). This is composed from another structural device – U shape-on-baseline

Concentricity, collinearity or *parallelism* (see Figures 8.5, 8.6 and 8.8) emerge as children learn to plan the spacing of lines; a conceptual achievement based on earlier rhythmically patterned actions. *Going through* (see also Figure 8.8) is another dynamic passage of movement which can be represented in drawing when parallel groupings are established.

Higher and lower

Gradually, higher and lower relations are mapped onto the drawing surface. For example, Joel at 2 years 8 months draws a 'nose' above a 'foot'. Gradually, a vertical axis is established and sometimes co-ordinated with a horizontal axis. This is the case in Figure 8.9, a drawing by Ben (3 years 4 months) which shows a man climbing down a rope from a helicopter to rescue people from another helicopter crashed in the sea. The man is shown at various instances in his descent – a development based upon earlier investigations of sequential displacement through time; in hopping games, for example, or making dots in a linear series.

Figure 8.9 Drawing by Ben at 3 years 4 months. A man is shown descending a rope, in stages, from a helicopter to rescue people from another helicopter crashed in the sea. Ben combines all the basic structures to describe events within a space in which vertical and horizontal axes are co-ordinated.

Theme and variation

Each time the child transfers the same pattern of movement from one medium to another, some new aspect or quality of that structure is revealed. There are important differences between making a rotation with a felt-tip pen, or a big brush, or spinning in three dimensions of space. Making your rotation in electronic paint is different again (Matthews and Jessel, 1993a and b). A mouse-driven, microcomputer paintbox programme is very different in important respects from traditional media. Colours do not mix or run out; the drawing surface is separate from its display; the display unit may only show a portion of your drawing action; and operating a mouse requires the co-ordination of several schemes. Yet John Jessel and I found that very young children (between 1 year 10 months and 3 years 10 months) carried robust marking strategies – horizontal arc, push–pull and rotation – from traditional drawing media to a very different drawing device which they had not seen before.

However, these drawing strategies are only generalized categories and different media will elicit variations. The computer paintbox is a good example. The children quickly adapted their actions as they detected this new medium's possibilities and constraints. For example, actions in the third dimension do not affect the quality of electronic painting to the extent that similar actions made in physical paint will. This meant that the children tended to disuse the vertical arc and discovered other uses for lifting the mouse - replacing it in better positions for drawing, for example. In the many interactions between deep structures and different media, one can see a play of theme and variation, as deep structures reveal different aspects of their characters.

Clusters of actions

In representation, stable topological relations, like inside and outside, generally precede higher and lower relations, which in turn generally precede projective relations. However, it is wrong to think that these structures appear in a completely linear sequence. They appear in clusters, with one or other system predominating for a period of time until it is superseded by another (see Matthews, 1990, 1994b for more detail). Vertical and horizontal trajectories, for example, may be glimpsed alternating with rotational movement. Then, the pattern changes, and we see children actually combining what were initially separate actions.

Similarly, there is an important shift from making actions in the round to the ability to encode these relations and axes on the drawing surface. However, it should not be inferred that this is a one-way, hierarchical process, from primitive 'embedded' thinking to supposedly more sophisticated symbolic thought. A drawing may be the prototype for an action. Take the example of continuous rotation once more: Hannah (1 year 7 months) draws elliptical shapes with bread and chocolate spread, synchronizing a song, 'Eeeeeeee'. This leads her to spin and twirl in space with her entire body. From this age, Hannah's continuous rotations flow between drawing and dance. She experiments with rotation as an expressive structure, whirling around on the spot, her plastic pants in outstretched hand or, at 1 year 9 months, with a flailing tape-measure. She sometimes punctuates the end of the rotational sequence by falling down. This is an example of the combination of two initially separate actions. Three months later she is drawing a rotation again, saying 'round'. From a variety of very different rotational experiences, she abstracts the invariant feature they all share - 'roundness'. Two months later she is drawing a closed-shape on her hand and saying it is 'daddy's watch'. Later still, she draws the core and radial (Athey, 1990), a combination of closed-shape with attached lines – an important 2D structure we will describe shortly in more detail.

Developments

As the child matures, so the specifications he or she encodes about spatial and temporal relations change. These changes come about probably because of revolutions occurring in the CNS in relation to the environment. As forms are combined with each other they suggest further structural possibilities whilst simultaneously specifying similar relations in the world. This is made possible by the child's discovery and application of the surprisingly limited number of structural principles described above.

We have already noted the important closed-shape. I mentioned the encoding of inside and outside relations, but closure has other uses too. The child can use it to represent a face of an object or else the entire volume of the object, irrespective of viewpoint (Willats, 1985). This may seem subtle but the difference is actually very important. Which way we interpret the drawing will influence strongly the way in which we interact with the child.

Linear attachment

Important as the closed-shape is, it is only one of a family of structural principles which the child discovers and uses from about 2 years 5 months. A general *attachment* of lines to each other and to other shapes occurs. Angles, dots, arcs, sections and ends of lines are used by the child as targets for further clustering of marks, and especially the anchorings of lines (see Figure 8.6). Noticeable is a tendency toward a *perpendicular attachment* of lines (see Figure 8.7).

Different sets of cues vie for the child's attention when attaching lines. These landmarks include the child's own body position and movements, and external landmarks or local orientation cues (Freeman, 1980). Sometimes there is a fluid balancing act between different sets of attractors. External landmarks or local orientation cues include the edges of a piece of paper, or the marks themselves as they appear upon it. These gradually come to be considered and used as bases and baselines.

The decisions and influences involved in the so-called 'perpendicular bias' – visual, motor, intellectual – are complex (Bremner, 1985), but I agree with Willats (1986, personal communication) that a factor contributing to this tendency might be the child seeking the maximum visual contrast of forms that this linear junction offers. Later, other structural-symbolic options might be available but, for the present, the right-angular join is not so much a bias, rather an important early rule in an internal programme designed to move the child toward increasing differentiation of form.

Core and radial

A special instance of right-angular attachment is when lines are joined to the closed-shape (see Figure 8.5). This is the core and radial, which I mentioned earlier. The child's targeting of lines oscillates between different sets of cues, so that this core and radial form (Athey, 1990) may have its rays drawn between longitudinal and lateral lines – the edges of the sheet of paper perhaps, or possibly an internal reference frame of X and Y co-ordinates. Or else all cues other than the closed-shape itself are ignored, and the lines arranged at different points of the compass, departing from the perimeter line at around 90 degrees (Matthews, 1994b) (see Figure 8.10).

Figure 8.10 A clock drawn by Hannah at 4 years 8 months. The *compass-array* at centre is a special case of core and radial in which angular variation is being mastered

With the core and radial, the child has combined what were initially separate drawing actions and shapes: a rotation and single lines. The linear-attachment principle and the core and radial are developmentally significant, because the child is now in a position to generate whole families of hybrid forms.

How the world is constructed in a child's drawing

The act of drawing plays a key role in alerting the child to the presence of invariant forms and relations within the environment. In a very real sense, the world is constructed in the child's use of visual media, and in the unfolding structures which are generated upon the drawing surface.

In some of the observations cited above (for example, in Hannah's rotations) we can see a further dimension to deep structure. Not only is the same structure investigated through a range of media at a particular time in the child's life, this investigation is also repeatedly shifted to new levels of cognition as the child grows older. This is the vertical-decollage model proposed by Athey (1990) in which what has been learnt at one time in one way is later investigated all over again in new ways, transformed by revolutions in thinking.

Observations of Joel provide another example. At six months he starts to become aware of the spatial relation inside–outside. By thirteen months he is filling and emptying all manner of containers. At two years he represents these relations in two dimensions, making closed-shapes into which nuclei are dotted. Six months later, this structure has acquired rich representational potential when he uses it to represent a 'baby in 'ere . . . a baby in the water', and at three years when it represents 'babies in mummy's tummy'. At four years the same spatial and emotional themes are reiterated when Joel enacts being born, by bursting out from inside a cardboard box.

Projective relations: in-front-of and behind

Even projective relations *in-front-of* and *behind* are glimpsed during the so-called 'scribbling stage'. When children (at around 3 years) cover or 'hide' one layer of paint with another, they may be forming an understanding of this relation. They are building upon a 'peek-a-boo' scenario which can be traced back to an even earlier relationship with their caregiver. When paint is used, the occlusion of one layer behind another is accomplished by the physical nature of the pigment. However, within a matter of days this understanding may be shifted to a more conceptual level when children use linear means alone to represent one object behind another (Matthews, 1983, 1990).

Gradually, the notion of an occluding boundary *emerges*, which means that children conceive of the boundary of a shape as being the edge of an object which conceals a further object. This in turn leads some children to encode *hidden line elimination*, where lines are purposely omitted to show that one's line-of-sight to the further form is interrupted by a nearer form. It is ironic that much experimental psychology conceals these representations, because they are exactly the kind which the psychologists are seeking!

Views of objects

Other projective relations are achieved when children use a single line to represent a totally foreshortened plane, and a closed-shape as a plane seen at a 90 degree line-of-sight, or 'face-on'. (These are precisely the kinds of understanding Piaget and Inhelder (1956) thought children below 4 years did *not* possess.) Some projective relations are encoded as a by-product of action representation. Representational actions made in play with, for example, toy figures in a miniaturized world, are carried over to drawing media. Movement passages enacted with a marker against paper leave configurative profiles which in turn specify views or aspects of scenes or events.

Hannah (3 years 3 months) uses two contrasting actions to represent rainfall. She uses a zig-zagging line to suggest a sheet of rain falling down through a vertical plane at 90 degrees to the line-of-sight of the observer. Then she repeatedly stabs the pen (vertical arc) against the paper, suggesting the impact of individual raindrops seen from directly above (or below?). By making these actions she represents two views of 'rainfall' (Matthews, 1990, 1994a).

Another example is when Joel (2 years 11 months) enacting, with the tracing of his pen, climbers going around and over a mountain, arrives at a plan and elevation of the mountain (Matthews, 1983, 1990, 1994).

Speech as image: symbol and sign

When children synchronize vocalizations to their drawing actions they may be starting a long investigation about how sounds we make with our mouths are encoded on the drawing surface. Actions and marks are 'written' and 'read' in different ways. The child investigates the difference between symbols and signs; how a drawn shape can represent the shape of a perceived object in the world, or how they can represent ideas we have in our heads or the words we utter. Frequently, pictorial symbols and arbitrary signs appear in a single drawing. It is as if the child is exploring the boundaries between very different semiotic systems (see Figure 8.8). It may be necessary for children to stretch the boundaries between different semiotic systems in this way, and teaching provision should allow them to do so. Nancy Smith (1979) points out that it may be necessary for children's symbol formation that it be initially amorphous.

Interaction and provision

It should be clear by now that we are dealing with a process which, although driven by a powerful inner programme, nevertheless does require a certain kind of support from the interpersonal environment.

Experience and research show that representational systems do not develop in a social or cultural vacuum. On the contrary, in such a context they wither and die. Both *laissez-faire* and rote-learning approaches have deleterious effects on children's development. On the one hand, where all is tolerated, so all is ignored. On the other hand, teaching methods which attempt to train skills by artificially separating them from their context in emergent representational systems effectively remove the purpose and meaning which drive children toward skill acquisition.

Children are quickly affected by negative atmospheres, and artificially imposed parameters on their symbolization will eventually have their destructive effect. We frequently notice curtailed development in drawing, but precisely the same kind of negative teaching environments contribute to the death of mathematical development in many people (Hughes, Shuard and Ginsburg, 1986). Rote-learning of reading and writing limit many people's language use too (Deterding, 1994, personal communication). But mathematics, language and drawing each have potential paths of development, and in some children we see these routes actualized. While so many people's development in drawing is crippled, it is a curious conclusion indeed to infer from this, as Hagen (1985, p. 59) does, that 'there is no development in art'. This may be so on a world scale but it is certainly untrue about the individual.

We know that the development of the different symbolic skills does not derive from general-purpose semiotic ability. Rather, there are specialist centres in the brain creating multiple channels of intelligence (Gardner, 1984; Jackendoff, 1994). However, once these systems are up-and-running they do interact with each other. Drawing can make an enormous contribution to many aspects of cognition, including mathematical, linguistic and spatial understandings. The environment which represses drawing is likely to be one that curtails other aspects of learning and development too. So what is the right kind of educational environment?

Interaction

Research shows that activities tend to be prolonged, extended and developed by the child where there is an interested, responsive adult close by who supports, consolidates and affirms what the child is doing (Bruner, 1980).

To have any meaningful dialogue with children about their expressive and representational actions, it is first necessary to identify and then cue into processes unfolding in the child. It is then possible to talk to children of any age about, for example, their drawings in terms of form and content. One can draw upon one's resources with reference to structures the child is either exploring or moving toward. Earlier I mentioned the example of the rotating child, who will enjoy stories and rhymes about going around.

The interaction between the teacher and the child may be extremely subtle. Sometimes it is silence that is required, the teacher being as unobtrusive as possible. Even here though, the teacher should still observe and record the key representational actions of the child, for it is this information which will guide future interaction and provision. Sometimes nothing more than encouraging facial expressions and gestures – if they arise from a genuine appreciation of the child's efforts – are required. Again, there are occasions when one would choose to immerse children in words and ideas, or hold a continuous conversation with them. In interaction of many forms and levels, the amount of words is not the key feature. What is important is that an aware and interested companion is occasionally close by or obtainable.

Children may well be surprised, interested, even delighted to learn that shapes and forms they produce *can* be described and discussed in a meaningful way. The teacher helps in this way to bring these understandings to the consciousness of the child; to help him or her to realize them. In describing shapes, forms and spatial relations, the child and teacher are often describing mathematical relations. In describing an adventure in a drawing, one is constructing narrative.

Even fairly basic responses made by a tired teacher will be effective if they are genuine. Nick MacAdoo (1990, personal communication) has pointed out that the remark to a three-year-old, 'That's an exciting zig-zag line, Jason', may seem fairly banal, but even here there are several implicit levels of meaning. Firstly, the child knows the adult is interested. Secondly, he is learning that a certain kind of line can be mathematically assigned to the group 'zig-zag'. This is an objective definition of this type of line which, he will learn, people will agree about. At a further level, he learns something about the line which is not given in its mathematical classification, and about which there may be interesting differences of opinion. This is the expressive and aesthetic quality of this line conveyed by the noun-classifier 'exciting'.

Even in simple exchanges like this, one is helping to extend the reflective and critical side of development. This is far, far better than smuggling in to the child's world paraphernalia of the adult art-world as part of the National Curriculum critical-studies component. We are already seeing the sabotaging of the child's internal agenda with, for example, Monet's bridge and water lilies appearing in the water and sand trays, and in play and painting areas of nurseries (Bruce, 1995, personal communication). Even with the slimmed-down curriculum of the post-Dearing era, this kind of practice may well continue – and, no doubt, be reviewed in art-education journals as exemplars of good practice. In reality such schemes will undermine the formation of a true reflective dimension of art-practice. Interaction does not consist, at nursery level or any other level of education, of arbitrarily imposed projects according to some pre-envisaged paradigm. It makes little difference whether one makes children build Monet's bridge or Easter Bunnies, this approach will hijack children's representational processes.

Events in the drawing and events in the world

In talking to a child about a 'jagged edge' or a 'swirling line' in a drawing we are using terms which simultaneously refer to experiences in the external world. It is, however, necessary for the teacher to know when he or she is using language to describe what is happening in the drawing and when words describe events or objects in the *external world* (see Willats, 1985). For instance, a shape 'in-front-of' another shape in a drawing is very different from a shape 'in-front-of' another in the world. By being clear about the way we describe events in reality and events represented, we build up children's understanding of the relationship between signifier and signified and the language with which to describe this relationship. We clarify the means, possibilities and – equally important – the limits of a medium as a vehicle for thought. In this way we are giving children more power and control over their forms of representation.

This points to the reasons for knowing about both the subject-area and child development. There is often a spurious argument between those who conceive of the curriculum in terms of the subject-content and those who advocate child-centredness. We need to know about the content of the subject-area, but not as a body of knowledge to be transmitted to the child. The content of the discipline is only important insofar as it contains instruments, processes and experiences which will promote development in the child, as this book is designed to demonstrate. Reciprocally, we need to know about development and how it interacts with what is available within the subject-area.

Teachers at nursery or any other level in education should be neither mere providers of equipment nor passive observers; not just transmitters of knowledge but 'experienced learners' (Blenkin, 1985, personal communication) who are involved with and partake in children's discoveries themselves.

Provision

Provision is not about the mere installation of equipment, but what is done with it. However, it is possible to make a few basic points about provision.

Children should have access to both horizontally inclined surfaces and vertical ones. Therefore, both easels and tables should be available. Standing at an easel offers the possibilities of movement of the entire body whilst drawing; sitting at a table means one can relax, contemplate one's drawing, look at the drawings of other children and discuss these with them. The interaction between children is vital. Sometimes they are very good teachers of each other, perhaps because they are closest to the kinds of issue their peers might confront in representation. This works best if the adult teacher has helped to create an atmosphere where it is natural to discuss all forms of representation without disdain or prejudice.

Several tables grouped together, making a large surface area around which several children can work, allow for interaction between them. Children should have the opportunity of painting on a large scale where the entire body is utilized.

Felt-tip pens, pencils, crayons should all be freely available. The children can be shown quite easily (in most cases!) how to use them and look after them, even at nursery level. Think about the different ways paint can be contained and transported. You do not have to stick to a manufacturer's designed kit. Make a collection of all useful containers for pigment. Take the lids off the paint-pots so that children can actually see the colours and learn how to mix them – a completely absorbing activity in itself for many children – and they also learn not to spill them.

Understandings made across media

Do not have any preconceptions about what toys, art or educational media actually are. Cardboard boxes and apple cores can be pivotal objects; many materials make marks. Why should drawing have to leave a trace anyway? Let the children help redefine the medium.

Opportunities should be arranged for the transportation of understandings from one medium to another. If drawing boards and paper are available in places other than the routine painting area, say, near the construction toy area, valuable transpositions between understandings made in four-dimensional play and two-dimensional media will occur. A design process may emerge in this way, as children move between construction and drawing.

Traditional media and electronic paint

It is also important to remember that different media elicit variations in children's performance (Golomb, 1992, 1993). Some constraints in children's actions thought to be related to general 'stages' in cognitive development turn out to be media-specific constraints. For example, it is sometimes said that children can only handle a few choices of colour.

With traditional pigment this may be so. Certainly there are practical problems in arranging for a large group of children to use more than a few pots of paint. However, with the computer paintbox, observations suggest it may be possible for the child to choose quite easily from hundreds, perhaps thousands, of colours (Matthews and Jessel, 1993a, 1993b).

Bring computers into the nursery. They should not be in a room of their own, facing a blank wall, separate from other media. Children from under two years of age can use them. Try placing them amidst other painting and drawing media. They should be protected from water, but it does not matter if they get paint on them.

Children can be given their own drawing books, which they may carry with them from one area to another. This also gives the child the sense of authorship, and over the days and weeks both the child and the teacher have a graphic record of development. To this end, do not take constructions, paintings or drawings away from children prematurely. Allow the child to take responsibility for his or her works. Let the child know where they are kept.

Presentation and display

Display the works in such a way, and at a physical level such that the child learns about his or her own development. Display and presentation should not simply be tacked on the end of children's activities but should offer the child valuable feedback about the consequences of his or her actions.

Some displays need time and attention spent on them by the teacher. Work has to be presented so as to maximize its visual qualities. However, means should be found for the immediate display of work, so that children see the effects of their paintings and drawings directly. This does not mean scrappy presentation; thought has to be put into it so that paintings etc. can be displayed quickly but effectively. Allow opportunities for the children themselves to display their own work.

There is not the space here to discuss presentation fully, but it is a vital part of interaction and teaching. Here are some main points to remember. Avoid contrived display where the children's real concerns become lost within the teacher's preconception. In this regard, think twice before destroying the formal and spatial integrity of a child's drawing with shears or guillotine. Most important of all, avoid implying in one's presentation that one representational mode is more worthy or valuable than another. The more attuned the teacher becomes to the nature of children's symbolization, the more he or she will realize that all levels and systems of representation have structure, validity and beauty.

Transformation and denotation

Attempts to co-ordinate two or more aspects of a scene may gradually cause the child to reconceptualize the drawing rules which hold the various elements of the drawing together. This might start to occur from age 4 years. Objects are drawn with reference to the drawing surface (Costall, 1991, personal communication) and involve visual percepts of the object combined with other kinds of knowledge not necessarily available within the optical array. This is rather different from the theory which splits *intellectual realism*, where children supposedly draw what they *know*, from *visual realism*, when children supposedly learn to draw what they *see*. Such a notion is sometimes blamed on Luquet (1927) but in fact he was an extraordinarily sensitive observer of children's drawing. The problem occurred when Piaget subsumed Luquet's ideas into his own theory and distorted them.

Defining and separating what is meant by 'seeing' and 'knowing' is fraught with problems. When children try to draw objects they use a combination of different kinds of knowledge. Some derive from scene-specific analysis (Pratt, 1985) – viewer-centred descriptions based on the observer's viewpoint to the object. Other kinds of knowledge derive from the main axes and features of the object irrespective of viewpoint, or object-centred descriptions (Marr, 1982; Willats 1990, personal communication). John Willats (1977, 1981, 1984, 1985) sees drawing development as essentially creative in a technical sense, depending, like language acquisition, on the child learning language rules, which change as he or she grows older. Willats, like Arnheim (1954, 1974) sees the child's drawing development not as triggered by better observation of nature so much as by his or her attempts to resolve the transformational and denotational ambiguities arising in the drawing.

This point is vital for anyone concerned with children's drawing at any level in education. Children's early drawings of the relations between and within objects and scenes seem strange only when we do not understand the representational systems they employ. Perfectly legitimate representational solutions offered by children are frequently confused (by teachers, artists and psychologists alike) with limited 'stereotypes' in need of correction by training children to 'look' more closely at nature. This assumption still underlies the National Curriculum in Art, despite attempts by some art-educators to challenge the notion of the superiority of a restricted type of observational drawing. In an otherwise sensitive and painstaking study, Van Sommers (1984, p. 173) makes this kind of mistake, going so far as to write of the 'tyranny' of graphic schemata, which he considers rigid strategies which actually retard development. It is strange to think of the vocabulary of early drawing in this way. It is like thinking that the child's early language is a barrier to his or her later language.

Though children do sometimes convey views of objects, they are very often attempting to encode structural relations which remain invariant despite movement of the object or movement of the viewer (Gibson, 1979). Moving around objects and moving the objects themselves (as in play with hand-held objects) reveals most, if not all, of their invariant properties. This is part of the cause of drawings which seem to show us several views of an object simultaneously.

Some people assume that children would show true views of objects if they only could, but it is more complex than that. The changes which occur in their drawings as they grow older reflect changes in their priorities about what constitutes the essential information to be encoded in a work (Light, 1985).

At certain points in development (from about 4 years), showing many views of an object may seem important to them; at other times they want to preserve the true shapes of objects. Perspectival representation distorts objects. Even when children are aware of projective relations and are capable of encoding them, they may avoid perspectival solutions because these sacrifice information about the true shape of objects.

There is an interesting multicultural and anti-racist dimension to discussion about drawing systems. Some people have thought that the Chinese or Indian artists painted the way they did because they did not understand perspective. This is completely erroneous. Chinese artists, for example, knew how to depict three-dimensional looking objects from a single viewpoint long before the supposed 'invention' of linear perspective in Renaissance Italy. The Chinese purposely avoided such devices because they were trying to convey, not physical space, but a transcendental one.

Whilst there are vast differences between adult artists and children, nevertheless children too use systems which best suit their representational intentions. The difference is that, in the case of children, the process is not conscious – the drawing systems they use fit into ecological niches in their development. We can certainly encourage children to draw from objects and scenes, when this has a basis in what the child is moving toward. But we should be cautious about overemphasizing the recording of viewer-centred arrays as if this was the only definition of drawing. This will cut across a developmental project much greater and more ambitious than producing skilful still-life drawings.

Copying

Because the child's construction of the visual world involves the interpersonal as well as the physical environment, this means that socially-mediated objects – including works of art and images of many kinds – are an important part of that development (Costall, 1985; Pratt, 1985). There have been some curiously inept arguments both for and against copying from the images of others. On the one hand, some have argued against copying so-called 'second-hand' images; on the other hand, copying from adult exemplars is often used as a form of oppression. Both advocates, for or against, misconstrue the issue. First of all, I want to differentiate between copying requested by the teacher and child-initiated, spontaneous copying. I will discuss the latter.

Many children – and these include some of our exceptional draughtspersons – benefit greatly from seeing how, for example, three-dimensions are translated into two in the drawings or images of others. With appropriate guidance children can use cultural models to gain insight into how representation operates within certain rule-bound constraints. Studying other people's pictures can help children understand, for example, how surface layout in the real world is cast – *projected* – onto the drawing surface. This does of course require that the teacher is in a position to discuss intelligibly the world's imagery, and also has an understanding of the child's development through representational systems.

Knowing something about the child's development helps us to predict the issues which the child is likely to address in visual representation. This means that we can plan the child's exposure to some things, and wait for, or ignore, others, because we will know *to some extent* that, only when certain structures are established in the child's own representation, will exposure to these things make any constructive difference. We will also know that forced exposure to some exemplars will cause damage, because the child does not have the necessary schemes in place.

As in language acquisition, the child, paradoxically, does not in fact copy whilst apparently copying! Rather, the child actively constructs according to internal programmes of enquiry (Jackendoff, 1994). They attend to certain formal features and ignore others, transcribing them according to the graphic and internal schemata which are already at their disposal, or to which they are moving. They notice exemplars and elaborations of the structures they themselves are generating. They only really adopt those which have a place in their descriptions of reality so far, or those which they realize can be used to extend these descriptions. Spontaneous, self-driven 'copying' is not usually arid and sterile but is part of the child's creative investigation of structure and content.

The child's search may well include studying available cultural models, anything from comics to computer graphics; from pictures in storybooks to perspective paintings; from bubble-gum cards to Cubism; to television's sequencing of events.

Emergent writing

A clear example of children's interpretation of a given model is children's early writing. Young children assimilate letter (and number) forms from the environment into their own emergent graphic schemata (see Figures

8.8 and 8.10). This means that they may attend to core and radial (Athey, 1990), closure, right-angular attachment and, later on, oblique angles. The orientation of individual letters may not initially strike children as significant, though an entire lateral line of words might. As the child may attend to various aspects of visual representation, so the child's focus may alternate between different aspects of written language. For example, the child might focus upon individual letter-forms using the structures described above; or else he or she might pretend to handwrite, using travelling zig-zags and loops, whilst pretending to read what is being written. Incidentally, this is not restricted to any particular language. For example, Chinese children I observed in Singapore produce emergent Chinese characters (Matthews, 1994b). Like their British counterparts, these children sometimes appear to use letter forms and pictorial types of configuration interchangeably. This does not necessarily mean of course that the child does not realize that letter-forms are different in some sense from other kinds of configuration, but it does show that they use them in a personal, symbolic, even idiosyncratic way. This suggests that any differentiation they do make between letter-forms and pictorial configuration is probably different from that made by adults. Detailed observation suggests that when children alternate between arbitrary, conventional signs and pictorial symbols, they may be trying to actively sort out how each type encodes reality.

Conclusions

In this chapter I have described a family of expression and representation of which drawing is one member. I have described drawing as a continuum which exhibits organizational and semantic characteristics right from the outset, even before so-called 'scribbling'. The educational implications of this are profound.

The transformations which early sensori-cognitive adventures of line undergo may seem chaotic but there is a structure within that chaos. Within a fluid play with visual media the child co-ordinates the shape, location and movement of entities. This play consists of the script-like as well as visual information from which the child's internal descriptions of the world are made. Bretherton (1984) has suggested that internal descriptions of objects may in fact be derived from internal event representations. If this is so, we see again the importance of dynamic representation.

Additionally the drawing becomes an unfolding scenario in which thoughts, feelings and actions of imaginary agents in imaginary worlds are enacted. Action representation epitomizes the beginnings of a dialectical relationship between the thinking child, the ever-changing parameters of the representational intention and the possibilities unfolding on the drawing or play surface (Wolf, 1989). The child's drawing is like a kind of window, but not in a sense in which that is usually intended.

This window does not merely open out on to a copy of a visual world; but, as Ray Jackendoff (1994) has said of language, is a window on thinking itself.

If we want children to become competent symbolizers, literate in the fullest sense of the term, and able to initiate and self-direct their own independent thinking, the formation of these early systems of representation must be encouraged and supported, especially by teachers.

There is a great deal of confusion about how far this process is universal and how far it is culturally-specific. Some of this confusion arises because many people are not yet able to differentiate between structure and content, decoration and denotation, expressive elements and structural principles. Interaction between the representational programme and various cultural settings will of course create differences (see, for example, Matthews, 1994b), as will gender and social class. These differences are not strongly apparent in the drawings of the very young, but tend to show up as the child matures. We need to know more about how these variables interact with this programme of expression and representation.

However, I think that the evidence shows that, at a deep level of description, this process is universal. Children are involved with concerns which are common and essential to all humans. These concerns are acultural and persist while adults' wars of words and weapons go on over their heads. If we take the trouble to look beyond superficial differences in their manifestation and learn about how representation is structured, how it becomes either developed or disturbed, we will perhaps have some control over our destiny and give children some control over theirs.

Suggested further reading

Matthews, J. (1994) *Helping Children Draw and Paint in Early Childhood: Children and Visual Representation*, Hodder & Stoughton, London.

9

The Development of
Mathematical Understanding

Marilyn Metz

Since the first edition of *Early Childhood Education* was published, many aspects relating to the teaching of mathematics in the early years have changed. We have seen the statutory implementation of a National Curriculum for mathematics, and we have endured major changes in the content and organization of this curriculum (DES, 1989, 1991; DFE, 1995a). We have also seen considerable changes in the ways in which assessments of children's mathematical understanding and knowledge are made, including the introduction, and several amendments, of formal assessment at the end of Key Stage 1. One result of these upheavals has been that early years teachers, especially those working at Key Stage 1, have understandably needed to concentrate heavily on curriculum content and on assessment. Planning has centred around the mathematical concepts outlined in the changing programmes of study within the mathematics National Curriculum documents. Assessment has concerned itself with attainment targets and statements of attainment, and of course with the end of Key Stage 1 formal assessment procedures.

What this has meant in practice is that the focus of the mathematics curriculum offered to the young child has undergone profound change; the pressure on early years educators is now to deliver the National Curriculum – whatever 'delivery' means! Whenever this term is used I am reminded of the sound of mail plopping onto the doormat. It has certainly been delivered (usually to the correct address) but the person doing the delivery has no guarantee that the contents of the envelopes will be read, understood or acted upon.

This is not the place to enter into a detailed critique of the National Curriculum for mathematics. Others have done this already (e.g. Dowling and Noss, 1990) and it is to be hoped that informed critical commentary on the underlying principles, form and content will continue. The most important practical implication of the continued presence of a statutorily imposed mathematics curriculum is that early years educators need to include specific content in their planning and their teaching, and that they need to see knowledge and understanding of, and mastery of skills related to this content as a goal for the children in their care. What the presence of this statutorily imposed mathematics curriculum does not mean is that the ways in which children develop their mathematical understanding have changed. Our understandings of how children develop mathematically may alter as fresh evidence is discovered through research and reflection (e.g. Steffe and Wood, 1990; Nunes, Schliemann and Carraher, 1993). Because of the inevitable pressure from National Curriculum demands to 'deliver' mathematics to young children it is critically important that early years educators remain aware of the findings of research and scholarship regarding children's mathematical development. The everyday teaching of mathematics in the classroom may appear to be intuitive and pragmatic, but even the most apparently trivial child–teacher interaction can be seen to have an underlying theoretical framework (Orton, 1987). As informed early years educators we need to be able to identify the potential tensions that exist between the requirements of the mathematics national curriculum and what we know about the young child's mathematical development.

This chapter will not provide answers, nor will it necessarily ease these tensions. What it aims to do is to review the state of our knowledge of early mathematical development, and thus provide teachers with information from which to develop sound starting points for the mathematical development of the children in their care. After all, mathematical development in the early years should not solely be related to National Curriculum requirements. There are fundamental and important aspects of mature mathematical understanding which can be best established in early years practice, in particular explorations of pattern, of logical thinking, sequencing and the development of the ability to generalize.

When children first enter our education system, they come with a wealth of mathematical experience and knowledge which they have gained in the first few years of their lives. These mathematical understandings are not necessarily organized in a way which would enable an adult to identify them as being contained within the academic subject labelled 'mathematics'. Many adults see mathematics as a body of knowledge, divorced in many respects from everyday life, and accessible only to those who, by virtue of specialist education, can be called mathematicians. Young children do not intuitively understand mathematical ideas in this formal, abstract way. They may be able to count accurately, but not be able to recognize the symbols conventionally used for numbers. They may be able to add and subtract, but not be able to represent these operations on paper in a recognizable form (Hughes, 1986). As teachers, we believe that learning mathematics is an important part of the young child's education, and thus in the nursery and first school classroom much emphasis is placed upon providing children with the skills and knowledge they require in order eventually to become mathematically competent members of our society. Part of the early years teacher's task is, of course, to introduce young children to the conventions of mathematics. Another role, however, and one which has a more fundamental and longer term goal, was suggested as long ago as 1982 in the Cockcroft Report, *Mathematics Counts* (DES, 1982c), and is still valid – that of opening the doors of mathematical discovery for the young children in our care.

Many mathematicians and mathematics educators will agree with Papert (1981) when he says that the fundamental difference between a mathematician and a young child learning mathematics is not essentially rooted in the amount of technical information they know, but in the fact that the mathematician is actively involved in 'doing', whereas the young child may not be. Introducing a young child to the vast and exciting field of mathematics means developing that child's already forming sense of pattern and order, as well as extending and refining her or his ability to think logically, and to compare, match and order the complex content of her or his environment. It also means enabling the child to become an active investigator, and helping her or him to 'do' mathematics rather than just learning about it. Building upon this early mathematical knowledge in a way in which the young child is actively involved is an essential role of the teacher of young children.

Having emphasized the importance of active investigation, which we shall see is an essential element of Piagetian and post-Piagetian approaches to mathematical development, it is also necessary to examine critically some commonly-held notions about the nature of mathematics and the learning of mathematics. Unless we do this we cannot understand the difficulties children have in coming to terms with school mathematics and therefore we shall not be able to approach the teaching of mathematics in an informed and considered way. Burton (1990) identifies several features of a model of mathematics that is commonly adhered to, and provides arguments to counter dependence on them. These features are worth considering here.

The first is a belief in the simplicity of mathematics. It is often assumed that the so-called body of knowledge we label as mathematics is carefully structured from the simple to the complex. To some extent we can see this reflected in the organization of the content of the mathematics National Curriculum. Following from this assumption there is another that states that because mathematics proceeds from the simple to the complex, the teaching of mathematics begins by being a simple task and develops in complexity. Burton argues, however, that a distinction must be made between the mathematical content of something being taught, and the nature of the learning task itself. As we shall see later in the chapter, although, for instance, counting is a relatively simple activity, the task of learning how to count is complex. For young children to extend their mathematical understanding, their existing knowledge needs to be restructured in order to incorporate the new ideas. This restructuring is both difficult for the children and presents a challenge for the teacher – that of presenting the new ideas in a way that will enable the children to make meaningful connections with their existing frameworks and also enable them to make the necessary changes in their frameworks.

The second element of Burton's analysis that bears consideration is the belief that learning takes place more effectively if children are enjoying themselves. This is probably true, but it does not mean that learning *will* take place if children are enjoying themselves. Here, as with all aspects of early years education, mathematical or not, the active intervention of the teacher is of crucial importance. Added to this, we also need to ask what enjoyment is in the context of learning, and how it may be best sustained. Yes, learning can be enjoyable, but it can also involve need, application, frustration, and impatience. If we deny these emotions in the context of young children learning mathematics, then we sterilize the subject.

Burton's third feature is a belief in the reality of mathematics. Mathematics is often seen as an objective body of knowledge, abstract and absolute. If we combine this with the belief, taken from many different theoretical models, that children need to experience concrete examples of abstract mathematical ideas in order to understand the abstract essence of the mathematics, then we have a model which approaches abstract 'reality' through practical activity with real materials. There is no fundamental argument about the importance of active involvement with real materials in early years learning. But we do need to ask 'What does "concrete" mean to young children?'. In an environment where ideas may be presented via television, video games and computers, it becomes necessary to consider whether such easily available everyday images exist in the same way as bricks, balls, bicycles or bats do for the young child. It may be that experience of such untouchable, non-concrete images alters the ways in which young children's mathematical ideas develop. Papert (1980) has certainly argued that this is the case. What we are really doing, however, when we offer children objects to manipulate in order to develop their mathematical thinking, is not a concrete example of an abstract idea, but a concrete representation of an idea that remains abstract, however many differing kinds of representation are made. It is important to remember this when considering the examples of classroom provision that are mentioned later in this chapter. We also need to remember that a child will bring her/his own interpretation to any concrete representation, and that sometimes this can lead to more complexities than conclusions.

Burton's fourth and last feature is the 'empty vessel' belief. If we see mathematics as a codified body of knowledge, the child as starting formal education empty of any mathematical concepts, and the role of the teacher as filling the child with this body of mathematical knowledge, then we shall approach mathematics learning and teaching in a highly mechanistic and hierarchical manner. We have only to glance at research findings concerning children's informal mathematical knowledge (e.g. Nunes, 1993) to see that the young child certainly does not begin her or his formal education in mathematics empty of mathematical ideas and skills. We also only need to reflect upon any one mathematical teaching experience to become aware of the fact that effective mathematics teaching is not a case of 'filling up' the child with information. What is often more fruitful is to look at where the 'leaks' occur. No child-centred or developmental model of education has a place for a belief in the child as an empty vessel and we need to be keenly aware of this when working mathematically with young children.

Much of our knowledge of the development of the young child's mathematical thinking stems from the work done by Piaget (1896–1980). There is no doubt that since his writings became available (around the 1960s) in English, his findings have had a profound effect on early childhood education in general and on our perception of the mathematical development of the young child in particular and have also acted as a springboard for further research. Since his death, and indeed for some years before that, his work has been the subject of criticism from various sources, e.g. Vygotsky, Bruner, Bryant, Donaldson, Ausubel. Readers are referred to Sutherland (1992) for some detail regarding Piaget and his critics. A fundamental belief, however, held by both Piaget and his critics, is that the young child's development takes place through an active involvement with the environment. The details of that active involvement, together with the role of language, of the adult and of the social situation in development vary, depending on the theoretical stance taken. For the early years teacher in England this fundamental belief is the mainstay of her/his practice. Indeed, the influence of Piaget is still very strong in most if not all early years classrooms in the country. It is important, however, to remember that Piaget's findings have been criticized and developed. Although his important findings are still on the whole very relevant to good early years practice, there are other factors which need serious consideration.

As we shall see later in the chapter, the activity-based model of learning that Piaget put forward has been refined by Donaldson (1978) and Hughes (1986). Experimental work carried out by them emphasizes the importance of the child's interpretation of meaning of the activity for subsequent success. Re-contextualizing some of Piaget's experiments, young children's success rate improved. The important message to be read in this work is that for effective learning to take place, it must be presented within a context that is familiar and has meaning for the young child.

Piaget's model of development has been challenged by Bruner (Sutherland, 1992) in other ways. Although Bruner agrees with Piaget that constructive play should be an essential feature of the early years, he takes issue with Piaget over the concept of readiness. Bruner's interventionist approach centres on the child and her/his needs, but also emphasizes the importance of the challenges that teachers set children in order to enable them to develop their ideas. Bruner's spiral curriculum reflects his belief that any topic can be taught effectively to children of any age in an intellectually respectable form; his starting point remains a Piagetian one: the child. The brief report of a case study in Metz (1985) is a small example of the spiral curriculum in action in the learning of mathematics.

Donaldson's emphasis on meaningfulness, Bruner's ideas regarding intervention, together with Vygotsky's identification of a 'zone of proximal development' (Sutherland, 1992) all emphasize the importance of the active nature of the role of the early years teacher. Differing from Piaget, his critics have shown that sensitive and informed structuring of a situation, together with open and carefully framed questioning, can facilitate learning and accelerate the mathematical understanding of the young child. The implications for the ways in which early years teachers approach the teaching of mathematics are very clear.

Part of the role of mathematics teaching in the early years is to provide a sound foundation for the development of skills associated with the knowledge about, and manipulation of, our number system, but, all too often, this identification of 'mathematics' with 'numeracy' clouds our own understanding of what mathematics is, and what it can be in the first few years of schooling. To restrict the teaching and learning of mathematical skills to the limited field of number is to ignore much of the mathematical knowledge which the young child brings with her/him when s/he enters the education system. The most current version of the mathematics National Curriculum (DFE, 1995a), with its strong emphasis on number during Key Stage 1, may well add more pressure to perceive mathematics as numeracy; this is a danger that early years educators need to heed.

Having said this, however, it seems to me to be important to attempt to tailor this chapter to the realities of the present-day early years curriculum and the needs of the early years educator. Given that number and the development of numeracy is an important dimension of growing mathematical understanding and also given that the overwhelming wealth of research into the young child's mathematical development is in the field of number, I make no excuses for the fact that the largest section of this chapter concerns itself with number concept development.

Number

As I have already mentioned, many adults, when asked about mathematics, reply in a way that shows the questioner that they identify mathematics with arithmetic. In many respects, however, although number is a very important unifying dimension in mathematics, it is not used in the everyday world without reference to something concrete. We add, but we might be checking our change in the supermarket, or working out how much fabric we need for new curtains, or deciding how much food we need to prepare a meal for six people, and how long it will take to cook. There is almost always a practical context in which to place operations on numbers. We need to bear this in mind as we look at the young child's development of number concepts.

Some of the many mathematical skills which the young child brings into the nursery or first school concern the ability to make sense of our number system. Ginsburg (1977) has perceptively documented and commented upon the child's struggles to understand the apparently arbitrary nature of numbers in our culture. He talks of learning to count as 'a song to sing', and he sees this song as very special, to be learned in a particular way, and one which has no end. A child learns that 'one, two, three' is not the same as 'two, one, three', and he or she also finds that as soon as he or she succeeds with one part of this song, a new part is introduced – indeed, the counting numbers do have no end; there will always be another number, one larger than the very largest you can think of, or say.

For the young child, this task must seem enormous and unmanageable, and yet children do learn to count, and often manage to do so before they enter the nursery. The strategies which Ginsburg (1977) identified as being significant in order to succeed in this massive task are important ones – those of looking for order and pattern, and coping with just a little of the task at a time. So children may well manage 'one, two, three' before they attempt 'four, five, six', and so on. The search for pattern and hence predictability takes a little longer. Our counting numbers do not reflect any pattern until we pass 'twelve', and then 'twenty'. But from then on, the task is made much easier. There is an identifiable rhythm in the tens: 'twenty, thirty, forty, fifty, etc.', and within the tens: 'twenty-one, twenty-two, thirty-one, thirty-two, etc.'. How often have you noticed that a young child will need prompting when he or she reaches nineteen or fifty-nine, but can then count on comfortably until at least twenty-nine or sixty-nine?

The position is somewhat different for children learning to count in some cultures where the number symbols and names differ from the ones we use. In China number symbols have a clear regularity, as do the number names. There are symbols for one to ten; eleven is written and said 'ten one'; twenty-three is written and said 'two ten three'; eighty-nine is written and said 'eight ten nine', and so on. Therefore, from one to one hundred, there is a clear and repeatable pattern with no irregularities.

There is some evidence to show that young Chinese children do not have the same difficulties as described above when learning the number names and to count. This may also be true in cultures where the number symbols and names have more or less regularity than ours. It would be interesting to know, for instance, how French children cope with learning number names, where 'seventy' is 'sixty-ten' and 'eighty' is 'four-twenty'.

We have so far only discussed the learning of number names and their correct sequencing. Learning to count involves more than this. Gelman and Gallistel (1978), in a classic piece of work, identified five criteria that need to be fulfilled before one can say that the counting of items in a collection has been successfully achieved. These are as follows:

- *The one-to-one principle*: each and every item is given one, and only one, number name.
- *The abstraction principle*: what the objects in the collection are is irrelevant. They can vary in all sorts of ways; the important aspect is that they all belong to the collection being counted.
- *The stable-order principle*: the number names are used in an unvarying order: one, two, three, four, etc., not two, three, four, one.
- *The cardinality principle*: the final number name denotes the number within the collection. If, for instance, the collection has six items in it, when 'six' is reached, this gives the number of items in the set.
- *The order-irrelevance principle*: it does not matter in which order the items in the set are counted. As long as all the other criteria are adhered to, the final count reached will be the same.

Gelman and Gallistel's work has shown that, although these five criteria may appear to adults to be relatively self-evident, they are not to the young child, and moreover s/he finds it difficult to adhere to all of the criteria at any one time. Learning to count is an excellent example which refutes the belief in simplicity (Burton, 1990). Apparently a simple activity, the learning task involved is identified here as a complex one, and involves the young child in attending to a considerable number of features in order to be successful.

Learning to count is not the only way that numbers become familiar to the young children. They will meet and use the same words used in a variety of ways, with different meanings. They will hear and see number words used as names: 'The 41 bus stops outside Woolworth's', 'We live at number 80'; as adjectives: 'I have three buttons on my anorak', 'My bike has two wheels'; and also as objects to manipulate: 'One and one is two'. It is this last use of the number words which we, as teachers, seek to develop in the young child, initially through experience of the number properties of concrete sets, but eventually aiming at the young child's understanding of number in the abstract world of mathematics.

Hughes, in his book *Children and Number* (1986), has looked closely at the very young child's understanding of number and number operations, and has highlighted some of the problems which seem to occur when we ask young children to handle numbers without reference to concrete objects, and when we introduce our culture's symbols for numbers to them. He has identified a gap which seems to be present between a child's abstract understanding of number, and her or his ability to represent this understanding in the formal language of mathematics. He argues that children need to be helped to develop ways of bridging this gap, so that firm links may be established between the knowledge based on concrete experience that the child is sure of, and the abstract nature of the language or arithmetic.

The kinds of links which can be made must be rooted fundamentally in the young child's realm of understanding, and this is initially founded in experience of the concrete. In manipulating objects, collecting sets of things together, combining and partitioning these sets, counting and recounting the objects within the sets and sub-sets, the child begins to learn about the way in which counting words can also be used to describe a set – in other words, the number of objects in a set becomes a way of describing that set mathematically. The number word that describes the set represents a mathematical property of that set. The members of a set of objects, for example, may have several properties: they may be all made of wood, they may be all circular, and there may be eight of them. The properties of that set can be seen as 'wooden-ness', 'circular-ness' and 'eight-ness'. Another set might have other properties: the objects in this second set may all be plastic and square, but there may also be eight objects. So, though the properties of 'plastic-ness' and of 'square-ness' are not shared with the first set, the property of 'eight-ness' is.

Being able to see number as a property of a set is a complex ability which Piagetian theory argues needs, as a precondition, the attainment of the concept of conservation of number – that the number of objects in a given set does not vary, however the objects might be physically arranged. There has been much criticism of Piaget's approach to the young child's understanding of number concepts, and various alternative models have been postulated. It does seem clear, however, that the concept of conservation is important, though not the final stepping-stone to achieving a complete understanding of the concept of number. What is essential to remember is that, although this concept is important, it does not mean that, once he or she is able to conserve number, a young child is therefore able to handle the idea of number in the abstract. Although conservation is important, a child often needs to make an easy connection between her or his experiences of number and the representations of number in the world of concrete objects in order to build on this concrete world and eventually handle abstract mathematical ideas comfortably.

What we have looked at so far is the cardinal aspect of number – where a child can count the members of a set of objects and arrive at a stable and accurate number to describe that set. There is another element involved in the understanding of number which is important – the ordinal aspect. Here a child needs to be able not only to count 'one, two, three', but to order 'first, second, third'. Piagetian research on the conservation of number involved investigating the development of both of these. To decide whether two sets are equivalent in number property, it is necessary for a child either to count the members of each set, or to arrange the members of one set in one-to-one correspondence with the members of the other set. In the latter case, the child is handling the ordinal property of the sets – matching the first to the first, the second to the second, and so on. Piaget's experiments which focused on the ordinal aspect of number highlighted the fact that a child's understanding of number involved both the ordinal and cardinal aspects, in a close relationship with each other.

In the very first years of education a teacher may be primarily concerned with the young child's ability to recognize the number property of a set and to order the members of that set, but what is also important is fostering the child's ability to perform operations on number – to add, subtract, multiply and divide. The findings of Hughes (1986) show us here that the gap between a child's understanding of operations on number and her or his ability to express this understanding in formal mathematical language is very important for the teacher to be aware of. To enable the teacher to help the child to bridge that gap we need to look at the strategies which the young child might develop in order to be able to perform these important operations, and to understand that these strategies are important tools in the development of an understanding of number concepts as a whole.

Looking at the formal presentation of operations on number, we may well assume that the symbolic representation which we use is quite unambiguous: $2 + 2 = 4$, $8 - 3 = 5$, $9 \div 3 = 3$, $4 \times 2 = 8$, all look very straightforward. But when we look at the meaning of these apparently clear representations, we see that the situation is not as simple for the young child as we might think.

Much research has been carried out with the aim of trying to understand how the young child interprets operations on number and to establish the level of complexity of each kind of interpretation. If we look briefly at the possible meanings which the operation of addition might have, we shall perhaps be able to get some idea of the difficulties the young child must begin to cope with, and also gain some awareness of the complexity of our role as the teacher.

From a review of research, Dickson, Brown and Gibson (1984) have found that the operation of addition can be seen in five different ways. The first can be described as the union of sets: 'This vase holds four red flowers and three yellow ones; how many are there all together?' The second involves combining sets: 'The vase holds four red flowers and I put three more flowers in it; how many are there in the vase now?' The third interpretation involves a comparison: 'One vase has four flowers in it, and the other has three more than the first; how many flowers are in the second vase?' The fourth way of viewing addition is sometimes called complementary subtraction: 'I take four flowers out of the vase, and now I have three left; how many did I have at the beginning?' The final meaning that can be placed on addition has been labelled vector subtraction: "This morning I threw three dead flowers away, but this evening I have four more than I had yesterday; how many flowers did I pick today?'

A reading of these five interpretations of addition tells us not only that addition can be understood in different ways, but also that there are varying degrees of complexity represented here. There is some evidence that, for young children, the first two interpretations are the most straightforward, and that the last seems to be the most complicated. And yet they can all be symbolically represented by the simple mathematical expression $4 + 3 = 7$.

Interpretations of the meaning of subtraction are also varied and differ in their complexity, as do those for multiplication and division. It therefore seems clear that a young child cannot be said to have fully understood any of the four operations when only one or two of the meanings that can be placed on these operations have been grasped. And given that understanding grows slowly, one of our roles as teachers of young children must be to establish the nature of the child's understanding at any given time, and build on that situation. One of the tools we can use to do this is to ask for 'stories about sums', which allows the child to tell us what the mathematical expression means to her or him. The examples given above which illustrate different ways of interpreting the expression $4 + 3 = 7$ attempt to explain these differences by telling a story about the sum. What these stories do is represent the abstract mathematical expression in a real-life situation, and attempt to make sense of it in this way.

It is important, therefore to realize that before a child can make sense of the symbolic representation of a mathematical expression, he or she needs much experience of representing the four operations in practical situations, with real objects. The environment of early years education is rich in resources to support this development, not only in the materials specifically produced to assist the growth of mathematical thinking, but also in structured play materials of all kinds. A child's knowledge of number and number operations can be enhanced and grow from her or his spontaneous involvement in all kinds of activities with help from the adult. In the home-corner the early years teacher might ask: 'Are there enough chairs for everyone here to sit down?'; 'How many more vegetables will fit into this saucepan?'; 'Will there be any knives left over?'. Miniature worlds can equally well be used in a similar way, and teacher involvement in the child's construction play or activities with sand and water can highlight her or his knowledge of number and its properties. It is not enough, however, simply to ask 'How many?'; or 'Will there be any left over?'. We need to intervene further and ask such questions as 'How do you know?'; 'Can you show me?'; 'What do you think the answer will be?'; 'Why?'; 'Are there any others that have the same number – more – fewer?'. Remembering the importance of the child's interpretation of the activity (Donaldson, 1978), the early years teacher also needs to listen with great care and with no preconceptions to the child's answers and explanations and to ask for clarification if what the child says is not clear to the adult. In this way we are better able to tune into the child's meaning and not be tempted to impose our own on the situation.

We must remember that children are born into a world full of mathematics, and from the moment of their birth are exploring and making their own sense of this world. New-born babies' first physical movements and their continual exploration, via their senses, of the new kind of space around them, are their highly personal investigations of how things exist in relation to themselves and how they fit together in relation to each other. And so it would make sense for us to look next at the development of spatial concepts in young children and how this development can be enriched and refined in their early years at school.

The development of spatial concepts

As mentioned before, one of the fundamental factors underlying Piagetian developmental theory, as well as that of other developmental psychologists such as Bruner, Vygotsky and Donaldson, and a fundamental tenet supporting early childhood education in general, is that a child learns through interaction with the environment. Knowledge develops and extends through an active investigation of the concrete. Before ideas and knowledge can be handled in an abstract way, experience is needed of representations of these abstractions with real objects in real situations, and, through the compilation of information gathered in such contexts, generalizations will eventually be made and abstractions develop.

One important element of Piaget's theory of the development of spatial concepts highlights this active involvement with the real world, and distinguishes between what he has identified as perception and representation. Perception relates to the knowledge of objects obtained from direct contact with them; representation is concerned with the ability to create a mental image of an object – to recall it, in the absence of the object itself. A child's perceptual ability develops from the moment of birth, in what Piaget calls the 'sensori-motor' period of the first two or so years of life. The ability to represent an object, in Piagetian terms, only begins to develop later, perhaps a little before a child enters nursery education, and is not fully developed until much later, when a child has already entered the junior stage of her/his primary education.

The Piagetian theory of the development of spatial thinking has contributed a great deal to our understanding of a young child's mathematical development, despite the fact that there are many criticisms of his theoretical model. Without going into any great detail, these criticisms may be summarized as follows. First, the distinction between perception and representation which Piaget saw as discrete, is now thought of as a much more blurred area, so that perception is now seen as not differing in kind from mental imagery, but perhaps differing more in degree. Secondly, and a criticism which has been made of Piaget's work in other areas than that of spatial thinking, as we have already seen, many of his experiments have produced quite differing results when apparently trivial changes have been made. In *Children's Minds*, Donaldson (1978) discusses much of this research in detail, and one of her major arguments rests on the meaningfulness of the experimental situation for the child himself or herself. As part of her important and significant critique, she argues that Piaget's experiments often placed the child in a context which held little meaning for her or him, and that when this factor is changed, the results alter also. Therefore the careful provision of the tools best suited to a young child's explorations of space and shape needs to be a major consideration in the early years classroom. Alongside this careful provision comes teacher awareness of what to expect when the child investigates the structured environment.

One of the most fruitful areas in which to develop spatial thinking is that of structured play situations of all kinds. Home-corner play, for instance, when carefully resourced, can develop concepts of shape and size – 'Which plates shall we need for tea, which for a snack?' 'Will this saucepan be large enough to cook all these vegetables?' 'How can we fit all these knives into this drawer?' Working with a miniature world such as a farm can develop other important spatial concepts – 'Can the farmer see all the sheep in that field from where she is standing now?' 'Which animals can the farmer see if she is standing at the farmhouse door?' The world of construction provides a plethora of opportunities as well – 'Are there enough bricks to build the rest of this wall so that it is as high as the rest?' 'How can you construct a wall which won't fall down easily?' 'Will you be able to get through this doorway without bending down?' As discussed in the above section on number, early years teachers need also to continue to listen, to question further and to ask for clarification.

Alongside high quality intervention the emphasis also needs to be placed on the care with which materials are chosen in all of the early years activity areas. In the home-corner, for example, different sized plates, different sized knives, and an assortment of vegetables of various sizes as well as several different saucepans will be needed in order to explore the examples I have chosen. In the same way, the provision of materials to create varying landscapes for the farm is needed so that the spatial concepts which this particular miniature world can develop may be fully exploited. And there are many different kinds of construction equipment available, so that the answers to questions such as the ones suggested can not only be investigated, but also compared and contrasted. The careful and caring choice of materials in all these examples is to some extent predetermined by the children themselves; by their developmental level and their motivation to engage in creative play with these materials. But the teacher's focus must not only be on obtaining this engagement, it must also be aimed towards the development of the child's mathematical understanding within the context presented to her or him. This development can best be encouraged by the provision of a quality of open-endedness. Only one size of plate in the home-corner, only one selection of vegetables, only one possible landscape for the miniature world of the farm, or only one assortment of Lego bricks or large construction bricks – all these will restrict the answers to any possible questions and, as a consequence, the depth and richness of the child's mathematical thinking and the potential scope for her or his development.

Measurement

Implicit in a young child's play activities, alongside her or his exploration of number and space and shape, is much involvement in and exploration of another important area of mathematics – that of measurement. Before children come to nursery or school, they will have had a wealth of experience comparing, contrasting, ordering and matching many different objects. In their private play, as well as play alongside friends and adults, and in all the activities of everyday life, they will have been told how much they have grown, made decisions about whether a particular toy is too long to fit a given space, perhaps decided that a certain cup doesn't hold enough for them, seen that there was wallpaper left over when a room had been decorated, been cajoled into hurrying up 'because we haven't got very much time'. All these experiences create the foundations for the development of a sense of measurement.

Measurement has many different aspects. If asked, most adults would probably define measurement in terms of quantifying linear properties in some way; noticing how tall a particular vase is, or how many metres of material it will take to make a dress, or perhaps how far Birmingham is from Southampton. But in each of these examples aspects other than linear measurement are involved. If you need to find out how much a vase will contain, the linear measurement of its height will not be the most useful information to have – more useful will be a measure of its capacity; a tall thin vase will have a smaller capacity than a tall fat one.

In the same way, measuring fabric in linear measure disguises the fact that dressmaking is concerned with covering area – the area of the body. Convention alone demands that we think in terms of a linear measure – metres – although the total area of cloth is the more important measure. And if you are travelling from Birmingham to Southampton, although you may know the distance in miles between these two places, a more useful measure might well be that of time – someone informing you that the trip will take you about three hours by car will have given you more useful information than telling you the number of miles you will travel.

Perhaps these few examples give you a sense of the complexities of measuring in the adult world. If we look at them again, we see two other sources of complexity and of sophistication – both of which often cause problems when we look at the early development of concepts of measurement. The first relates to the units with which we measure. In the everyday world of adults, we are familiar with the standard conventions in measuring which, because they are used universally, have come to hold a position more important than they actually deserve when viewed from a developmental standpoint. In measuring capacity, for instance, we use litres, pints, millilitres, cubic centimetres etc.; in measuring length we use centimetres and metres, and in measuring distance we use miles or kilometres. We tend to forget that these units are all arbitrary; they exist only to be convenient tools for the accurate communication of measures, and do not exist as separate entities in themselves. We call them 'standard units' only because they have an internationally recognized meaning.

The second source of problems is related to the first, and centres round the level of sophistication in measurement in the world today. Increasingly the standard units of measurement have become more and more refined, so that great emphasis is now placed on the accuracy of measurement, to the detriment of the history of the development of measuring tools and, through this history, the need to see a tool as fitted to its task. The child now is born into this refined and complex world, and there is a danger that we will assume that he or she is also born with an intuitive sense of measuring which is closely related to the sophisticated models of measurement that the world uses. This is not so, and we need to be always aware that the young child needs to spend much time developing concepts fundamental to the understanding of measurement in all its varied and related aspects before he or she can come to terms with not only our adult conventions of standard measuring units, but also the high degree of refinement which our measuring system has. Therefore we need to look at those important concepts which lie at the foundation of understanding measurement.

Again, we turn to Piaget and the important contribution his work has made to our understanding of what is fundamental to the measuring process. In Piagetian theory, two important preconditions have been identified – those which he identifies as the concepts of conservation and transitivity.

The concept of conservation contains the essential notion of invariance – that certain aspects of a situation always remain the same. The amount of substance in a ball of clay remains unvaried, whether the clay has a spherical shape or is rolled out into a long, thin ribbon. The length of a path remains the same whether I walk along it or run. The amount of liquid in a given container does not vary, whether it remains in the original container, or is poured into one which is taller and fatter. The idealized concept of transitivity involves the use of a moving middle term as a measuring device. A child demonstrates that he or she has an idea of transitivity when he or she can use a stick, for instance, to measure the length of a line of bricks, and then construct a second line of the same length, using a different starting position.

Piaget argues that young children up to about six or seven very often display no grasp of either conservation or transitivity. The amount of clay in a ball will be judged as being less than the amount of clay present when the same ball is rolled out into a ribbon; when using measuring tools, they will be overlapped or left with gaps between them; they will judge that a space is bigger when it takes longer to walk across it than it is when they run along the same route. According to Piaget it is not until towards the end of the early years of education that the concepts of conservation and transitivity develop, and the child will then be able to begin to use measuring devices with some meaning, and to understand what measuring means, whether he or she is dealing with mass, weight, time, area, capacity, volume, angle or linear measure.

We must not, however, expect the young child to conserve all these different aspects of measurement at the same time. Research and theoretical opinions vary as to the order in which conservation of these concepts occurs. Piaget's findings support the notion that the concepts of length and area develop first, around six to seven years, and then those of mass (at seven or eight) and weight (at nine or ten) are acquired; not until about eleven or twelve years of age does a child grasp the idea of conservation of volume. Other research findings somewhat cloud this picture, and it does not seem definite that these concepts develop in the order stated above, or that there is not a great deal more age variation than Piaget claimed (Dickson, Brown and Gibson, 1984). One has to remember, as with all of Piaget's work, that his experiments took place at a particular time and within a specific social context and alongside a model of educational practice which present-day early childhood educators would not subscribe to. Despite this lack of clarity, however, and the inevitable constraints that surround any developmental research, it is clear from research work that young children do not develop sophisticated concepts of measurement in their early years of education. We need

to be ever sensitive to this fact, and to take special care over the provision
we offer in this area of a child's mathematical development.

The early experiences offered to young children will form the foundation of their concepts of conservation and transitivity. What is again
essential here is children's active involvement with many different kinds
of materials in the context of their everyday lives. During their pre-school
life, frequent everyday opportunities will arise in which to investigate the
properties of different substances, and to start to develop the idea of conservation. Playing in the bath, rolling out pastry or dough, and running
and walking around different kinds of open spaces; these are some
important and valuable activities. The teacher's role in the early years is
in part to develop and extend these play situations – with sand and water,
clay and plasticine, and many kinds of physical activity in large spaces
– and to provide the equipment which will focus the child's attention on
the concepts of conservation and transitivity. Together with this careful
provision of equipment, it is also important to direct the child's attention
sensitively – by working alongside her or him, and by questioning and
responding to the child's replies, as part of the all-important
child/teacher dialogue.

Language and mathematics

One of the essential factors in all of these practical situations is the use
of language to discuss and explain what is happening. The teacher needs
to listen to the child, and then to discuss with her or him, starting from
the child's interpretation and exploring all possibilities. Before children
start nursery or school, their mathematical experiences will have been
almost exclusively expressed through talking rather than writing, and
through listening rather than reading. If we as teachers build on this foundation, it will mean that children start from the known, can celebrate their
knowledge and will therefore enter the realm of the unknown with more
security and confidence. Listening and talking with children in the early
years will enable them ultimately to come to terms with our conventions
of recording and manipulating mathematical ideas.

The importance of the role of questioning has been mentioned before
but needs, in the context of language and mathematics, to be reiterated.
For early years teachers to ask themselves 'Why am I questioning?';
'What do I want to know?'; 'How is my question being interpreted?' is
an essential part of a successful child–teacher interaction. It is not only
the young child who is in a learning situation in the early years classroom, but also the adults, who need constantly to reflect on their role,
their interactions with children and whether their behaviours are effective in developing the mathematical thinking of the children in their care.

Looking a little more closely at the relationship between language and
mathematics, we see that there are several different perspectives to be

considered. One is the relationship between the young child's language development and her or his mathematical development; a second is concerned with the language of mathematics itself and the young child's understanding of the formal expression of mathematical ideas; and a third covers the area of language as communication, and the problems that arise when words which are in common use are also used with specific mathematical meanings. These three dimensions are closely interlinked, and the following discussion does not attempt to separate them.

As mentioned above, the young child's very early experiences of mathematics are centred around oral language, both speaking and listening. We have emphasized the importance of the child's search for pattern and predictability in her or his mathematical understanding. The search for pattern in counting may be seen to have a parallel in the young child's language explorations. We can see that pattern is an important guideline when, for instance, a child is learning to use the past tense in verbs, and chooses 'bringed' or 'runned' instead of 'brought' or 'ran', having over-generalized that the addition of -ed to a verb will produce the past tense. Adults understand the meanings of these over-generalizations. In the same way we need to highlight the fact that we cannot rely solely on a child's ability to express himself or herself verbally as a clear reflection of that child's level of mathematical understanding. We must remember that the language of mathematics can be sophisticated, complex and abstract, and that the child starts from the concrete world and will need to make many representations within the real world of the intricacies of the world of formal mathematics. We have touched upon some of these intricacies when discussing the interpretation of addition, and we need to be aware of them, and of the many others, at all times.

We use the language of mathematics all the time: 'Would you like more?'; 'Is this long enough?'; 'How many are there all together?'. In these examples the use of the words 'more', 'long', 'how many all together?' would appear to be fairly clear in meaning. But now consider 'I saw a very odd thing today', and 'Seven is an odd number'; and 'What is the difference between a frog and a toad?', and 'What is the difference between eight and one?'. In each of these examples, it is clear that the mathematical meanings of the words 'odd' and 'difference' are not the same as the everyday meanings. Yet the words themselves are the same. These are only two examples of the important and potentially confusing part language plays in mathematical development.

Much of the research that has been done into language and mathematics has focused on mathematical meanings, and also upon difficulties which the child has when confronted with the need to interpret these meanings. Analysis of mathematical meanings is essential, and until we are aware of the problems inherent in the interpretation of these meanings we will not be able to effect secure understandings. I do, however, feel that an overemphasis on 'problems and difficulties' does a great deal to mask our awareness of what the child really does understand. This, together with an attitude towards mathematics which subscribes to the four beliefs identified by Burton (1990) and does not, as Papert (1981) and many other mathematics educators do, view it as a creative activity to engage in, tends to lead us to concentrate on instruction in order, as it were, to put the facts straight in the child's mind, and not to facilitate learning from the child's position of strength – what he or she is confident of understanding. It reflects a view of education as content rather than as a process of development, a view from the perspective of the knowledge to be acquired rather than from that of the human mind to be developed.

We can only come to terms with what the child understands through some form of communication with her or him. That communication may be through listening and talking, or through reading and writing. In any form, a language of some kind needs to be used. We have touched upon the ambiguities inherent in spoken language when it is used as a tool for mathematical communication. There are also ambiguities present when we look at written language as a means of sharing and exchanging mathematical ideas, and we need to be sensitive to these as we introduce the symbols of mathematics to young children.

Ginsburg (1977) points out that although children learn to read and write the numerals 0 to 9 fairly easily, things become more complicated for them with the numerals from 10 onward. Our written number system includes the concept of place value as an important organizing factor. When we write, for instance, three hundred and forty-two in numerical form, we write the symbols 2, 3 and 4 in a specific order: 342. The position, or place, that the symbol takes in the sequence gives us all the information we need to interpret its value, and this powerful mathematical convention is understood implicitly by adults. Young children do not come by this understanding automatically; what they very often do is apply the patterns and rules which have worked for spoken numbers to representing these numbers in written form. We may well see a young child write three hundred and forty-two as 300402. If we then only read this, and do not listen to it being read, we are perhaps likely to misunderstand the error that appears to have been made. Making a fairly simplistic generalization, it could be argued that, just as children learn about the conventions in language through both using them and talking about them, so they need to learn about the conventions in the symbolic representation of mathematics, not only by using them but also by talking about them and their use of them. This is equally true of the symbols we use for mathematical operations, +, - , ÷ and ×, as it is of our written numerals.

It is often stated that mathematics can be viewed as a language. Pimm (1987) takes this as his starting point in a detailed analysis of the role and uses of language in mathematical education. He argues that mathematics can be seen as a language in several ways. Mathematical language may be seen as part of English or of any other language, may be viewed as a kind of shorthand which is internationally used and understood, or, thirdly, mathematics may be considered a language in its own right. Whichever interpretation we choose, we as teachers are concerned to help our students to understand mathematical meanings. To do this, we need to be able to communicate, in speech or writing, by talking or listening. Unless we can communicate, and foster communication in children, we shall never be able to know whether mathematical understanding is developing.

Conclusions

In this outline of mathematical development in the early years, some issues have not been discussed at all while others have been only lightly touched upon. For instance the potential of calculators and computers in the learning and teaching of mathematics has not been addressed. This is not an indication that these tools are considered unimportant, rather that a full discussion of the issues surrounding their use would need much more space than is available here and would need to include an exploration of their role in perhaps modifying our perception of what concrete experience with real materials means. Several points, however, still remain to be mentioned. One which is possibly of overall importance concerns the framework within which mathematical development takes place.

The examples that I have used to illustrate various points have been chosen to emphasize the fact that the development of mathematical think- ing can best be fostered in situations where it is set in contexts which have meaning and interest for the young child. Teachers of young chil- dren begin with a great advantage. The classroom environment in the early years should contain much which is motivating for the young child. Imaginative play situations, construction materials, painting, sand and water all contain the potential for enriching mathematical development. Our role as teachers includes learning how to structure these activities in order to highlight those factors which will develop mathematical con- cepts for the child, as well as planning effective interventions and inter- actions with the child and the environment. In deciding on the structure, perhaps the most important factor is to create an environment which will be familiar to the child, but will also be stimulating and provocative, and will motivate her or him to experiment. In doing this, we need to be ever sensitive to whom we are teaching, and to all the needs of the children, not simply those which centre on mathematical development. We need to ask ourselves many questions, some of which will be: 'What math- ematical concepts can I be sure the child understands?'; 'What concept(s) am I attempting to develop?'; 'Am I presenting these concepts in a

cultural, social and linguistic context which is familiar to the child?';
'Does the context I have chosen favour boys rather than girls?'; 'In choosing this context, am I respecting the child's previous experiences and building on them?'. There are not always clear-cut answers, but in searching for them, and even in asking the questions themselves, we shall be seeing the mathematical development of the young child in the context of her or his development as a whole.

Suggested further reading

Hughes, M. (1986) *Children and Number: Difficulties in Learning Mathematics,* Blackwell, Oxford.

Nunes, T., Schliemann, A. D. and Carraher, D. W. (1993) *Street Mathematics and School Mathematics,* Cambridge University Press, Cambridge.

Steffe, L. P. and Wood, T. (eds.) *Transforming Children's Mathematics Education,* Laurence Erlbaum Associates, Hillsdale, N.J.

10

Learning Through Science in the Early Years

Roy Richards

In the first edition of this book I began by saying: 'there is still a need to convince many teachers and parents of the valuable role scientific experience can play in a young child's development'. That was in 1987 and in the short space of time since then the National Curriculum has brought a ready acceptance by all that science shall be done in our primary schools. However, then as now there still needs to be an exemplification of what such experience should be and why it is valuable.

Almost from the moment they are born young children show an interest in their world. Certainly a one-year-old goes everywhere, touches everything in sight, pulls books off shelves, stuffs things in the mouth, falls over things. 'He (or she) wears me out' is the cry from the parent's lips. Parents would not have it otherwise. They take delight in their offspring's curiosity and warm to the child's lively 'pranks' because they know that the child is finding out and learning about the world in a meaningful way. As a child begins to talk parents enthuse over developing powers of speech and attempt to answer the child's questions in a desire to encourage the innate willingness to explore and learn. Some parents do this better than others but, however well they do it, this is the foundation stone on which the nursery and infant school must build in order to nurture a child's burgeoning curiosity, sense of wonder and willingness to explore the world. To neglect this desire for discovery is unwise. Not only is it the root of a developing scientific awareness but it is probably the most powerful force for learning in the whole of education. It is, as Jacob Bronowski (1959) once said of science, 'the search for truth which gives us two satisfactions . . . One is the sense of wonder at the world: how finely knit the world is, we say, how beautiful. The other is the sense of identity with the world: how wonderful to become part of it by understanding.' This search for truth is innate in us all, young as well as old.

Children's thinking

Helping with the cooking, playing about with things in the sink or bath, watching a snail crawling along, digging things up in the garden, there are a thousand and one things in an infant's day many of which are part of the continuing exposure to things scientific. Many educationalists believe that such exposure helps children's cognitive development. Children's thinking is very different from adults'. The study of how it develops into an adult form is an intriguing and fascinating one. We know something about the development of thought through the work of Piaget and others. This must make us reflect on the kinds of scientific experience we can offer children. Wynne Harlen (1991, pp. 126–7) writes:

> Whether one believes that [the mental characteristics of young children] cluster into well-defined 'stages' between which there is a distinct qualitative change, or whether the change is regarded more as a continuous development, makes no difference to the accuracy of the description of children's thinking at various points. Both research and teachers' experience confirm the broad features of the thinking of five-, six- and seven-year-olds. Those that are most relevant to scientific development can be summarized as follows.
>
> They cannot 'think through' actions (unless these are very familiar ones, often performed) but have to carry them out in practice. This makes for severe restrictions on reasoning. For example, if they pour water from one container to another of a different shape in which its quantity may appear to have changed they will affirm that it has changed. They cannot imagine the water being poured back and therefore realize that its quantity must have remained the same.
>
> They take but one point of view of events, their own. They do not take another's point of view or realize that a different viewpoint can make things look different, unless they physically move to the other position. Even then they may not realize that it is a different view of the same thing.
>
> They focus on one aspect of an object or situation at a time. Thus their judgement of the amount of water in the container takes into account one dimension, probably the height the liquid reaches, not the height and the width of the container.
>
> They tend not to relate one event to another when they encounter an unfamiliar sequence of events. They are likely to remember the first and last stages in the sequence, but not the ones in between. For example, a six-year-old, after watching sand run through a timer, was reported as being able to draw the timer and its contents at the beginning and end, but not in between. Given five drawings of the timer as the sand was running out he could not arrange them in sequence (Harlen, Darwin and Murphy, 1977).
>
> The results of actions not yet carried out cannot be anticipated. Whereas older children could work out, for instance, that if they increase their size of step they will take fewer steps across the room, the five- or six-year-old will have to get up and do it.
>
> There are clear consequences of these points for the sorts of activities the children will be able to learn from. The children's limitations are obvious. It will be no use expecting them to see patterns in events until they have begun

to connect events in a sequence; the notion of a cause being related to an effect is still developing, so the idea of separating two or more variables to test the effect of each separately is still a long way off; their limited experience will mean that their ideas tend to be based on few very specific instances, selectively observed, having little explanatory power as far as new experience is concerned.

Equally clear are the indications for the kinds of experience that are appropriate at this age. Action and thinking are closely related to each other, reflecting their even closer identification at an earlier, pre-school stage. Thus infants need to be able to act on things, to explore, manipulate, describe, sort and group them. First-hand experience and exploration of objects in their immediate environment is the chief aim of teaching science to infants.

What is of value in presenting scientific activities?

Young children actively exploring are using their senses to make observations about their world and ordering and interpreting those observations. In doing so they develop their sense of curiosity, talk about things with the teacher and with one another, raise questions and eventually make records through painting, modelling, pictorial representation, writing and so on.

Observing – using the senses

It is vital to develop the full use of the senses. Infant teachers are adept at this. A rich classroom environment, coupled with an active exploration of the world outdoors gives children many things to look at and handle. Blindfolded children can attempt to identify things by touch, lifting and generally handling things as well as simply feeling them. Can they distinguish between lemon peel, orange peel and grapefruit peel? Can they tell emery-paper from sandpaper? Tape recording the children's speech as they do so is revealing. A playback discloses their confidence, hesitation and search for the correct words and phrases. What about the texture of things? Are they rough, smooth, waxy, greasy, furry, sharp, prickly, crumbly, ridged, angled, moulded, carved? What shape is the object? Is it a cube, a pyramid or a sphere? Irregular shapes are fun! Looking at how easily they topple, trying to balance them, seeing how the weight is distributed, all add to the interest. Even the temperature of objects can be explored. Wool and expanded polystyrene will feel warmer than metals. Yet are they really warmer? Are the objects damp? Are they hard? Pressing, twisting or scratching objects such as Plasticine, putty, rubber, balsa wood, beech, metals, chalk, limestone, granite, present further suitable experiences.

'Listening walks' are popular where the noises heard are noted down and then talked about. Often the use of a portable tape-recorder helps recall the sounds, and the odd emphasis of the sounds that the mechanical tape brings gives added effect and interest. Different places produce different sounds; the playground, the High Street, a supermarket, a wood, a church, a bedroom, a waterfall, all evoke different atmospheres. Can you hear a pin drop? This is the chance for a scientific test. Will it matter what the pin is dropped on? Does it matter what height it is dropped from? Does it matter how far away it is?

How many common bird-songs can be recognized? The sounds of thrush, blackbird, sparrow, starling and a few other common birds should become part of the 'vocabulary' of any child. Sometimes just the listening is enough, for as Pestalozzi said, 'Lead your child out into nature. Teach him on the hill-tops and in the valleys, there he will listen better. But in these hours of freedom let him be taught by Nature rather than by you. Let him fully realize that you with your art do nothing more than to walk quietly by his side. Should a bird sing or an insect hum on a leaf, at once stop your talk. Birds and insects are teaching him. You may be silent'. The primordial senses of smell and taste also bring their pleasures. Who can ever forget the smell of new-mown hay or kippers cooking? Pleasant and unpleasant smells, country smells and city smells, household and garden smells, all give cause for sorting and separating. Children often know the smells of dandelions, marigolds and pansies which we as adults have invariably forgotten. Tasting things and smelling things need care. There are dangers to beware of, such as those that berries, seeds, tablets, medicines and cleaning fluids can bring. However, with proper supervision there is a whole world here for exploration. Can children distinguish the taste of apple, pear, banana, grape, onion, chocolate, coffee, tea, orange squash and so on when blindfolded? Can they group things into sweet, sour and salty tastes? Can they tell margarine from butter or saccharine from sugar? In all such cases fair tests will need to be thought out and tried.

Who can see best? Which colour combinations are good to use for signs and which are bad ones? Have you tried yellow symbols on white paper or black letters on purple? Each day brings new things to explore. Of course we normally use our senses in combination with one another and relate the sensations together in our memory. Children will do this well when school staffs produce the experiences and provide the materials and equipment to help the children employ their senses in every way.

(Richards, 1983, pp. 101–2)

All such experience leads to the skill of being able to make observations, to order those observations, to finding certain observations will group together (for example, most leaves seem to be green, water always runs downhill), and eventually to interpreting observations to make simple predictions (for example, a pet snail may always go to rest at night in a certain place in the snailery; if I put it in the centre of the snailery when I go home from school I can predict it will be back in its resting place in the morning).

Questioning

Many of the questions that children ask can be answered by direct testing.

Will water go through cloth? Through wood? Through soil?
Why does the holding end of a spoon get hot?
Is John's toy car faster than Jim's?

Why is the bricklayer putting a dampcourse between the bricks?
Are all the tree leaves the same size?
Why is it cooler under a tree than in the open?
Why do roadmen wear orange jackets?
Do children hear better than adults?

The important thing is to pick out such questions in day-to-day living, to engineer situations where similar questions can occur or, sometimes, even to pose such questions deliberately. Then teacher and children can sit down together and devise ways of finding answers to the questions. This is the heart of scientific method and one of the most difficult yet most rewarding aspects that children and adults have to indulge in.

(Richards, 1983, pp. 103–4)

Of course, children will ask some questions that are almost rhetorical, not requiring an answer, and some questions that need a straight, brief answer. However, it is questions such as those outlined above which are valuable from a scientific point of view, and these need discussing with children so that they try to find the answer for themselves by inquiry. The more that children can be involved in proposing the inquiry the better.

Communicating

In any busy classroom children will work together, sometimes as a class and sometimes in small groups. It is important that interaction and communication occur. When children are talking and writing together this happens. It can also happen in many other ways. Tape-recordings, charts, graphs, pictures, pieces of writing, stitched books or models, all displayed and used in the classroom help interpersonal communication. This is especially true when groups or individuals are given the opportunity to tell the class about a particular piece of work or bring a problem forward for communal discussion and approbation. This can also help individuals to express themselves clearly and interact with others who possess different experiences or hold different points of view.

(Richards, 1983, pp. 104–5)

Initially communication among infant children is essentially oral, with questioning and pictorial forms of communication playing a part. Gradually this extends to making accurate descriptions, commenting on results, and eventually to written accounts, block graphs and making conclusions.

Measuring

Measuring refines observing, questioning and communicating. At first this may be done by simple means such as comparing equal lengths, then comparing things which are longer than others, shorter than others and so on. As children develop they measure with arbitrary units such as handspans and eventually come to measure with standard units such as metres and millimetres. With experience children's measuring becomes more and more accurate. Development also continues as they deal with mass, capacity and time. Science helps enormously in a practical investigation of the environment for it gives children interesting, real things to measure. Rulers, calipers, graduated jugs, scales, timers, all begin to be meaningful in a child's life. Things like hand lenses are useful too; whilst not strictly used for measuring things they do help open up a new world. The enlargement of newsprint, the skin on the back of the hand, cloth or a snail's tentacles intrigue and fascinate children, helping them understand that world even more.

Classifying and recognizing pattern

Children exploring sort and separate things. Sharing sweets or conkers, matching cups and saucers to people having tea, putting farm animals into groups, help to develop an appreciation of sets and sub-sets, and such work begins to lay a foundation for the understanding of classificatory systems in science, as well as being an early prelude to understanding of number. Coupled with observation, measuring, questioning, discussing (and with a strong lead from the teacher), patterns may begin to appear. At first this will be tentative but by the time they leave the infant school many children will recognize relationships even if they have difficulty trying to describe them in a formal way. Infants looking after snails will become aware of the spiral shell which is but a short step to looking at other things such as springs and screws, bindweed, coiled ropes, pea tendrils, electric light filaments, even the arrangement of florets in a dandelion to find such pattern repeated.

Investigating and making fair tests

There are many activities in an infant classroom which lead to investigation. Water play, cooking, the home-corner, the sand tray, simple gardening and plant growing, and so on are all fruitful activities for finding out about things. With the nursery and reception class the teacher tends to pose the problems; often this is done simply by providing suitable materials and apparatus, for example, various sized and shaped containers to pour water from one thing to another. How many cupfuls of water to fill the teapot? How many teapots to fill a bucket? Tentative ideas on capacity begin to form. As children grow older they begin to suggest ways to find answers to problems. Six- to seven-year-olds may even make suggestions about things they would like to find out about, and help decide how they would like to go about the work.

There is usually, in any busy infant classroom, much investigation. What infant children have difficulty in deciding is which factors, or variables as a scientist would say, influence any current investigation. Indeed they are often not capable of doing so. The teacher has to control this by restricting the sets of materials available. An example may make this clear. Television advertisements used to claim that it was difficult, if not impossible, to tell a certain kind of margarine from butter. Is this really so? How could a fair test be devised? The children's reaction might be to get some margarine, get some butter and taste them. Indeed, with many infant children this might be sufficient for there would be a good interaction situation, some tasting and talking, and perhaps some simple recording of what is discovered. However, some infants might be capable of having their mental abilities stretched a bit further. If teacher thinks aloud 'I wonder if it's wise to try just one butter and one margarine. Perhaps we should choose two of each? Does it matter what we try them on? Does it matter in what order we taste the butters and the margarine? Does it matter if some are salty and some are not?', then a much more stringent, scientific approach to things becomes possible. It would have to be handled very carefully to have meaning to infants. All the variables thrown up in the questioning could be investigated but the teacher would have to sort them for the children, taking them one at a time. That is to say, try two butters and two margarines first. Then try the effect of different substrates for the fats, then try salted and non-salted fats. Infants are capable of making much more radical progress in this sort of work than they are often credited for, but it does need patient, skilled teaching where the teacher acts as guide, and yet stands back at that magical moment when children make the first tentative steps at identifying one or two variables, deciding which is relevant and explaining how it might be controlled.

It is also true that conclusions can often be reached from the result of such investigating. However, what is interesting, and extremely valuable, is that a scientific way of thinking is being inculcated in children's minds. It is a way of thinking that can be applied to many situations. Given time and experience children should be able, as they progress through the primary school, to find answers to problems by practical testing that are as fair and rigorous as anyone could make them. The roots of such a capability begin in the infant school.

In terms of the new National Curriculum for science (DFE, 1995e, pp. 2–3) this capability is stated as:

* *Systematic enquiry*	Pupils should be given opportunities to:
	a) ask questions e.g. 'How?', 'Why?', 'What will happen if . . . ?;
	b) use focused exploration and investigation to acquire scientific knowledge, understanding and skills;
	c) use both first-hand experience and simple secondary sources to obtain information;
	d) use IT to collect, store, retrieve and present scientific information.

	Pupils should be taught to:
* Communication	a) use scientific vocabulary to name and describe living things, materials, phenomena and processes; b) present scientific information in a number of ways through drawings, diagrams, tables and charts, and in speech and writing – as well as give due regard to science in everyday life, the nature of scientific ideas, and health and safety.

Specifically, in terms of 'Experimental and Investigative Science' the new National Curriculum says:

	Pupils should be taught:
* Planning experimental work	a) to turn ideas suggested to them, and their own ideas, into a form that can be investigated; b) that thinking about what is expected to happen can be useful when planning what to do; c) to recognize when a test or comparison is unfair.
* Obtaining evidence	a) to explore using appropriate senses; b) to make observations and measurements; c) to make a record of observations and measurements.
* Considering evidence	a) to communicate what happened during their work; b) to use drawings, tables, and bar charts to present results; c) to make simple comparisons; d) to use results to draw conclusions; e) to indicate whether the evidence collected supports any prediction made; f) to try to explain what they found out, drawing on their knowledge and understanding.

Scientific ideas

There has been a growing attempt in recent years to define the nature of the scientific experience that should be included in any infant programme. Of course one would not want very young children to study nuclear physics or photosynthesis but could some reasonable representation of content be stated? The danger in doing so is twofold; first, it could lead to a stereotyped curriculum and, secondly, it could lead away from an emphasis on developing the scientific skills of observing, questioning, communicating, measuring, classifying and recognizing patterns, and investigating and making fair tests. Emphasis over the last twenty years has rightly been placed on using these processes of science to develop children's conceptual understanding and scientific attitudes, and this emphasis should remain foremost in our minds. However, the processes cannot develop divorced from a content. At a simple, pragmatic level Bertrand Russell's statement that 'We are creatures of Earth; our life is part of the Earth, as we draw our nourishment from it. To the child even more than to the man it is necessary to preserve some contact with the ebb and flow of terrestrial life' gives us a strong lead. Infants will be interested in the rocks, pebbles and soil around them (one never ceases to marvel at how muddy they can get!), and in the plants and animals associated with that soil. Here is a good basis for much work. Certainly they are interested in anything that moves, be it a wriggling worm, rain-water running in a gutter, or a Dinky toy speeding down a slope. They love things that make a noise, splashing in and out of puddles, baking bread, playing in the sink, chasing shadows. Surely it is here in an infant's surroundings that we should look for the nature of our scientific experiences. Attempting to define scientific ideas in terms of 'light travels in straight lines' or 'the faster an object moves, the more energy it has', can be a useful academic exercise for the teacher but it draws attention away from the essential nature of a young child's world and importantly shifts the centre of focus of how things should be explored. The more clinical the analysis the more clinical the approach could tend to become!

The Schools Council Science 5/13 unit *Early Experiences* (Richards, 1972) very much took activities that would occur fairly naturally around the children, activities to do with:

Sunny day things
Doing things
Listening to things
Comparing things
Growing things
Cooking things
Looking after things
Looking at things
Rainy day things
Wintry things.

The more recent text, *An Early Start to Science* (Richards, Collis and Kincaid, 1986), takes a similar line with activities to do with:

1. *Some themes*
   Myself
   Music and other sounds
   Gardens and gardening
   Colour
   Time
   Shadows
2. *Some collections*
   Shells

> Stones and pebbles
> Bricks and blocks
> Seeds
> Fasteners
> Bottles and jars
> Toy animals

3. *Some water play*
> Feeling water
> Wet and dry
> Collecting rainwater
> Looking at, smelling and tasting water
> Changing the shape of water
> Measuring water
> Squirting water
> Floating and sinking
> Adding things to water
> Out of doors

4. *Some home play*
> Comparisons and matching
> Making dolls' things
> Looking after dolls
> Caring for sick dolls

5. *Some other things*
> Balancing things
> Flying things
> Electrical things
> Transport things
> Shiny things.

The National Curriculum took hold of what the scientific content should be, starting with 17 Attainment Targets and going through a number of changes to settle on 4, of which the three 'knowledge' based ones are:

- *life processes and living things*
  life processes of animals and plants, classification, variation and living things in relation to their environment;
- *materials and their properties*
  grouping and changing materials;
- *physical processes*
  electricity, forces and motion, light and sound.

Much can be said about what is included and what is left out. Much can be said about the language – for example, 'pupils' not 'children', and 'children should be taught' with its emphasis on telling rather than on finding out. Much can be said about the set programme drawing teachers away from the valuable exploratory work that so often comes from making use of chance happening and pursuing a programme where children very genuinely want to know the answer. However, set against this, there is for the first time a laid-down statutory curriculum which all schools must follow rather than the somewhat patchy science curriculum which often occurred in first schools in the past.

Using resources

The key to providing good scientific experience for young children lies in the provision and proper use of resources. This is not to say that we write off to scientific suppliers for long lists of apparatus and materials; even if we had the money this would probably be counterproductive. Specialized equipment often comes between children and understanding and it can isolate the science from a child's real world. It is much better to use the things that children are already familiar with in their daily lives, and which they are already in the habit of using. Thus a squeezy bottle may be converted into a container for gathering rainwater, or a drip-timer for timing events, or tub for growing seeds, or as a 'jet-gun' used to squirt water across the playground to investigate how the liquid moves. The first task therefore is to gather things; plastic bottles, jars, tin-cans, pebbles, shells, matchboxes, cotton-reels, disused kitchen equipment – all and everything. The next job is to store it, and then finally to use much of what has been gathered to make further apparatus.

The more children can help design 'manufactured' pieces of apparatus the better. It helps them to realize that they can learn about the real world through their own activities. A simple home-made wind-vane will provide experience of wind direction each day, whilst a kite helps demonstrate the pull of that wind. The top cut from a plastic water container makes a temporary home for tadpoles; one funnel at each end of a garden hose makes a good speaking tube. Of course quite a number of things will need to be purchased, especially measuring equipment.

The Schools Council Learning Through Science text, *Science Resources for Primary and Middle Schools* (Richards *et al.*, 1982) gives copious lists of materials and equipment that can be collected, bought and made. Here, it is suggested that these should be:

(a) equipment for arousing and maintaining children's curiosity – from Lego or plastic Meccano to garden tools and plant pots;
(b) equipment for collecting specimens and data – from boxes, plastic bags and medicine droppers to spirit levels and secateurs;
(c) equipment for housing animals – from jam-jars to formicaria and wormeries;
(d) equipment for aiding the development of inquiry skills – from Plasticine to egg-timers and kitchen scales;
(e) equipment for the scientific aspects of topic work – a long list from balloons, pop-guns, parachute toys, etc., for a topic like 'Air and

airborne', to kaleidoscopes, coloured filters and prisms, etc., for a topic such as 'Colour';

(f) equipment for aiding communication – everything from chalk and felt pens to Polyfilla and poppet beads.

Such equipment needs proper storage, and whilst much of it would be used on a day-to-day basis in the classroom there are very many things that would only be used from time to time. These are better stored in a central school resource area open to all. The proper establishment of such a resource and its day-to-day use have exercised many infant schools of late, and their rationale is discussed in *Science Resources for Primary and Middle Schools* (Richards *et al.*, 1982).

The teacher's role in developing scientific processes has already been discussed, and indicates how the use of all these materials and equipment is of paramount importance. Children need to be brought into contact with the resources. They need to handle them, look at them, be left time to stare and talk, to play, to feel the shape and texture of things, to absorb how heavy things are, how warm or cold they feel, how the colour of things appears to change in different lights – indeed at times just to think their own thoughts so that they can come to terms with the richness of their surroundings. Children differ. Some take longer than others to absorb things. Talking is vital; both children talking and teacher talking. The children will want to talk about the things around them, and will hear others around them talking. It is the skill of the teacher that helps develop the ability to talk and listen. This is when the teacher begins to bring about real learning, and in many instances this can reach a high level of achievement. Scientific exploration lends itself enormously to talking situations, it provides things to talk about and things to help children find out more about their surroundings, it helps them to make sense of their environment. Some children understand more than others, some children see things in a different way from others. All have something to contribute and their contribution as they talk helps us see what sense children are making of the things we have put them in contact with, and what sense they are making of problem-solving situations. Of course, the teacher talks too, intervening at times, sometimes questioning, sometimes adding a comment, sometimes leading discussion. Whole-class discussions, from time to time, are important because they bring a corporate sharing of experiences and often bring a verbal repetition of what has happened at other times in the day or week, a time for children to think again about experiences and to share that thinking with one another. As the interaction and talking develop so too does the sophistication of the experiences. The resources concerned with measurement of length, capacity and volume, mass and time will need to be employed, and again the teacher's skill in gradually introducing these will come into play. All this provision, coupled with skilled teaching and open discussion, can lead to the sort of classroom where children show proper respect for one another and where one moves from the rudiments of freedom of thought and expression to a real cementing of these values.

Conclusions

Science with young children consists of fostering the primary drives present in all infant children. That is to say:

(a) exploration of their environment with the attendant gathering of experience at first hand;
(b) manipulation of objects and materials;
(c) observation of things around them;
(d) comparison of one thing with another;
(e) measuring things;
(f) questioning, arguing, communicating about things;
(g) testing things out, taking part in simple problem-solving activities;
(h) looking for patterns in things, seeking for relationships.

The development of such skills goes hand in glove with gaining knowledge of the everyday world around children. It is in this world that we look for the content of the work – in stones and pebbles, bricks and blocks, baking a cake or chasing a shadow, albeit we now have to relate this world to the demands of the National Curriculum. However, all these, and many, many more, experiences can have value so long as the teacher challenges the children and draws out the scientific aspects of such experience. Resources are all-important, but prime amongst them are the everyday bits and pieces surrounding children, for specialized equipment often comes between children and understanding and can isolate the science from a child's real world. Exploring the environment by using the science skills enumerated in this chapter enables children to develop a scientific approach, inquiring minds and an awareness, interest and concern for the things of their world.

Suggested further reading

Harlen, W. (1991) *Teaching and Learning Primary Science* (Second edition), Paul Chapman, London.
Richards, R., Collis, M. and Kincaid, D. (1986) *An Early Start to Science*, Macdonald, London.

11

The Contributions of Physical Activity to Development in the Early Years

Pauline Boorman

All children deserve the opportunity to become confident and competent in controlling their moving bodies.

(Roberton and Halverson, 1984, p. iii)

This chapter is concerned with movement and its contribution to the total education of each child. In reviewing current practice, the chapter will consider how far physical education (as it is taught in first and infant schools), and opportunities for physical play in the nursery, measure up to the criteria of our concept of education. It will also emphasize the significant but inseparable contribution that movement can make to the development of each child – not as something separate from what happens in the classroom, but as a vital medium for learning and expression.

The main reason for avoiding using the term 'physical education' in the title of this chapter is its obvious association with prescribed subject content. By specifying the areas of activity within physical education at Key Stage 1 as gymnastics, games and dance, the Dearing review of the National Curriculum (SCAA, 1995b; DFE, 1995f) has somewhat confirmed this view. It has formalized what is already timetabled in the infant school as large apparatus, music and movement, small apparatus or playground games, and this is significant in that it perpetuates what is often very narrowly conceived and associated with a limited subject area. The wording of the current orders outlining what 'should be taught' at Key Stage 1 conjures up visions of very specific activities; traditional 'competitive games', performance of gymnastics skills (for example different ways of rolling), and 'set' dances all of which are associated with older children, or even adult physical activities.

The ways in which this aspect of the curriculum is often viewed almost inevitably divorces the physical aspects of development from the rest of the child's experience in school, and thus reinforces the classical dualism of mind and body: 'the feeling that children's minds are nurtured in the classroom while PE lessons take care of their bodies' (Fowler, 1981, p. 37). Partly through this separateness and the consequent stress on physical outcomes there has been an underestimation of the contribution of movement or physical activity to the whole educational process. The narrow and limited perceptions of physical activity often detract from the significant and wider effects of movement in any environment – at home, in the nursery, in the playground, in the corridor or in the classroom – all of which form part of the picture of each child's developing powers.

In reality it is impossible to separate one facet of growth or development from any other, so interrelated and interdependent are they within the complexity of human development and behaviour. Hence the separation within school represents an artificially created division along subject lines which disguises the notion of education as 'a process in which psychomotor, cognitive and affective factors all interact during a life span' (Zaichkowsky, Zaichkowsky and Martinek, 1980, p. vii). Arguably, there are no purely physical activities. Cognitive, physical and emotional growth need to develop alongside one another – each contributing to the other. None can be neglected in a holistic approach. Healthy physical development is an inseparable part of the whole process, and needs to be recognized and understood in those terms. It is such an all-pervasive attribute that it is taken for granted all too often, and it has not been subjected to scientific study as much as it might have been (Holt, 1975, p. iii). In the literature on child development, even where physical development is discussed, it is characterized by detailed accounts of the progressive changes in motor behaviour: indicating motor milestones, and the charting of development.

As Laszlo and Bairstow (1985, p. 26) indicate, there is no shortage of this 'what happens when' account of motor development, which in consequence leads to certain expectancies that assume special importance or lead to unfair comparison and competition between children. More often, however, this physical aspect of a child's development is ignored altogether so that only cognitive/intellectual development is considered important. To be meaningful in educational terms, such literature must incorporate and recognize movement as an inextricable part of the whole process of child development. We cannot underemphasize any part of that process.

Yet if we consider current practice and look carefully at some of the PE sessions which take place in our schools, we still find that despite the recognition of physical education as a foundation subject within the National Curriculum, the physical activities and experiences of children are often isolated, underrated, underestimated, underdeveloped and certainly may not be as imaginative, beneficial or purposeful as we might hope. Although there are inherent dangers in generalizing, it could be said that three approaches towards the 'teaching' of PE still tend to predominate and all reveal a number of inadequacies.

Inadequacies in current practice

The laissez-faire approach

In the first instance it is generally assumed that young children need little encouragement to be active, seem to enjoy physical activity and are constantly on the move. On this assumption, recognition of the importance of movement is tacitly given by the provision of areas for gross motor play in the nursery school and by the allocation of a larger space at special times in the infant school. However, little attempt is made to use these in a coherent fashion to help children explore their movement potential. Children's needs for exercise and physical play, it seems, are assumed to take place naturally, at break times, lunchtime or after school. PE then is often considered to be little more than a diversion from academically respectable experiences or pursuits, and in many instances physical activity or the PE lesson is seen merely as an opportunity for letting off steam; an aimless expression of surplus energy, as Herbert Spencer (1855) would have us believe.

For many teachers, the demands of the National Curriculum, with its attendant assessment requirements, particularly for the 'Division One' subjects (Whitehead, 1992), have tended to squeeze out the time that is available for the less 'academic', and some would say lower status subjects (Goodson, 1983; Kirk, 1992). Perhaps as Piaget (1969) suggested, reasons why play was neglected are reasons why PE tends to play a somewhat Cinderella role . . . it was thought play was devoid of functional significance, no more than relaxation – a frivolous pastime.

This attitude is often clearly visible in the nursery class or school, where movement between indoors and outdoors or even between climbing or large construction activities and other activities indoors may be carefully restricted to organized 'patches' of the day when the 'work' for the day has been completed. Compare this with the flexibility of time and individual choice afforded pupils to follow through their interests in the 'classroom'. There are sometimes 'supervisory' reasons for modifying the free-flow arrangement, but the area for gross motor play is often bottom on the list of priorities, and does not always reflect the full range of learning opportunities, in planning or in practice.

Similarly, whereas provision for a variety of other activities is carefully planned, observed and evaluated, outside 'the classroom' the teachers' efforts, it seems, are frequently directed to providing a safe environment. Apparatus is erected and checked (rightly so) but often with little thought and planning for the opportunities and experiences it provides. In many instances areas are crowded with a great deal of the available apparatus in what may be thought to be a stimulating and challenging environment, yet this may almost prevent some forms of free movement or role-play and may frighteningly overwhelm and bewilder some children. The assumption is 'that expensive pieces of indoor and outdoor play equipment will aid effectively in the development and refinement of the children's movement abilities' (Gallahue, 1989, p. 481). When staff are outside only for short periods of time doing 'duty' in what is seemingly a less significant environment, what messages are given to children about the importance of the activities? In these circumstances the teacher's role is usually only supervisory and allows no opportunity for, or acknowledgement of, the need for positive teacher involvement, whether in observation and evaluation of children's movements or for positive interaction. Yet these times are excellent opportunities for pupils to develop socio-emotional, cognitive and physical skills, and are consequently deserving of much more teacher observation and input.

Similarly, in the infant school the teacher's role is all too often predominantly a supervisory one, limited to ensuring fair turns or preventing accidents, with little thought given to how learning in this environment can be promoted and extended. In some instances it is frequently said to be 'too cold' or 'too windy' to go outside to use the larger playground space, yet children are sent out at every possible play-time, for free play. Sometimes because of timetabling difficulties, use of small apparatus becomes a seasonal activity limited to only a few lazy, hazy days of summer when everyone wants to be outside! Teachers (and children) are often too involved in prestige classroom activities and forsake physical activity rather than arrange an exchange.

Alternatively a tape may be switched on and children are coaxed and encouraged to respond to an anonymous voice. Although these tapes present some very valuable movement experiences for children and supply much-needed sound accompaniment, the teacher is denied the opportunity to respond to ideas, movements or needs of the children within his or her class. The rather detached role of the teacher may also be illustrated in situations where large apparatus is arranged and erected by others – by the school-keeper, by older children, or by other teachers – and hence may not be designed to provide opportunities for, or to develop the experiences and natural capacities of particular children. 'Too often children are turned loose on various forms of equipment and expected magically to develop efficient forms of movement behaviour on their own' (Gallahue, 1989, p. 481).

The teacher has a crucial role in guiding children towards appropriate challenges. However lavish and well equipped the environment, much depends on the skills of adults in involving and interacting with each child. We need to help children develop confidence in a wide variety of situations and to extend their imagination and ingenuity in movement terms, but there seems to be an unwillingness on the part of teachers to meddle in children's physical activity and many are fearful of interfering, or stopping the flow of activity. Unfortunately the development of confidence, competence or increased understanding does not come automatically from free play. 'If we were to leave children completely alone to find out everything for themselves this would be a long and wasteful process and one from which they would be likely to get little of value' (Downey and Kelly, 1975, p. 162).

In the 'physical' environment discovery learning could indeed be a long, often painful process. To ensure progress, learning experiences and activities need to be both satisfying and challenging so that children can be nurtured and guided through developmentally appropriate experiences. It is often assumed, however, that no special measures are needed to educate children to crawl, to walk, to run and to jump. Because these are some of the most obvious changes in infancy and because they occur in an apparently similar sequence in all infants, motor development has traditionally been attributed to maturation alone. (Zaichkowsky, Zaichkowsky and Martinek, 1980; Gallahue, 1989). For these reasons these skills and other 'physical' aspects of a child's development have often been left to maturation, that is, to chance. Biological maturation does exert a major influence on the time and sequence of such motor events but we perhaps forget the interest, encouragement and help given by parents in fostering these earlier skills which need to be nurtured and developed rather than taken for granted. 'The genetically controlled sequence of growth and maturation . . . only defines the potential for development' (Malina, 1973, pp. 55–6).

Developmental sequences are not automatic beyond rudimentary levels and the realization of potential is strongly influenced by experience. For some children many components of motor development become arrested at early developmental levels (Gallahue, 1989). We presume that because they know how to walk and run when they enter the school system, little attention needs to be given to developing these and other motor patterns. As we all know, when performance is unsatisfactory or unsatisfying there is a tendency to avoid situations which contribute to the defeating cycle. 'The component is not used because it has not developed and it cannot develop because it is not used' (Roberton and Halverson, 1984, p. 141).

In this way, involvement in some or all actions or forms of movement may produce a negative spiral for some children who are then less likely to seek participation and for whom it is less likely that performance will be satisfying when indeed they do get involved (Griffin and Keogh, 1982, p. 214). The practical concern for parents and teachers of young children must be to maintain a positive spiral of movement involvement to enable both girls and boys to respond and react to their environment in a competent and confident way. This may require positive strategies (clothing, timing, sharing, grouping) to enable opportunities to become successful experiences for all children. This will influence each individual's persistence and involvement in movement situations and will help to develop the feeling of competence which is an important part of their self-esteem. It would seem that for children, once basic locomotor, postural and manipulative actions have been attained, very precise, fine motor movements (e.g. writing) are emphasized at the expense of gross motor movements. Indeed, 'the capability to execute purposive movements is often taken for granted and only the acquisition of specific skills is considered an achievement' (Laszlo and Bairstow, 1985, pp. 1–2), for example dressing, writing, riding a bicycle. The assumption is that gross motor development is complete by the end of the primary years. Clearly this is not the case, and physical learning, like learning of all types, continues throughout life as we modify and adapt our actions to meet different circumstances. Many people, however, only become 'aware of difficulties when perceptual and motor factors have to be integrated to form a new combination, when learning a new activity like driving a car' (ibid.), or realize the many advantages of efficient movement when they lose it or when they see others who are immobile (Holt, 1984).

Concentration on skills learning

Another major inadequacy in current practice is that very often the only forms of gross motor development which are recognized or encouraged are those requiring the acquisition of very specific or specialized sports or other skills. This approach tends to concentrate on the physical outcomes, particularly the acquisition of recognizable, traditional skills like forward rolls or catching and throwing. Within this approach subject-content is traditionally divided into separate activities, and this has been reinforced by the National Curriculum for PE with its 'subjects within a subject' approach. The 'content' of these lessons is given predominance over the developmental base, with expectations in each area narrowly conceived. Planning in this view focuses upon the end-product – skills associated with games players, gymnasts, dancers – rather than upon the quality and value of the educational experience to the individual child's cognitive, emotional and physical development. If great care is not taken, the process of developing confidence and competence becomes secondary to the production of certain outcomes, largely assessed in terms of skilled performance.

Such an approach, with its narrow conception of excellence, is inherently competitive and hence PE is rapidly rejected by many children who soon recognize their failure in its terms. We are not in the early years, or in fact at any other stage of schooling, concerned with producing international sportsmen and women, although the emphasis on 'competition' in the current orders for games, even at Key Stage 1, might suggest that PE's primary function is indeed to lay the foundations for future sporting success.

Within such a view, objectives are clearly prescribed and seen in terms of functional and recreative efficiency, the acquisition of skill in achieving fitness and health and/or, in social adjustment and emotional health (Kane, 1976). Unfortunately, although lip service is given to the latter two aims, in practice they are simply assumed to be outcomes from participation in, for instance, games. There is no attempt to evaluate these factors in relation to individual children; instead the concentration is almost exclusively in terms of subjective assessment of motor skills and, more recently, levels of fitness. Clearly such an instrumental approach focuses upon achievement in terms of pre-specified criteria or standards. The inevitable 'comparisons between children at the level of tasks and activities can be misleading. Differences in task proficiency could reflect different opportunities for practising the skill, and different interests and motivation, yet the norms and expectancies that are quoted when considering motor development are often at this level' (Laszlo and Bairstow, 1985, p. 4). The idea of chronological stages is endemic in the type of class-teaching methods usually adopted in PE in which the content or material of the lesson is paramount. Many interpretations of planning to meet the requirements of the National Curriculum reflect just this kind of approach. All are based on the needs of the mythical 'average' child.

In programmes for games great emphasis is placed on specific skills like bounce and catch, throw and catch. Traditionally games have been associated with predetermined rules, teacher commands (when the teacher plans actions and gives specific instruction), prescribed practices and set skills and techniques; hence the technique charts itemised in nearly every games book or set of guidelines. Even in the infant school the teacher sees the teaching of technique as the critical part of the lesson whether it be helping individuals to catch a ball or whether it be instructing the whole class – 'a strategy wholly successful in dividing the school population into those who can and those who cannot do the activity' (Bailey, 1983, p. 11). The emphasis is almost always on the end-product. For young children this involves acquiring basic skills as groundwork for participation in later major team games – adult-imposed ideas of games technique – hence 'skills training', when part of a lesson is devoted to learning new skills – usually restricted to those most appropriate to those major games like throwing overarm, bouncing or hitting. Within this part of the lesson one or two basic skills are taught to the class, often within a pre-specified time and with limited ways of practising – based on a prescribed hierarchy for 'average' performers (e.g. rows of pairs of children all throwing underarm and catching – some fumbling, some frustrated by the limitations of the experience). These methods treat the skills very much in isolation and without reference to the context in which they may be used. The 'games for understanding' and 'games making' approaches have helped teachers to become aware that 'traditional methods have tended to concentrate on specific motor responses (techniques) and have failed to take account of the contextual nature of games' (Bunker and Thorpe, 1983, p. 1). Although reference to these approaches have now been removed from the games programme of study (SCAA, 1995b), it does not preclude these activities as a means of developing children's experience of games playing.

Traditional methods also provide children with little opportunity to think for themselves. A child who is so used to following the directions and instructions of the teacher may well become too dependent on being 'fed' information or ideas by the teacher. It is a situation which results in mindless physical responses, and although there may well be a place for this sort of response activity on occasions (to encourage children to use their bodies to full capacity, for example), it cannot be called 'education' except in the sense that all experiences could be educational. Indeed it might well reduce children's independence of action and make it very difficult for them to be thoughtful and flexible in any movement situation. Teacher-dominated methods are also often limited in providing successful experiences for everyone. With an imposed, predetermined model of what performance should be, or what it looks like, some children will have inevitable difficulty and will feel that 'they can't' or say that they 'don't know how'. All too often we see children pressed into preconceived adult versions of activities – using bat and ball as in tennis, rather than reducing an option and ensuring success by keeping the ball and manoeuvring it with the bat on the floor.

This approach shows a lack of concern or awareness for children's physical development, often ignoring the vast differences in young children's experiences, abilities and interests and the need to build up confidence to develop each individual's manipulative skills. The approach shows a lack of concern for children's cognitive development in a situation which prescribes an approach suggesting a passive acceptance by the children of what they are told to practise – or do – and a lack of concern for their socio-emotional development. It is not surprising therefore that in 'physical education' the teaching of specific motor skills is seen to be often separated from the wider aspects of children's development (Blenkin and Kelly, 1981, 1987).

Misunderstanding of 'child-centredness'

These inadequacies so far described have illustrated fairly common, but rather extreme, versions of approaches to the teaching of physical education in the early years. Another approach which is seen frequently in current practice might perhaps be even more worrying. As with most other aspects of the primary curriculum, PE has adopted a philosophy that espouses the values of the 'child-centred' approach. However, despite the 'educational' ideals which are often articulated in the introductions of books or curriculum guidelines, these ideals are usually followed with very prescriptive plans involving 'movement training' which emphasizes what 'should be taught' to year 1 or year 2 children, often in lesson-by-lesson formats, and with lists of skills which are to be incorporated in each theme.

Similarly, many writers advocate the exploration of equipment by children through playing with a wide variety and range of objects which gives lots of opportunity for hands-on experience to develop hand-eye co-ordination and concepts of time and space. Also they recognize that the direct teaching of a limited number of skills in a competitive framework is inappropriate for young children because 'each individual has his or her own unique timetable for the development and acquisition of movement abilities' (Gallahue, 1989, p. 7). Children have had such varied experiences before coming to school, have a wide range of interests and very individual styles of learning, yet often are treated the same in attempts to teach skills. Clearly, certain skills like learning to swim or learning to do a headstand for example, may be easy to define in terms of objectives, but, by using such narrow terms, we belie the complexity of this situation and this results in such skills being superficially 'done'.

If the skills are to be learned then they should be developed much more closely in relation to the needs and interests of the individual children concerned. A prescribed lesson-by-lesson scheme of work for a whole class of children cannot come to terms with the methodology inherent in a truly developmental approach. Similarly, there are many facets of current approaches to the practice of teaching PE, which despite the ideology of child-centred education have the effect of promoting the subject and skills training. If one looks at how lessons are sometimes structured and taught we might well question the 'educational' label which is attached. When children are told exactly what to do we lose opportunities for them to think as well as do. To give a practical example, the arrangement of apparatus, if it is linear in form, often reduces initiative and spontaneity in children's responses. They resort to following and copying, often at increasing or decreasing speeds and this does not help them to cope effectively, resourcefully and flexibly with their ideas or the environment. In fact, as Betts and Underwood (1992) highlight, it may result in children sitting or standing waiting for turns, or for instructions, for large proportions of the lesson.

Constraints

In the school situation, there are of necessity many constraints on the ways in which we are able to encourage young children to be physically active. In contrast to the classroom, the need for space and therefore a new location often means that what happens in the hall or playground is perceived very differently from what happens in the classroom. In fact PE is usually the first subject in the infant school to be timetabled.

Certainly there is a conflict between the constraints of class teaching and the needs of individual children. The separateness of these sessions, with the attendant narrow focus of attention, stems partly from this change in location when classes take turns to use the hall or larger playground space. An added constraint upon the way we teach is the rigid, traditional division of physical education into separate, compartmentalized experiences which occur at set times each week. To young children it's all 'Pee Yee'. They get changed and they move about and it's almost incidental whether they are sometimes on large apparatus or sometimes playing with small apparatus. Certainly the traditionally arranged timetable which, for example, advocates one lesson of large apparatus on Tuesdays, one lesson of dance on Wednesdays and one lesson for playground games on Fridays, may well be too rigid. Similarly, days when the large apparatus is set out for a day or half a day for use by several classes unfortunately severely reduces the options available to each individual teacher and his or her class within this type of lesson. It restricts the ways these activities can be developed with the children.

Somehow, in surroundings that are remote from the classroom, PE is seen as something different, something special, and often frightening for teachers who are rightly concerned about teaching the whole class in a big space, frequently with different sorts of apparatus. These concerns and feelings depend to some extent on a teacher's previous feelings about this aspect of the curriculum. Sometimes these may be feelings of pleasure in observing and helping young children to enjoy their movement, but more often concern or anxiety predominates and the physical activity lesson becomes an ordeal. It is probable that much of their anxiety may result from concern over difficulties of control when dealing with a whole class involved in predominantly one sort of activity – physical activity – at the same time, often moving around and using apparatus.

These factors and the limitations imposed by safety regulations, particularly when apparatus is used, mean that there are some constraints on the way we teach. Class size, space, safety and equipment often prevent an ideal or more individual approach, yet these are often excuses for setting up a very teacher-dominated environment. Often there is overconcern for regimentation and teacher organization which reduces each child's involvement and individuality to a minimum. Clearly, a lesson planned and taught in this way is extremely prescriptive, with little if any opportunity for individual children to do other than respond in a very precise way to the tasks set. A major problem then for this kind of approach is that a challenge, which if given to an individual child might be highly relevant and appropriate, when posed as a class activity becomes inappropriate and too prescriptive.

Thus far, some of the problems which relate to content and matters of organization have been emphasized. What is of vital importance, however, is that the activities themselves 'are of less importance than the ways they are used as process vehicles for educational outcomes' (Kane, 1976, p. 81).

Towards a more positive view of the role of physical activity in the development of the child

Most children enjoy being physically active and often explode with energy once allowed to move in a larger space. Holt (1984, p. 9) suggests that this is just as well as there is 'no better way to promote their muscular development and physical health'. Few would doubt the young child's need for vigorous activity which is generally held to be an important factor in the growth and development of children (Gallahue, 1989; Malina, 1986). Yet many four-year-olds in infant schools are denied sufficient access to the outside environment where they can use their motor and other skills. Perhaps it is time to consider a much more flexible use of the playground and 'playtime', particularly for the reception classes. There has been a growing realization of the importance of physical activity for children, as well as adults (Gallahue, 1989), and great concern for the fitness of our youngsters.

Recent research (Armstrong and Bray, 1991; Armstrong and McManus, 1994) has revealed the likelihood of an increase in cardiac problems amongst today's children as they reach adulthood because they do too little exercise – not enough to maintain the physical and organic development which is essential for healthy living: 'the voluntary activity patterns of the children studied [six- to seven-year-olds] may not be adequate in terms of duration and intensity to promote cardiovascular health' (Gilliam *et al.*, 1981, p. 67). This is a concern for everyone, yet there is an assumption that through their play children get plenty of activity. It must be realized that with increasingly sedentary life-styles (cars and other modes of transport, flats or restricted living space, television, computers and video games – and the need for supervision of young children in their play, in the park or in the street) opportunities for physical activity within school have an important contribution to make. Timetabled physical education lessons cannot satisfy a child's total exercise requirements but there is a vital need, not only for adequate provision for movement, but also to develop opportunities for children to be engaged in strenuous physical activity in enjoyable and purposeful ways, so they can begin to develop a concern and understanding for their own physical well-being.

Physical education, however, should not just be equated with physical fitness. For the young child, movement is an important means of self-discovery (Whitehurst, 1971). However repetitive, aimless or even reckless it may seem to adults:

> a child enjoys discovering what his body can do. He tries out the normal range of bodily actions and, with an inventive mind and mobile joints, is eager to

discover less conventional actions to extend his range . . . He tests himself out in movement. He can find out how it feels to balance on narrow surfaces at increasing heights, or to drop from a height, to sail through the air or to up-end himself. He uses movement as a means of learning about himself and the physical world.

(DES, 1972, p. 5)

The sensations and feelings of daring, fun and exhilaration are an important part of these early experiences and cannot be separated from the physical actions themselves.

Free play and physical activity, however, do not necessarily develop a high level of body awareness or movement competence within a child. We need to find ways to provide opportunities for each child to gain a growing awareness of his or her body – to stimulate possible ways of using the body through a variety of activities, in a variety of circumstances, through experiment, suggestions or guidance. The sixth and often forgotten kinesthetic sense (knowing by feeling) is that through which movements of the body are experienced. It is important for the sense of balance, for relaxation, for developing the ability to move with control, precision and clarity, for the body to be lithe, agile, responsive, skilful and efficient – whether digging, painting, jumping or running for the bus! 'The emphasis on the "wholeness" of the child is exemplified by the concept of body awareness' (Hoffman, Young and Klesius, 1981, p. 41), and this becomes apparent in activities that require hand dominance and an awareness of laterality and/or directionality. An incomplete conception of direction and space may create later difficulties, for example in coping with handwriting or with traffic (Holle, 1976). Thus 'the development of perceptual motor abilities involves the complex interaction of perceptual, motor and cognitive processes' (Gallahue, 1982, p. 294) and many therapeutic, sensori-motor, perceptual or movement programmes have tried to demonstrate their virtues on concept readiness and cognitive functioning (Delacato, 1959; Frostig, 1969; Kephart, 1971; Cratty, 1972).

The ability to move about also opens up great opportunities for children to explore their environment. Motor skills are the child's 'special tools for experimenting and expanding his environment' (Flinchum, 1975, p. 2). It is a medium of learning that is direct, spontaneous, and which provides immediate feedback which is possible without dependence on words:

By using their bodies in a variety of situations, such as climbing in and out of boxes, balancing on planks, rocking on see-saws and so on, children develop spatial awareness and begin to conceptualise dimension, distance, height, speed, weight and balance. On a small scale indoors block building enables children to estimate size and shape and appreciate height and length.

(Choat, 1978, p. 24)

There are indeed many activities which come under the label 'physical' education but which may be helping the child to develop in many different ways (Dowling, 1976, p. 80). In fact we might even question the educational validity of the term which 'it is suggested implies an undesirable limit to the processes and effects of bodily movement' (DES, 1972, p. 8). 'Movement seems to be very important for a young child – for his pleasure, to enable him to learn about the world around him, and for him to develop normal emotional patterns' (Holt, 1975, p. 6).

Many researchers too have shown how motor development influences social and emotional development. Gallahue (1989) discusses the relationship between motor development and the development of self-concept and self-confidence. Cratty (1972) argues that a child who cannot control his or her movements adequately develops a poor self-concept and encounters difficulties in social and emotional adjustment. Motor abilities and movement skills are only one avenue by which self-image may be enhanced. It is, however, a most important one for children because so much of their daily life experiences are centred round the need for efficient and effective movement (Gallahue, 1989, p. 356). We need to recognize that social and emotional experiences encountered in movement must be evaluated in terms of the child's whole development. It is how each child reacts to the total situation which is important. The outdoor play area or the physical education lesson provides very different environments from the classroom and therefore offers unique opportunities to develop social awareness and responsibility – opportunities for co-operation, collaboration, sharing, for developing consideration and feelings of belonging.

Some criticisms of Piaget's stages of development (Brown and Desforge, 1979) have suggested that it has often lowered teacher expectations of the sorts of co-operative activity that children were able to engage in during their early years, but if we look at the kinds of 'games' which children play on their own without adult supervision (Opie and Opie, 1969) they reflect a sophistication which many would not dream was possible:

> they seldom need an umpire; they rarely trouble to keep scores, little significance is attached to who wins or loses, they do not require the stimulus of prizes, it does not seem to worry them if a game is not finished . . . they like games in which there is a sizable element of luck so that individual abilities cannot be directly compared . . . they like games that restart almost automatically to give everyone a new chance.

> (Opie and Opie, 1969, p. 2)

'The opportunities movement offers for developing language and imagination as well as more social skills of discipline, co-operation and self-awareness have not always been fully appreciated' (Kent County Council, 1982, p. 1) let alone recognized or developed. In dance particularly, movement is a unique, direct and valuable means of expression and representation, and a most natural and spontaneous learning medium for young children. They can explore and begin to understand words through their actions, and equally refine their actions through the use of words. 'They spontaneously use words to accompany themselves and will suggest colourful words like "swirling" or invent new ones like "clumping" ' (Shreeves, 1990, p. 19).

Having briefly explored the various facets and contributions of physical activity to development in the early years, 'it is important to recognize the role of movement as a common denominator of the total development of the child, and its integrating function. Movement is bound up with physical, intellectual and emotional development and a child's doing, thinking and feeling may be examined in movement terms' (Brearley, 1969, p. 83).

More specific methodological principles which underlie practice

If we can recognize and apply some basic education principles to our teaching of 'physical' education, it means that rather than our being concerned with instrumental objectives, where skills and content of lessons 'take over', or alternatively leaving physical development to maturation, the principles can be implemented in different ways while still allowing the 'individuality of teachers to find expression in ways they apply this or that principle to their own situations' (Wright, 1986, p. 44) to meet the needs of their own children.

Time for physical activity should not have to justify its importance or be regarded as a frill. Each child does need the widest possible range of movement experiences – some will be favoured by some children, others by other children (and there are the obvious dangers of mixing activities – flying quoits or bean bags and upside-down children). Different demands are made by different activities, different interests and abilities can be stimulated and extended, and can make a special contribution to each child's developing powers. A varied and imaginative movement programme can promote enjoyment and satisfaction in vigorous movements of the body.

The sheer experience of 'doing' is very valuable in itself and, whenever possible, situations should enable children to be participating and involved in some way for most of the time. Opportunities need to be provided, for example, for them to have one piece of 'apparatus' each so they have 'hands-on' experience – to enable them to explore and practise in individual ways without waiting for others. Team games can be utterly frustrating or very exciting and, if they are used at all, should be used with smallest possible numbers in each team to ensure maximum participation. Certainly we need to avoid large-sided games where all but a few children are left on the fringe or left waiting for their turn – while others follow the ball like bees round a honey pot – desperate for their chance to be part of the action. On large apparatus we need to try to avoid queues and unnecessary waiting, and by the arrangement of the apparatus enable children to exercise their ingenuity and inventiveness. The phrase 'active participants' in their own learning is well worn in its application in classroom situations but not one which has been questioned in movement. A child who is thinking and suggesting is involved, as opposed to one who passively accepts an idea or task as in mindless drill or physical training. Thus it is important that opportunities are provided for individuals to make their contribution, whether suggesting their words or feelings, showing their ways of answering a task, or thinking through the process of how to get on the apparatus in a different way, thus reinforcing attitudes that every pupil has something worthwhile to give to enrich the collective experiences of the group. Almost without exception, sessions should include some opportunities for choice or free play to enable children to practise, consolidate or try out more actions of their own.

What is equally important, however, is that activities are not left too open-ended, too vague, or with too many choices for too long. Too much choice can be intimidating, even confusing in a free, open environment; where to go, what to do, whom to look at. Children, therefore, often need help to make choices between viable alternatives, to build up their experience of choosing and acting on those choices. Very often they need a clear focus for their attention, a task or an idea to try out or think about in movement terms. A task or problem which is too vague or open-ended may, after a while, be taxing even for the most agile and may not direct the child's attention to what is possible, thus allowing less scope for individual variations, rather than encouraging exploration of a diversity of actions. The setting of uniform tasks for a whole class, unless they respond to the specific needs of that class at a particular time, is likely to be too prescriptive and tends to control, stifle and restrict responses, allowing little individuality or spontaneity. We need to recognize the child's growing need for autonomy and self-expression and find ways in which we can help children to begin 'to tackle open-ended situations in systematic and informed ways, guiding their thinking along divergent rather than convergent lines' (Wright, 1986, p. 46), and helping their understanding, not just in terms of set skills or information, but in an awareness of themselves and others. Often a child wants to initiate or try some action which they have seen others doing (TV, playground, peers or adults). The teacher may need to intervene in a way which enables the action to be successful, offering an option, modifying the approach, giving timely advice or making a teaching point, which may be pertinent to an individual or small group, or sometimes the whole class.

An important element is the way we communicate our expectations and feelings to the child as 'significant others'. It is important to use positive encouragement, in a caring and meaningful way. If 'good' and 'well done' are applied too liberally without reasons or acknowledgement, the praise eventually becomes meaningless and devalues our role. If used too sparingly, children will not get the support and encouragement they need to feel successful or to build their self-confidence. Thus the circulation of the teacher, moving among, being near and encouraging individual children, although seemingly an impossibility in some circumstances, is a vital link to give children the security to move independently. Realistic expectations and a proper sequencing of activities or suggestions are crucial in determining a child's sense of success or failure. 'When tasks are too easy and success too cheap little development takes place – when tasks are too difficult and achievement impossible, frustration and reinforcement of a negative concept are likely to follow' (Frost, 1973, p. 36).

Thus it is essential that activities should be planned on the basis of a thorough understanding of the child's current stage of development and needs (a difficult task with as many as thirty in the class). The use of exploratory or problem-solving approaches to movement activities or to learning new skills is a method which can be adopted and which facilitates a more individual approach to PE. A movement environment must like any other learning environment have an atmosphere of success and satisfaction. It needs to be fun. Success is very important particularly in the initial stages of learning and it is one of the greatest contributors to development – the more successful the child is, the more wholeheartedly he or she enters into the situation. This again suggests the necessity of a more individual approach since success is relative to the interest and ability of the individual concerned. Personal experiences reveal our tendency to continue those activities in which we are successful.

It is, in most schools, greatly to be regretted that the constraints of timetabling do not permit greater flexibility in terms of when, and for how long, activities should take place. Given the problems which might arise from total flexibility of timetable arrangements and therefore a consequent need for some structure, more flexibility would give opportunities for interests to be followed through, or activities to take place, which were much more closely related to children's precise needs at a particular time. In this way activities might be developed in successive lessons while ideas and interests are still buoyant rather than wait until the following week. Some continuity or routine, however, is important to give children the security to build up familiarity, to enable them to explore more fully and to build on their experiences.

Above all, the activities need a movement environment which is fun, without fear of failure or rejection, which preserves and develops as far as possible the playful elements within physical activity but retains the thrill, and a feeling of mastery or accomplishment that comes from succeeding at activities which challenge courage, control and imagination. We need to provide opportunities for learning and expression through the medium of movement, and these need to be planned in constructive and thoughtful ways as for other activities. We need to provide a variety of stimulating movement experiences and these should make balanced demands on capacities which contribute to our basic educational principles but which retain the unique emphasis on promoting motor development. We need to help children to improve and understand their own movement – both by encouraging them to explore and think about movement, and by guiding them to discover efficient and effective movement for themselves, whilst retaining the spontaneity, excitement and autonomy of some of their 'natural' movements, and play situations. It is an approach which considers 'attitude, confidence, development and opportunities as the key aspects', and 'focuses upon the individual first and does not seek to impose a set of... activities upon the pupil' (Williamson and Hickling, 1978, p. 100).

Conclusions

'Through movement and play children learn more than motor skills, they learn to employ cognitive strategies, to understand their psychological self and how to interact with other children' (Zaichkowsky, Zaichkowsky and Martinek, 1980, p. 11). What it is hoped has been emphasized here and elsewhere in this book is the need for a holistic approach which encompasses considerations of the cognitive, physical, social and emotional development of the child. Attention has been focused on some extreme and apparently contradictory features and inadequacies that exist in current practice in both the *laissez-faire* and the skills/subject-based approaches. Some of the narrow aspirations and uncertainties associated with this area of the curriculum have been discussed, but we have tried to focus in a much more positive way on the developing experience of the child. Through keen observation, sensitive interaction, timely guidance and careful evaluation every teacher can make a positive response to children's movement; not just by setting up an environment and letting things happen, but by seeking opportunities to extend the experience of children. With a thoughtful, constructive approach towards these special times and by efficient organization, without dominating the activities, we can enable a diversity of actions and attempt to retain the individuality and spontaneity in a young child's movement. By including opportunities to develop initiative, imagination and independence of action we can enjoy the growing movement competence and confidence of each child and can appreciate the profound effect physical activity can have at every stage, and on every aspect of development. Such an approach focuses first upon an understanding of the child and sees physical activity as a potentially rich source of educational experiences which offer many opportunities for individual children to develop (Almond, 1983).

Suggested further reading

Gallahue, D. L. (1989) *Understanding Motor Development, Infants, Children, Adolescents*, Brown and Benchmark, Indianapolis.

Kelso, J. A. S. and Clark, J. E. (1982) *The Development of Movement Control and Coordination*, Wiley, New York.

Roberton, M. A. and Halverson, L. (1984) *Developing Children – their Changing Movement*, Lea and Febiger, Philadelphia.

BIBLIOGRAPHY

ALBSU, (1995) *Read and Write Together*, ALBSU/BBC Publications, London.

Almond, L. (1983) Aspirations in physical education, *British Journal of Physical Education*, 14 April, p. 94.

Archambault, R. D. (ed.) (1965) *Philosophical Analysis and Education*, Routledge & Kegan Paul, London.

Armstrong, N. and Bray, S. (1991) Physical activity patterns defined by continuous heart rate monitoring, *Archives of Disease in Childhood 66*, pp. 245–7.

Armstrong, N. and McManus, A (1994) Children's fitness and physical activity – a challenge for Physical Education, *British Journal of Physical Education*, Spring, pp. 20–6.

Arnheim, R. (1954; 2nd edn, 1974) *Art and Visual Perception: A Psychology of The Creative Eye*, University of California Press, Berkeley.

Association of Teachers of Mathematics (1985) *Some More Lessons in Mathematics with a Microcomputer* (SLIMWAM 2), Association of Teachers of Mathematics, Derby.

Athey, C. (1980) Parental involvement in nursery education, *Early Childhood*, December, pp. 4–9.

Athey, C. (1981) Parental involvement in nursery education, *Early Childhood Development and Care*, Vol. 7, no. 4, pp. 253–67.

Athey, C. (1990) *Extending Thought in Young Children: A Parent–Teacher Partnership*, Paul Chapman, London.

Atkin, J. and Bastiani, J. (1985) *Preparing Teachers to Work with Parents: A Survey of Initial Training*, University of Nottingham School of Education.

Baddeley, P. and Eddershaw, C. (1994) *Not So Simple Picture Books. Developing responses to literature with 4–12 year olds*, Trentham Books, Stoke-on-Trent.

Bakhtin, M. (1968) *Rabelais and his world*, Harvard University Press, Cambridge, Mass.

Bailey, L. (1983) Anyone for tennis? Game, set and match, in L. Spackman (ed.) op. cit.

Barnes, D. (1976) *From Communication to Curriculum*, Penguin, Harmondsworth.

Barney, D. (1976) Kindergarten four-year-olds' concept of reading, knowledge of books and print, in D. B. Doake and B. T. O'Rourke (eds.) op. cit.

Barrett, G. (1986) *Starting School: An Evaluation of the Experience*, AMMA and Centre for Applied Research in Education, Norwich.

Barrett, G. (1989) *Disaffection From School? The Early Years*, Falmer, London.

Barrs, M. (1992) The tune on the page, in K. Kimberley, M. Meek and J. Miller, (eds.) op. cit. pp. 16–28.

Barrs, M. and Pidgeon, S. (eds.) (1993) *Reading the Difference: gender and reading in the primary school*, CLPE, London.

Barrs, M. and Thomas, A. (1991) *The Reading Book*, CLPE, London.

Barthes, R. (1974) *S/Z*, Hill & Wang, New York (originally published 1970, Seuil, Paris).

Bartholomew, L. and Bruce, T. (1993) *Getting to Know You*, Hodder and Stoughton, London.

Bayliss, S. (1986) Bringing parents into the equation, *Times Educational Supplement*, 3 January.

Benton, M. and Fox, G. (1985) *Teaching Literature, Nine to Fourteen*, Oxford University Press, London.

Berger, J. (1972) *Ways of Seeing*, Penguin and BBC, Harmondsworth.

Bernstein. B. (1973) *Class, Codes and Control*, Routledge & Kegan Paul, London.

Beruetta-Clement, J., Schweinhart, L. J., Barnett, W. S., Epstein, A. S. and Weikart, D. P. (1984) Changed lives: the effects of the Perry pre-school programme on youths through age 19, *Monographs of the High/Scope Educational Research Foundation*, no. 8, pp. 16–28.

Bettelheim, B. (1975) *The Uses of Enchantment. The Meaning and Importance of Fairy Tales*, Thames & Hudson, London.

Betts, M. and Underwood, G. (1992) The experiences of three low motor ability pupils in infant Physical Education, *The Bulletin of Physical Education*, 28.3, pp. 45–56.

Bickerton, D. (1981) *The Roots of Language*, Ann Arbor, Karoma.

Biemiller, A. (1970) The development of the use of graphic and contextual information as children learn to read, *Reading Research Quarterly*, Vol. 4, pp. 75–96.

Bierley, M. (1983) The development of a record-keeping system, in G. M. Blenkin and A. V. Kelly (eds.) op. cit.

Bissex, G. L. (1980) *GYNS AT WRK: A Child Learns to Write and Read*, Harvard University Press, Cambridge, Mass. and London.

Blenkin, G. M. (1980) The influence of initial styles of curriculum development, in A. V. Kelly (ed.) op. cit.

Blenkin, G. M. (1983) The basic skills, in G. M. Blenkin and A. V. Kelly (eds.) op. cit.

Blenkin, G. M. (1988) Education and development: some implications for the curriculum in the early years, in W. A. L. Blyth (ed.) op. cit.

Blenkin, G. M., Edwards, G. and Kelly, A. V. (1992) *Change and the Curriculum*, Paul Chapman, London.

Blenkin, G. M., Hurst, V. M., Whitehead, M. R. and Yue, N. Y. L. (1995) *Principles into Practice: Improving the Quality of Children's Early Learning, Phase One Report*, Goldsmiths' College, University of London.

Blenkin, G. M. and Kelly, A. V. (1981; 1987) *The Primary Curriculum*, Paul Chapman, London.

Blenkin, G. M. and Kelly, A. V. (1983) The education of teachers, in G. M. Blenkin and A. V. Kelly (eds.) op. cit.

Blenkin, G. M. and Kelly, A. V. (eds.) (1983) *The Primary Curriculum in Action*, Paul Chapman, London.

Blenkin, G. M. and Kelly, A. V. (eds.) (1992) *Assessment in Early Childhood*

Education, Paul Chapman, London.

Blenkin, G. M. and Kelly, A. V. (eds.) (1994) *The National Curriculum and Early Learning*, Paul Chapman, London.

Blenkin, G. M. and Yue, N. Y. L. (1994) Profiling early years practitioners: some first impressions from a national survey, *Early Years* Vol. 15, no. 1, pp. 13–22.

Bloom, B. S. (ed.) (1956) *Taxonomy of Educational Objectives. 1: Cognitive Domain*, Longman, London.

Blurton-Jones, N. (1967) Rough-and-tumble among nursery school children, in J. S. Bruner, A. Jolly and K. Sylva (eds.) op. cit.

Blyth, W. A. L. (1965) *English Primary Education: A Sociological Description: Volume 11: Background*, Routledge & Kegan Paul, London.

Blyth, W. A. L. (ed.) (1988) *Informal Primary Education Today: Essays and Studies*, Falmer, Lewes.

Bower, T. G. R. (1971) Early learning behaviour, *Times Literary Supplement*, 7 May.

Bower, T. G. R. (1974), *Development in Infancy*, Freeman, San Francisco.

Bower, T. G. R. (1977) *The Perceptual World of the Child*, Fontana/Open Books, London.

Brearley, M. (ed.) (1969) *Fundamentals in First School*, Blackwell, Oxford.

Bremner, J. G. (1985) Figural biases and young children's drawings, in N. H. Freeman and M. V. Cox (eds.) op. cit.

Bretherton, I. (1984) Representing the social world in symbolic play: reality and fantasy, in I. Bretherton (ed.) op. cit.

Bretherton, I. (ed.) (1984) *Symbolic Play*, Academic Press, London.

British Association of Advisors and Lecturers in Physical Education (1986) *Strategies for Change in Physical Education*, Congress Report, Codicote Press, Hitchin.

Britton, J. (1983) *Prospect and Retrospect. Selected Essays of James Britton*, Heinemann, London.

Bronowski J. (1959) The search for truth, *Education Review*, Vol. 11, no. 2.

Brown, A., Bricknell, D., Groves, L., McLeish, E., Morris P. and Sugden, D. (eds.) (1984) *Adapted Physical Activities*, Hartnoll, Cornwall.

Brown, G. and Desforges, C. (1979) *Piaget's Theory: A Psychological Critique*, Routledge & Kegan Paul, London.

Browne, A. (1993) *Helping Children to Write*, Paul Chapman, London.

Browne, N. (1993) From birth to sixteen months, in M. Barrs and S. Pidgeon (eds.) op. cit. pp. 38–45.

Bruner, J. S. (1964) The course of cognitive growth, *American Psychologist*, Vol. 19, pp. 1–15.

Bruner, J. S. (1966; 1968) *Toward a Theory of Instruction*, Norton, New York.

Bruner, J. S. (1972) Nature and uses of immaturity, in J. S. Bruner, A. Jolly and K. Silva (eds.) op. cit.

Bruner, J. S. (1975) The ontogenesis of speech acts, *Journal of Child Language*, Vol. 2, pp. 1–19.

Bruner, J. S. (1980), *Under Five in Britain. (Oxford Pre-School Research Project, 1)*, Grant McIntyre, London.

Bruner, J. S. (1981) The pragmatics of acquisition, in W. Deutsch (ed.) op. cit.

Bruner, J. S. (1983) *Child's Talk: Learning to Use Language*, Oxford University Press, Oxford.

Bruner, J. S. (1984) Language, mind and reading, in H. Goelman, A. Oberg and

F. Smith (eds.) op. cit.

Bruner, J. S. (1986) *Actual Minds, Possible Worlds*, Harvard University Press, Cambridge, Mass.

Bruner, J. S. (1990) *Acts of Meaning*, Harvard University Press, Cambridge, Mass.

Bruner, J. S. and Haste, H. (1987) *Making Sense: the child's construction of the world*, Methuen, London.

Bruner, J. S., Jolly, A. and Sylva, K. (eds.) (1976) *Play – First Role in Development and Evolution*, Penguin, Harmondsworth.

Bryant P. and Bradley L. (1985) *Children's Reading Problems*, Blackwell, Oxford.

Bunker, D. and Thorpe, R. (1983) A model for the teaching of games in the secondary school, in L. Spackman (ed.) op. cit.

Burghardt, G. H. (1984) On the origins of play, in P. K. Smith (ed.) op. cit.

Burton, L. (1990) What could teacher education be like for prospective teachers of early childhood mathematics – with particular reference to the environment, in Steffe L. P. and Wood T. (eds.) op. cit.

Bush, H. and Silver, B. (1994) *Why Cats Paint: A theory of Feline Aesthetics*, Ten Speed Press, Berkeley, California.

Bussis, A., Chittendon, E., Amarel, M. and Klausner, E. (1985) *Inquiry into Meaning: an investigation of learning to read*, Lawrence Erlbaum Associates, Hillsdale, NJ.

Butler, D. (1979) *Cushla and Her Books*, Hodder & Stoughton, Sevenoaks.

Cannon, W. B. (1932) *The Wisdom of the Body*, Norton, New York.

Carter,R. (ed.) (1990) *Knowledge about Language and the Curriculum*, Hodder & Stoughton, London.

Centre for Language in Primary Education (CLPE) (1987) *Language Matters 2 & 3*, CLPE, London.

Centre for Language in Primary Education (CLPE) (1988) *The Primary Language Record*, CLPE, London.

Centre for Language in Primary Education (CLPE) (1989) *Language Matters 1*, CLPE, London.

Centre for Language in Primary Education (CLPE) (1990) *The Primary Learning Record*, CLPE, London.

Chambers, A. (1993) *Tell Me. Children Reading and Talk*, Thimble Press, Stroud.

Chapman, L. J. and Czerniewska, P. (eds.) (1978) *Reading: From Process to Practice*, Open University Press, Buckingham.

Choat, E. (1978) *Children's Acquisition of Mathematics*, National Foundation for Educational Research, Windsor.

Clark, M. M. (1976) *Young Fluent Readers*, Heinemann Educational, London.

Clark, M. M. (ed.) (1985) *New Directions in the Study of Reading*, Falmer Lewes.

Clark, M. M. and Cheyne, W. (eds.) (1979) *Studies in PreSchool Education*, Hodder & Stoughton, London.

Clay, M. M. (1975) *What Did I Write?*, Heinemann, London.

Coard, B. (1871) *How the West Indian Child is Made Educationally Subnormal in the British School System*, New Beacon Books, London.

Cochran-Smith, M. (1984) *The Making of a Reader*, Ablex, Norwood, New Jersey.

Commune di Modena (1979) *I Servizi Scholastici Di Base in Europa*, Commissione Nazionale per L'Anno Internazionale del Bambino 1979 e Regione Emilia-Romagna, Modena.

Condon, W. (1975) Speech makes babies move, in Lewin R. (ed.) op. cit.

Cook, E. (1976) *The Ordinary and the Fabulous. An Introduction to Myths, Legends and Fairy Tales* (2nd edn), Cambridge University Press.

Copple, C., Sigel, I. E. and Saunders, R. (1979) *Educating the Young Thinker: Classroom Strategies for Cognitive Growth*, Van Nostrand, New York.

Corbin, C. B. (ed.) (1973) *A Textbook of Motor Development*, W. C. Brown, Dubuque, Iowa.

Costall, A. (1985) How meaning covers the traces, in N. H. Freeman and M. V. Cox (eds.) op. cit.

Costall, A. (1994) The myth of the sensory core: the traditional versus the ecological approach to children's drawings, in C. Lange-Kuettner and G. V. Thomas (eds.) op. cit.

Court, E. (1987) Drawing on culture: some views from rural Kenya, A paper presented at a symposium on Social and Cultural Influences on Children's Drawings, Biennial Meeting of the Society for Research in Child Development, Baltimore, Maryland, 24 April 1987. Elsbeth Court, Institute of Education, University of London.

Cratty, B. J. (1972) *Physical Expressions of Intelligence*, Prentice Hall, Englewood Cliffs, New Jersey.

Crozier, W. R. and Chapman, A. J. (eds.) (1984) *Cognitive Processes in the Perception of Art*, North Holland, Amsterdam.

Curtis, A. M. (1986) *A Curriculum for the Pre-School Child. Learning to Learn*, NFER/Nelson, Windsor.

Czerniewska, P. (1992) *Learning About Writing*, Blackwell, Oxford.

Darwin, C. (1871) *The Descent of Man and Selection in Relation to Sex*, Murray, London

Darwin, C. (1872) *The Expression of the Emotions in Man and Animals*, Murray, London.

Davies, P. (1995) Issues concerning early childhood services in Wales (open letter to seminar of Nursery Education Liaison Group, House of Commons 22/3/95), Early Childhood Unit, Children in Wales, Cardiff.

Dearden, R. F. (1968) *The Philosophy of Primary Education*, Routledge & Kegan Paul, London.

Dearden, R. F. (1976) *Problems in Primary Education*, Routledge & Kegan Paul, London.

Delacato, C. (1959) *Treatment and Prevention of Reading Problems*, Charles C. Thomas, Springfield, Illinois.

Design Council (1987) *Design and Primary Education: The Report of the Design Council's Primary Education Working Party*, The Design Council, London.

Deutsch, W. (ed.) (1981) *The Child's Construction of Language*, Academic Press, London.

De Vries, R. with Kohlberg, L. (1987) *Programs of Early Learning: the Constructivist View*, Longman, New York.

Dewey, J. (1938) *Experience and Education*, Collier, New York.

Dickson, L., Brown, M. and Gibson, O. (1984) *Children Learning Mathematics: A Teacher's Guide to Recent Research*, Holt, Rinehart & Winston for the Schools Council, Eastbourne.

Doake, D. B. and O'Rourke, B. T. (1976) *New Directions for Reading Teaching*, New Zealand Educational Institute, Wellington.

Donachy, W. (1979) Parental participation in preschool education, in M. M. Clark and W. Cheyne (eds.) op. cit.

Donaldson, M. (1978) *Children's Minds*, Fontana/Collins, Glasgow.

Donaldson, M. (1992) *Human Minds: an exploration*, Penguin, London.
Donaldson, M., Grieve, R. and Pratt, C. (eds.) (1983) *Early Childhood Development and Education*, Blackwell, Oxford.
Dowling, M. (1976) *The Modern Nursery*, Longman, London.
Dowling, P. and Noss, R. (1990) *Mathematics versus the National Curriculum*, Falmer, London.
Downey, M. E. and Kelly, A. V. (1975; 1979; 1986) *Theory and Practice of Education*, Paul Chapman, London.
Drummond, M. J. (1995) Primary Update, *Times Educational Supplement*, 28 April.
Dunn, J. (1987) Understanding feelings: the early stages, in J. S. Bruner and H. Haste (eds.) op. cit.
Early Years Curriculum Group (1989) *Early Childhood Education: The Early Years Curriculum and the National Curriculum*, Trentham, Stoke-on-Trent.
Early Years Curriculum Group (1993) *Statement of Principles*, EYCG, London.
Early Years Curriculum Group (1995) *Four-Year-Olds in School: Myths and Realities*, EYCG, London.
Early Years Trainers Anti-Racist Network (EYTARN) (1995) *The Best of Both Worlds: Celebrating Mixed Parentage*, EYTARN, London.
Egan, K. (1986) *Individual Development and the Curriculum*, Heinemann, London.
Eisner, E. W. (1982) *Cognition and Curriculum: A Basis for Deciding What to Teach*, Longman, New York and London.
Eisner, E. W. (1983) Foreword, in N. R. Smith (1983), op. cit.
Epstein, D., and Sealey, A. (1990) *Where it Really Matters*, Development Education Centre, Sellyoak College, Birmingham.
Fagen, R. (1984) Play and behavioural flexibility, in P. K. Smith (ed.). op. cit.
Ferreiro, E. and Teberosky. A. (1982) *Literacy Before Schooling*, Heinemann Educational, Exeter, New Hampshire.
Fisher. K. A. (1980) A theory of cognitive development: the control and construction of hierarchies of skills, *Psychological Review*, Vol. 87. no. 6, pp. 477–531.
Fletcher, H. (1970) *Mathematics for Schools: Teachers' Resource Book*, Addison-Wesley, London.
Flinchum, B. M. (1975) *Motor Development in Early Childhood*, C. V. Mosby, St Louis.
Floyd, A. (ed.) (1981) *Developing Mathematical Thinking*, Addison-Wesley in association with the Open University Press, London.
Forster, E. M. (1962) (originally published 1927) *Aspects of the Novel*, Penguin, Harmondsworth.
Fowler, J. S. (1981) *Movement Education*, Saunders College Publishing, Philadelphia.
Fox, C. (1993) *At The Very Edge Of The Forest: the influence of literature on story and narrative by children*, Cassell, London.
Fox, G., Hammond. G., Jones, T., Smith, F. and Sterck, K. (eds.) (1976) *Writers, Critics and Children*, Heinemann Educational, London.
Freeman, N. H. (1980) *Strategies of Representation In Young Children*, Academic Press, London.
Freeman, N. H. and Cox, M. V. (eds.) (1985) *Visual Order: The Nature and Development of Pictorial Representation*, Cambridge University Press.
Freire, P. (1972) *Pedagogy of the Oppressed*, Penguin, Harmondsworth.
Frost, R. B. (1973) Physical education and self concept, *Journal of Physical Education*, Vol. 70, pp. 35–7.
Frostig, M. (1969) *Move Grow and Learn*, Follett, Chicago.

Gagne, R. M. (1969) *The Conditions of Learning*, Holt International, London.

Gallahue, D. L. (1982) *Understanding Motor Development in Children*, Wiley, New York.

Gallahue, D. L. (1989) *Understanding Motor Development, Infants, Children, Adolescents*, Brown and Benchmark, Indianapolis.

Galton, M., Simon, B. and Croll, P. (1980) *Inside the Primary Classroom*, Routledge & Kegan Paul, London.

Gardner, H. (1984) *Frames of Mind: The Theory of Multiple Intelligence*, Heinemann, London.

Garvey, C. (1977) *Play*, Fontana/Open Books, London.

Garvey, C. (1979) An approach to the study of children's role play, *Quarterly Newsletter of the Laboratory of Comparative Human Cognition* Vol. 1, no. 44, pp. 69–73.

Garvie, E. (1990) *Story as Vehicle*, Multilingual Matters, Clevedon.

Geertz, C. (1976) Deep play: a description of the Balinese cockfight, in J. S. Bruner, A. Jolly and K. Silva (eds.) op. cit.

Gelman, R. and Gallistel, C. R. (1978) *The Child's Understanding of Number*, Harvard University Press, Cambridge, Mass.

Gelman, R. and Gallistel, C. R. (1983) The child's understanding of number, in M. Donaldson, R. Grieve and C. Pratt (eds.) op. cit.

Gentry, J. R. (1982) Analysis of developmental spelling in GNYS AT WRK, *The Reading Teacher*, November, pp. 192–200.

Gibson, J. (1979) *The Ecological Approach to Visual Perception*, Houghton Mifflin, Boston, Mass.

Gill, D., Mayer, B. and Blair, M. (eds.) *Racism and Education: Structures and Strategies*, Sage and Open University, London.

Gillespie, A. (1986) An attempt to examine one teacher's interaction with her class, paying special attention to language. Unpublished dissertation, University of London, Goldsmiths' College.

Gilliam, T. B., Freedson, P., Geenan, D. and Shahraray, B. (1981) Physical activity patterns determined by heart rate monitoring in 6–7 year old children, *Medicine and Science in Sports and Exercise*, Vol. 13, no. 1, pp. 69–77.

Ginsburg, H. (1977) *Children's Arithmetic: How They Learn It and How You Teach It*, PRO-ED, Austin, Texas.

Goddard, D. (1985) Assessing teachers: a critical response to the government's proposals, *Journal of Evaluation in Education*, Vol. 8, pp. 35–8.

Goelman, H., Oberg, A. and Smith, F. (eds.) (1984) *Awakening to Literacy*, Heinemann, Portsmouth, N.H..

Golomb, C. (1974) *Young Children's Sculpture and Drawing: A Study in Representational Development*, Harvard University Press, Cambridge, Mass.

Golomb, C. (1991) *The Child's Creation of a Pictorial World*, University of California Press, Berkeley.

Golomb, C. (1993) Art and the young child: another look at the developmental question, *Visual Arts Research*, Vol. 19, no. 1, pp. 1–16.

Goodman, K. S. (1967) Reading: a psycholinguistic guessing game, *Elementary English*, 42, pp. 639–43.

Goodman, K. S. (1993) *Phonics Phacts*, Heinemann, London.

Goodman, K. S. and Goodman. Y. M. (1978) Learning about psycholinguistic processes by analyzing oral reading, in L. J. Chapman and P. Czerniewska (eds.) op. cit.

Goodman, Y. M. (1990) The development of early literacy, in R. Carter (ed.) op. cit.

Goodson, I. (1983) *School Subjects and Curriculum Change*, Croom Helm, London.

Gordon, P. and Lawton, D. (1978) *Curriculum Change in the Nineteenth and Twentieth Centuries*, Hodder & Stoughton, London.

Goswami, U. and Bryant, P. E. (1990) *Phonological Skills and Learning to Read*, Lawrence Erlbaum, Hove.

Gregory, R. L. (1977) Psychology; towards a science of fiction, in M. Meek, A. Warlow and G. Barton (eds.), op. cit. (originally appeared in *New Society*, 23 May 1974).

Griffin, N. S. and Keogh, J. F. (1982) A model for movement confidence, in J. A. S. Kelso and J. E. Clark (eds.) op. cit.

Groos, K. (1901) *The Play of Man*, Appleton, New York.

Gura, P. (1992) with the Froebel Blockplay Research Group, directed by Tina Bruce (1992) *Exploring Learning: Young Children and Blockplay*. Paul Chapman, London.

Hagen, M. A. (1985) There is no development in art, in N. H. Freeman and M. V. Cox (eds.) op. cit.

Halliday, M. A. K. (1975) *Learning How To Mean: explorations in the development of language*, Edward Arnold, London.

Halsey, A. (1980) Education can compensate, *New Society*, 24 January.

Hannon, P., Long, R., Weinberger, J. and Whitehurst, L. (1985) *Involving Parents in the Teaching of Reading: Some Key Sources*, University of Sheffield.

Harding, D. W. (1937) The role of the onlooker, *Scrutiny*, Vol. VI, pp. 247–58.

Hardy, B. (1977) Towards a poetics of fiction: an approach through narrative, in M. Meek, A. Warlow and G. Barton (eds.) op. cit.

Hargreaves, D. (ed.) *Children and the Arts*, Open University Press, Milton Keynes.

Harlen, W. (1991) *Teaching and Learning Primary Science*, Paul Chapman, London.

Harlen, W., Darwin, A. and Murphy, M. (1977) *Match and Mismatch: Raising Questions: Leader's Guide*, Oliver & Boyd for the Schools Council, Edinburgh.

Harste, J., Woodward, V. and Burke, C. (1984) *Language Stories and Literacy Lessons*, Heinemann, Portsmouth, NH.

Harvey, O. J. (ed.) (1963) *Motivation and Social Interaction*, Ronald.

Heath, S. B. (1983) *Ways with Words. Language, Life and Work in Communities and Classrooms*, Cambridge University Press.

Held, R. (1965) Plasticity in sensory-motor systems, *Scientific American*, Vol. 213, no. 5, pp. 84–94.

Held, R. and Hein, A. (1963) Movement-produced stimulation in the development of visually guided behaviour, *Journal of Comparative Physiology and Psychology*, Vol. 56, pp. 607–13.

Hetherington, E. M. (ed.) (1983) *Carmichael's Manual of Child Psychology: Social Development*, Wiley, New York.

Hillingdon Education and Social Services (1994) *Early Years Guidelines*, Hillingdon.

Hirst, P. H. (1965) Liberal education and the nature of knowledge, in R. D. Archambault (ed.) op. cit.; also in R. S. Peters (ed.) (1973) op. cit.

Hirst, P. H. (1974) *Knowledge and the Curriculum*, Routledge & Kegan Paul, London.

Hirst, P. H. and Peters, R. S. (1970) *The Logic of Education*, Routledge & Kegan Paul, London.

Hoffman, H. A., Young, J. and Klesius, S. E. (1981) *Meaningful Movement for*

Children, Allyn & Bacon, Boston, Mass.

Holdaway, D. (1979) *The Foundations of Literacy*, Ashton Scholastic, London.

Holle, B. (1976) *Motor Development in Children: Normal and Retarded*, Munksgaard, Copenhagen.

Holmes, G. (1977) *The Idiot Teacher. A Book about Prestolee School and its Headmaster*, Spokesman, London.

Holt, K. S. (ed.) (1975) *Movement and Child Development*, Spastics International Medical Publications, Heinemann, London.

Holt, K. S. (1984) Movement studies, in A. Brown *et al.* (eds.) op. cit.

Hubel, D. H. and Wiesel, T. N. (1962) Receptive fields, binocular interaction and functional architecture in the cat's visual cortex, *Journal of Physiology*, Vol. 160, pp. 106–54.

Hughes, M. (1986) *Children and Number: Difficulties in Learning Mathematics*, Blackwell, Oxford.

Hughes, M., Shuard, H. and Ginsburg, H. (1986) in Twice 5 plus the wings of a bird, Horizon, BBC TV, producer: Simon Campbell-Jones.

Hughes, M., Wikeley, F. and Nash, T. (1994) *Parents and Their Children's Schools*, Blackwell, Oxford.

Hughes, T. (1976) Myth and education, in G. Fox *et al.* (eds.), op. cit.

Hunt, J. McV. (1963) Motivation inherent in information processing and action, in O. J. Harvey (ed.) op. cit.

Hutt, C. (1966) Exploration and play in children, *Symposium of the Zoological Society of London*. Vol. 18, pp. 61–81.

Hutt, C. and Bhavnani, R. (1972) Predictions from play, *Nature*, Vol. 237, May; also in J. S. Bruner, A. Jolly and K. Silva (eds.), op. cit. pp. 216–19.

Isaacs, S. (1930) *Intellectual Growth in Young Children*, Routledge & Kegan Paul, London.

Isaacs, S. (1933) *Social Development in Young Children*, Routledge & Kegan Paul, London.

Iser, W. (1974) *The Implied Reader: Patterns of Communication in Prose Fiction from Bunyan to Beckett*, Routledge & Kegan Paul, London.

Iser, W. (1978) *The Art of Reading. A Theory of Aesthetic Response*, Routledge & Kegan Paul, London.

Jackendoff, R. (1994) *Patterns in the Mind: Language and Human Nature*, Basic Books, New York.

Jackson, A. and Hannon, P. W. (1981) *The Bellfield Reading Project*, Bellfield Community Council.

Jones, G., Bastiani, J., Bell, G. and Chapman, C. (1992) *A Willing Partnership: Project Study of the Home–School Contract of Partnership*, RSA/NAHT, London.

Joseph, C., Lane, J. and Sharma, S. (1994) No equality, no quality, in P. Moss and A. Pence op. cit.

Kagan, J. (1972) Do infants think?, *Scientific American*, Vol. 226, no. 3, pp. 74–82.

Kane, J. E. (ed.) (1976) *Curriculum Development in Physical Education*, Crosby Lockwood Staples, London.

Katz, L. G. (1977) *Talks with Teachers*, National Association for the Education of Young Children, *Washington, DC.*

Katz, L. G. (1980) Mothering and teaching: some significant distinctions, in L. G. Katz (ed.) op. cit.

Katz, L. G. (ed.) (1980) *Current Topics in Early Childhood Education*, Vol. III, Ablex, New Jersey.

Katz, L. G. (1994) Equality in practice, in Save the Children Fund op. cit., pp. 6–31.

Katz, L. G. (1995) *Talks with Teachers of Young Children: A Collection*, Ablex Publishing Corporation, Norwood, New Jersey.

Keel, P. (ed.) (1994) *Assessment in the Multiethnic Primary Classroom*, Trentham, Stoke-on-Trent.

Kellogg, R. (1969) *Analysing Children's Art*, Mayfield, Palo Alto, California.

Kelly, A. V. (1977; 1982; 1989) *The Curriculum: Theory and Practice*, Paul Chapman, London.

Kelly, A. V. (ed.) (1980) *Curriculum Context*, Paul Chapman, London.

Kelly, A. V. (1986) *Knowledge and Curriculum Planning*, Paul Chapman, London.

Kelly, A. V. (1994) Beyond the rhetoric and the discourse, in Blenkin and Kelly (eds.) (1994) op. cit.

Kelly, A. V. (1995) *Education and Democracy: Principles and Practices*, Paul Chapman, London.

Kelly, E. and Cohn, T. (1988) *Racism in Schools: New Research Evidence*, Trentham, Stoke-on-Trent.

Kelso, J. A. S. and Clark, J. E. (1982) *The Development of Movement Control and Coordination*, Wiley, New York.

Kent County Council (1982) *Lets Dance*.

Kephart, N. C. (1971) *The Slow Learner in the Classroom*, Merrill, Columbus, Ohio.

Kimberley, K., Meek, M. and Miller, J. (eds.) (1992) *New Readings: Contributions to an Understanding of Literacy*, A & C Black, London.

King, R. (1978) *All Things Bright and Beautiful? A Sociological Study of Infants Classrooms*, Wiley, Chichester.

King, S. (1989) Extracts from a discussion, in CLPE (1989) op. cit.

Kirk, D. (1992) *Defining Physical Education: the social construction of a school subject in post war Britain*, Falmer, London.

Klein, G. (1993) *Education Towards Race Equality*, Cassell, London.

Kohler, I. (1962) Experiments with goggles, *Scientific American*.

Kratwohl, D. R. (ed.) (1964) *Taxonomy of Educational Objectives II. Affective Domain*, Longman, London.

Kuczaj, S. (ed.) (1981) *Language, Cognition and Culture*, Erlbaum, Hillside, New Jersey.

Lange-Kuettner, C. and Thomas, G. V. (eds.) *Drawing and Looking: Theoretical Approaches to Pictorial Representation in Children*, Harvester, Hemel Hempstead.

Laszlo, J. and Bairstow, P. (1985) *Perceptual-Motor Behaviour*, Holt, London.

Lawton, D. (1973) *Social Change, Educational Theory and Curriculum Planning*, University of London Press.

Lawton, D. (1975) *Class, Culture and the Curriculum*, Routledge & Kegan Paul, London.

Le Guin, U. K. (1980, 1981) It was a dark and stormy night: or why are we huddling about the camp fire?, in W. J. T. Mitchell (ed.), op. cit.

Lewin, R. (ed.) (1974) *Child Alive*, Temple-Smith, London.

Lewis, D. (1990) The constructedness of texts: picture books and the metafictive, *Signal*, no. 62, pp. 131–46.

Li, A. K. F. (1978) Effects of play on novel responses in kindergarten children, *Alberta Journal of Educational Research*, Vol 24, pp. 31–6.

Lieberman, J. N. (1977) *Playfulness: Its Relationship to Imagination and Creativity*, Academic Press, New York.

Light, P. (1985) The development of view-specific representation considered from a socio-cognitive standpoint, in N. H. Freeman and M. V. Cox (eds.) op. cit.

Lock, A. (ed.) (1978) *Action, Gesture and Symbol: The Emergence of Language*, Academic Press, London.

Luquet, G. H. (1927) *Le Dessin Enfantin*, Alcan, Paris.

MacLean, K. (1987) Writing at home, in CLPE (1987) op. cit.

Mager, R. F. (1962) *Preparing Instructional Objectives*, Fearon, Palo Alto, California.

Malina, R. M. (1973) Factors influencing motor development during infancy and childhood, in C. B. Corbin (ed.) op. cit.

Malina, R. M. (1986) Physical Growth and Maturation, in Seefeldt, V. (ed.) op. cit.

Mandler, S. M. (1979) Categorical and schematic organisation in memory, in C. R. Puff (ed.) op. cit.

Marr, D. (1982) *Vision: A Computational Investigation into the Human Representation and Processing of Visual Information*, Freeman, San Francisco.

Marriott, S. (1995) *Read On. Using fiction in the primary school*, Paul Chapman, London.

Martin, T. and Leather, B. (1994) *Readers and Texts in the Primary Years*, Open University Press, Buckingham.

Matthews, J. (1983) Children drawing: are young children really scribbling?, Paper presented at British Psychological Society's International Conference on *Psychology and the Arts*, University of Cardiff, Wales, 1983.

Matthews, J. (1990) Expression, Representation and Drawing in Early Childhood. Unpublished Ph.D. thesis, University of London.

Matthews, J. (1993) Art in the National Curriculum: implications for early childhood education and care, *Nursery World* 8 April, pp. 18–20.

Matthews, J. (1994a) *Helping Children Draw and Paint in Early Childhood: Children and Visual Representation*, Hodder & Stoughton, London.

Matthews, J. (1994b) Deep structures in children's art: development and culture, *Visual Arts Research*, Vol. 20, no. 2, issue 40, pp. 29–50.

Matthews, J. and Jessel, J. (1993a) Very young children use electronic paint: a study of the beginnings of drawing with traditional media and computer paintbox, *Visual Arts Research*, Vol. 19, no. 1, issue 37, pp. 47–62.

Matthews, J. and Jessel, J. (1993b) Very young children and electronic paint: the beginnings of drawing with traditional media and computer paintbox, *Early Years*, Vol. 13, no. 2., pp. 15–22.

McCail, G. (1981) *Mother Start*, Scottish Council for Research in Education, Cheyne.

McIntosh, P. (1976) The curriculum of physical education – an historical perspective, in J. E. Kane (ed.) op. cit.

Meek, M. (1988) *How Texts Teach What Readers Learn*, Thimble Press, Stroud.

Meek, M. (1994) *Learning to Read* (Second edition), Bodley Head, London.

Meek, M., Warlow, A. and Barton, G. (eds.) (1977) *The Cool Web. The Pattern of Children's Reading*, Bodley Head, London.

Mehler, J. (ed.) (1983) *Infant and Neonate Cognition*, Erlbaum, Hillsdale, New Jersey.

Mehler, J. and Fox, R. (1985) *Neonate Cognition: Beyond the Blooming Buzzing Confusion*, Erlbaum, Hillsdale, New Jersey.

Merttens, R. (1992) *Times Educational Supplement*, 20 November.

Metz, M. (1985) Chairs for bears, *Micromath*, Vol. 1, no. 3, pp. 8–10, also in D. Pimm (ed.) op. cit.

Michaels, W. and Walsh, M. (1990) *Up and Away: Using Picture Books*, Oxford University Press.

Michotte, A. (1963) *The Perception of Causality, Methuen Manual of Modern Psychology,* Methuen, London.

Millar, S. (1968) *The Psychology of Play,* Penguin, Harmondsworth.

Miller, J. (1986) *Women Writing about Men,* Virago, London.

Minhas, R. (1994) OFSTED inspections and the centrality of equality of opportunity in raising standards, in Keel (ed.) op. cit.

Minns, H. (1990) *Read It To Me Now! Learning at home and at school,* Virago, London.

Mitchell, W. J. T. (ed.) (1980; 1981) *On Narrative,* University of Chicago Press.

Moss, P. and Pence, A. (eds.) (1994) *Valuing Quality in Early Childhood Services,* Paul Chapman, London.

National Childminding Association (1993) *Training: The Key to Quality,* NCMA, Kent.

Nelson, K. (1981) The syntagmatics and paradigmatics of conceptual development, in S. Kuczaj (ed.) op. cit.

Newson, L. (1979) Intentional behaviour in the young infant, in D. Schaffer and J. Dunn (eds.) op. cit.

Northumberland County Council (1993) *Maintaining the Balance,* NCC, Northumberland.

Nunes, T., Schliemann, A. D. and Carraher, D. W. (1993) *Street Mathematics and School Mathematics,* Cambridge University Press, Cambridge.

O'Connell, B. and Bretherton, I. (1984) Toddlers' play, alone and with mother: the role of maternal guidance, in I. Bretherton (ed.), op. cit.

Olson, D. R., Torrance, N. and Hildyard, A. (eds.) (1985) *Literacy, Language and Learning. The Nature and Consequences of Reading and Writing* Cambridge University Press.

Opie, I. and Opie, P. (1969) *Children's Games in Street and Playground,* Oxford University Press.

Orton, A. (1987) *Learning Mathematics – Issues, Theories and Classroom Practice,* Cassell Educational, London.

Osherson, D., Kosslyn, S. M. and Hollerbach, J. M. (eds.) (1990) *Visual Cognition and Action: An Invitation to Cognitive Science,* MIT Press, Mass.

Paley, V. G. (1981) *Wally's Stories,* Harvard University Press, Cambridge, Mass.

Paley, V. G. (1990) *The Boy who would be a Helicopter,* Harvard University Press, Cambridge, Mass.

Paley, V. G. (1992) *You can't Say, You can't Play,* Harvard University Press, Cambridge, Mass.

Papert, S. (1980) *Mindstorms – Children, Computers and Powerful Ideas,* Harvester, Brighton.

Papert, S. (1981) Teaching children to be mathematicians versus teaching about mathematics, in A. Floyd (ed.) op. cit.

Papusek, H. (1969) Individual variability in learned response in humans, in R. J. Robinson (ed.) op. cit.

Payton, S. (1984) Developing awareness of print. A young child's first steps towards literacy, *Education Review Offset Publication,* no. 2, University of Birmingham.

Pepler, D. J. (1982) Play and divergent thinking, in D. J. Pepler and K. H. Rubin (eds.), op. cit.

Pepler, D. J. and Rubin, K. H. (eds.) (1982) *The Play of Children: Current Theory and Research,* Karger, Basel.

Peters, M. and Smith, B. (1993) *Spelling in Context. Strategies of Teachers and*

Learners, NFER Nelson, Windsor.

Peters, R. S. (1965) Education as initiation, in R. D. Archambault (ed.) op. cit.

Peters, R. S. (1966) *Ethics and Education*, Allen & Unwin, London.

Peters, R. S. (ed.) (1969) *Perspectives on Plowden*, Routledge & Kegan Paul, London.

Peters, R. S. (ed.) (1973) *The Philosophy of Education*, Oxford University Press.

Petitto, L. (1987) Gestures and language in apes and children, a talk given to the Cognitive Development Unit of the Medical Research Council, London 28 May.

Piaget, J. (1951; 1962) *Play, Dreams and Imitation in Childhood*, Routledge & Kegan Paul, London.

Piaget, J. (1969; 1971) *Science of Education and the Psychology of the Child*, Longman, London.

Piaget, J. and Inhelder, B. (1956) *The Child's Conception of Space*, Routledge & Kegan Paul, London.

Pimm, D. (1987) *Speaking Mathematically – Communication in Mathematics Classrooms*, Routledge & Kegan Paul, London.

Pimm, D. (ed.) (1988) *Mathematics, Teachers and Children*, Hodder and Stoughton in association with the Open University, Sevenoaks.

Pinch, A. and Armstrong, M. (eds.) (1982) *Tolstoy on Education*, Athlone Press, London.

Popham, W. J. (1969) Objectives and instruction, in W. J. Popham *et al.*, op. cit.

Popham, W. J., Eisner, E. W., Sullivan, H. J. and Tyler, L. L. (1969) *Instructional Objectives*, American Educational Research Association Monograph Series on Curriculum Evaluation no. 3, Rand McNally, Chicago.

Poulton, G. and James, T. (1975) *Preschool Learning in the Community: Strategies for Change*, Routledge & Kegan Paul, London.

Pratt, F. R. (1985) A perspective on traditional artistic practices, in N. H. Freeman and M. V. Cox (eds.) op. cit.

Pre-school Playgroups Association (1991) *Early Chances – Eliminating discrimination and ensuring equality in playgroups*, PPA, London.

Puff, C. R. (ed.) (1979) *Memory, Organisation and Structures*, Academic Press, New York.

Pugh, G., De 'Ath, E. and Smith, C. (1994) *Confident Parents, Confident Children: policy and practice in parent education and support*, National Children's Bureau, London.

Read, C. (1986) *Children's Creative Spelling*, Routledge & Kegan Paul, London.

Richards, R. (1972) *Early Experiences. Schools Council Science 5/13 Project*, Macdonald Educational for the Schools Council, London.

Richards, R. (1983) Learning through science, in G. M. Blenkin and A. V. Kelly (eds.) op. cit.

Richards, R., Collis, M. and Kincaid, D. (1986) *An Early Start to Science*, Macdonald Educational, London.

Richards, R., Collis, M., Kincaid, D. and Bailey, H. (1982) *Science Resources for Primary and Middle Schools. Schools Council Learning Through Science Project*, Macdonald Educational for the Schools Council, London.

Roberton, M. A. and Halverson, L. (1984) *Developing Children – Their Changing Movement*, Lea & Febiger, Philadelphia.

Robinson, R. J. (ed.) (1969) *Brain and Early Behaviour*, Academic Press, London.

Rosen, B. (1991) *Shapers and Polishers. Teachers as Storytellers*, Mary Glasgow, London.

Runnymeade Trust (1993) *Equality Assurance in Schools: Quality, Identity, Society,*

Trentham, Stoke-on-Trent.

Save the Children Fund (1994) *Equality in Practice*, London.

Schaffer, D. and Dunn, J. (eds.) (1979) *The First Years of Life: Psychological and Medical Implications of Early Experience*, Wiley, New York.

Schaffer, H. R. (1974) Early social behaviour and the study of reciprocity, *Bulletin of the British Psychological Society*, Vol. 27, pp. 209–16.

Schieffelin, B. and Cochran-Smith, M. (1984) Learning to read culturally, in H. Goelman, A. Oberg and F. Smith (eds.) op. cit.

Seefeldt, V. (ed.) *Physical Activity and Well-Being*, Renton, VA, ASHPERD.

Sendak, M. (1977) Questions to an artist who is also an author, in M. Meek, A. Warlow and G. Barton (eds.) op. cit.

Sharp, C., Hutchinson, D. and Whettan, C. (1994) How do season of birth and length of schooling affect children's attainment in Key Stage 1?, *Educational Research*, Vol. 36, no. 2, pp. 107–121.

Shields, M. M. (1978) The child as psychologist: construing the social world, in A. Lock (ed.) op. cit.

Shields, M. M. (1983) The young child's representation of persons and the social world, the Dorothy Gardner Memorial Lecture, 23 April.

Shreeves, R. (1990) *Children Dancing* (Second edition), Ward Lock Educational, London.

Silver, P. and Silver, H. (1974) *The Education of the Poor*, Routledge & Kegan Paul, London.

Simon, T. and Smith, P. K. (1983) The study of play and problem solving in preschool children: have experimenter effects been responsible for previous results?, *British Journal of Developmental Psychology*, Vol. 1, pp. 289–97.

Siraj-Blatchford, I. (1994) *The Early Years: Laying the Foundation for Racial Equality*, Trentham, Stoke-on-Trent.

Siraj-Blatchford, I. (1995) Racial equality education: Identity, curriculum and pedagogy, in Siraj-Blatchford and Siraj-Blatchford (eds.) op. cit.

Siraj-Blatchford, I. and Siraj-Blatchford, J. (eds.) (1995) *Educating the Whole Child*, Open University Press, Buckingham.

Smith, B. (1994) *Through Writing to Reading. Classroom strategies for supporting literacy*, Routledge, London.

Smith, B. H. (1980; 1981) Narrative versions, narrative theories, in W. J. T. Mitchell (ed.) op. cit.

Smith, F. (1981) Demonstrations, engagement and sensitivity, in F. Smith (1983) op. cit.

Smith, F. (1982a) *Understanding Reading* (3rd edn), Holt, Rinehart & Winston, New York.

Smith, F. (1982b) *Writing and the Writer*, Heinemann, London.

Smith, F. (1983) *Essays into Literacy. Selected Papers and Some Afterthoughts*, Heinemann Educational, London.

Smith, F. (1988) *Understanding Reading. A Psycholinguistic Analysis of Reading and Learning to Read (Fourth Edition)*, Lawrence Erlbaum Associates, Hillsdale, NJ.

Smith, N. R. (1979) Developmental origins of structural variations in symbol form, in N. R. Smith and M. B. Franklin (eds.) op. cit.

Smith, N. R. (1983) *Experience and Art: Teaching Children to Paint*, Teachers College Press, Columbia University, New York.

Smith, N. R. and Franklin, M. B. (eds.) (1979) *Symbolic Functioning in Childhood*, Erlbaum, Hillsdale, New Jersey.

Smith, P. K. (ed.) (1984) *Play in Animals and Humans*, Blackwell, Oxford.

Smith, P. K. and Simon, T. (1984) Object play, problem-solving and creativity in children, in P. K. Smith (ed.) op. cit.

Smith, T. (1980) *Parents and Preschool*, Grant McIntyre, London.

Smith, T. (1987) *Changing Roles in Early Childhood Work*, Centre for Early Childhood, Froebel Institute, London.

Spackman, L. (ed.) (1983) *Teaching Games for Understanding*, Curriculum Development Centre, College of St Paul and St Mary, Cheltenham.

Spelke, E. S. (1985) Perception of unity, persistence and identity: thoughts on infants' conceptions of objects, in J. Mehler and R. Fox (eds.) op. cit.

Spelke, E. S. (1990) Origins of visual knowledge, in D. Osherson, S. M. Kosslyn and J. M. Hollerbach (eds.) op. cit.

Spencer, H. (1855) *The Principles of Psychology*, Longman, London.

Steffe, L. P. and Wood, T. (eds.) (1990) *Transforming Children's Mathematics Education*, Lawrence Erlbaum Associates, Hillsdale, N.J.

Stenhouse, L. (1970) Some limitations of the use of objectives in curriculum research and planning, *Paedagogica Europea*, Vol. 6, pp. 73–83.

Stenhouse, L. (1975) *An Introduction to Curriculum Research and Development*, Heinemann, London.

Stenhouse, L. (ed.) (1980) *Curriculum Research and Development in Action*, Heinemann, London.

Stern, D. (1977) *The First Relationship: Infant and Mother*, Fontana, London.

Styles, M., Bearne, E. and Watson, V. (1992) *After Alice. Exploring children's literature*, Cassell, London.

Sutherland, P. (1992) *Cognitive Development Today – Piaget and His Critics*, Paul Chapman, London.

Sutton-Smith, B. (1967) The role of play in cognitive development, *Young Children* Vol. 22, pp. 361–70.

Sylva, K. (1977) Play and learning, in B. Tizard and D. Harvey (eds.) op. cit.

Sylva, K. (1992) Quality care for the under-fives: is it worth it? *RSA Journal*, Vol. CXL, no. 5433, pp. 683–90.

Sylva, K., Roy, C. and Painter, M. (1980) *Childwatching at Playgroup and Nursery School*, Grant McIntyre, London.

Taylor, D and Dorsey-Gaines, C. (1986) *Growing Up Literate*, Heinemann, Portsmouth, NH.

Temple, C., Nathan, R., Burris, N. and Temple, F. (1988) *The Beginnings of Writing (Second Edition)*, Allyn and Bacon, London.

Tizard, B. (1977) Play: the child's way of learning?, in B. Tizard and D. Harvey (eds.) op. cit.

Tizard, B. (1987) Parent involvement – a no-score draw?, *Times Educational Supplement*, 3 April.

Tizard, B. and Harvey, D. (eds.) (1977) *Biology of Play*, Heinemann, London.

Tizard, B. and Hughes, M. (1984) *Young Children Learning; Talking and Thinking at Home and at School*, Fontana, London.

Tizard, B., Mortimore, J. and Burchell, B. (1981) *Involving Parents in Nursery and Infant Schools*, Grant McIntyre, London.

Tizard, B., Scofield, W. and Hewison, J. (1982) Collaboration between teachers and parents in assisting children's reading, *British Journal of Educational Psychology*, Vol. 52, pp. 1–15.

Torrey, J. (1969) Learning to read without a teacher: a case study, *Elementary*

English, 46, pp. 550–6.

Trelease, J. (1982) *The Read-Aloud Handbook* (UK edn 1984), Penguin, Harmondsworth.

Trevarthen, C. (1975) Early attempts at speech, in R. Lewin (ed.) op. cit.

Trevarthen, C. (1984) How control of movement develops, in H. T. A. Whiting (ed.) op. cit.

Trevarthen C. (1987) Motives for culture in young children: their natural development through communication. A paper presented at the International Symposium on the Nature of Culture, Ruhr-Universiteit, Bochum, September.

Trevarthen, C. (1993) Playing into reality: conversations with the infant communicator, *Winnicott Studies* no. 7, pp. 53–67, Karnac Books, London.

Troyna, B. and Hatcher, R. (1992) *Racism in Children's Lives*, Routledge & National Children's Bureau, London.

Tucker, N. (1981) *The Child and the Book. A Psychological and Literary Exploration*, Cambridge University Press.

Tyler, R. W. (1949) *Basic Principles of Curriculum and Instruction*, University of Chicago Press.

United Nations (1989) *Declaration on the Rights of the Child*, U.N., New York.

Van Sommers, P. (1984) *Drawing and Cognition: Descriptive and Experimental Studies of Graphic Production Processes*, Cambridge University Press.

Vygotsky, L. S. (1962) *Thought and Language*, MIT Press, Cambridge, Mass.

Vygotsky, L. S. (1966) Play and its role in the mental development of the child, *Soviet Psychology*, Vol. 12, no. 6, pp. 62–76.

Vygotsky, L. S. (1978) *Mind in Society. The Development of Higher Psychological Processes*, Harvard University Press, Cambridge, Mass.

Walsh, W. H. (1969) *Hegeliun Ethics*, Macmillan, London.

Watt, J. (1987) Continuity in education, in M. M. Clark (ed.) op. cit.

Weeks, A. (1987) School information brochures: a primary school survey, *Cambridge Education Journal*, Vol. 17, no. 1, pp. 61–2.

Wells, G. (1981) Becoming a communicator, in G. Wells (ed.) op. cit.

Wells, G. (ed.) (1981) *Learning through Interaction. The Study of Language Development*, Cambridge University Press.

Wells, G. (1983) Talking with children: the complementary roles of parents and teachers, in M. Donaldson, R. Grieve and C. Pratt (eds.) op. cit.

Wells, G. (1985a) *Language Development in the Pre-School Years*, Cambridge University Press.

Wells, G. (1985b) *Language, Learning and Education*, NFER/Nelson, Windsor.

Wells, G. (1985c) Pre-school literacy-related activities and success in school, in D. R. Olson, N. Torrance and A. Hildyard (eds.) op. cit.

Wells, G. (1987) *The Meaning Makers: Children Learning Language and Using Language to Learn*, Hodder & Stoughton, London.

Wells, G. and Nicholls, J. (eds.) (1985) *Language and Learning: An Interactional Perspective*, Falmer, London.

Werner, H. and Kaplan, B. (1963) *Symbol Formation*, Wiley, New York.

Werner, P. H. (1979) *A Movement Approach to Games for Children*, C. V. Mosby, London.

White, D. (1954) *Books before Five*, Council for Educational Research, New Zealand.

White, J. P. (1973) *Towards a Compulsory Curriculum*, Routledge & Kegan Paul, London.

Whitehead, A. N. (1932) *The Aims of Education*, Williams & Norgate, London.

Whitehead, M. R. (1980) Once upon a time? *English in Education*, Vol. 14, no. 1, pp. 45–58.

Whitehead, M. R. (1990) *Language and Literacy in the Early Years: An Approach for Education Students*, Paul Chapman, London.

Whitehead, M. R. (1992) Assessment at Key Stage 1: Core Subjects and the Developmental Curriculum, in G. M. Blenkin and A. V. Kelly (eds.) op. cit.

Whitehead, M. R. (1993) Born again phonics and the nursery rhyme revival, *English in Education*, Vol. 27, no. 3, pp. 42–51.

Whitehurst, K. E. (1971) What movement means to the young child, *Journal of Health, Physical Education and Recreation*, May, pp. 34–5.

Whiting, H. T. A. (ed.) (1984) *Human Motor Actions – Bernstein Reassessed*, Elsevier Science Publishers, Amsterdam, North Holland.

Willats, J. (1977) How children learn to draw realistic pictures, *Quarterly Journal of Experimental Psychology*, Vol. 29, pp. 367–82.

Willats, J. (1981) What do the marks in the picture stand for? The child's acquisition of systems of transformation and denotation, *Review of Research in Visual Arts Education*, Vol. 13, pp. 18–33.

Willats, J. (1984) Getting the drawing to look right as well as be right: the interaction between production and perception as a mechanism of development, in W. R. Crozier and A. J. Chapman (eds.) op. cit.

Willats, J. (1985) Drawing systems revisited: the role of denotation systems in children's figure drawings, in N. H. Freeman and M. V. Cox (eds.) op. cit.

Willes, M. J. (1983) *Children into Pupils: A Study of Language in Early Schooling*, Routledge & Kegan Paul, London.

Williamson, D. and Hickling, P. (1978) A swimming education model for ESN schools, *British Journal of Physical Education*, Vol. 9, no. 4, pp. 100–1.

Winnicott, D. W. (1971) *Playing and Reality*, Penguin, Harmondsworth.

Wolf, D. (1989) Artistic learning as conversation, in D. Hargreaves (ed.) op. cit.

Wolf, D. and Fucigna, C. (1983) Representation before picturing. Transcript of symposium presentation; Symposium on Drawing Development, British Psychological Society International Conference on *Psychology and the Arts*, University of Cardiff.

Wood, D. (1988) *How Children Think and Learn*, Blackwell, Oxford.

Wood, D. J., McMahon, L. and Cranstoun, Y. (1980) *Working with Under Fives*, Grant McIntyre, London.

Woodhead, M. (1985) Pre-school education has long term effects but can they be generalised?, *Oxford Review of Education*, Vol. 11, no. 2, pp. 133–55.

Wright, C. (1992) Early education: Multiracial primary school classrooms, in D. Gill, B. Mayer and M. Blair (eds.) op. cit.

Wright, J. (1986) Gymnastics – principles into practice, in British Association of Advisors and Lecturers in Physical Education, op. cit.

Young, M. F. D. (ed.) (1971) *Knowledge and Control*, Collier Macmillan, London.

Zaichkowsky, L., Zaichkowsky, L. and Martinek, T. (1980) *Growth and Development: The Child and Physical Activity*, C. V. Mosby, London.

Zammarelli, J. and Bolton, N. (1977) The effects of play on mathematical concept formation, *British Journal of Educational Psychology*, Vol. 47, pp. 155–61.

Official publications referred to in the text

Board of Education (1931) *Primary Education* (The Hadow Report), HMSO, London.

Central Advisory Council for Education (1963) *Half Our Future* (The Newsom Report), HMSO, London.

Central Advisory Council for Education (1967) *Children and Their Primary Schools* (The Plowden Report), HMSO, London.

Department for Education (1995a) *The National Curriculum*, HMSO, London.

Department for Education (1995b) *English in the National Curriculum*, HMSO, London.

Department for Education (1995c) *Art in the National Curriculum*, HMSO, London.

Department for Education (1995d) *Music in the National Curriculum*, HMSO, London.

Department for Education (1995e) *Science in the National Curriculum*, HMSO, London.

Department for Education (1995f) *Physical Education in the National Curriculum*, HMSO, London.

Department for Education and Employment (1995) *Discussion Paper on Quality Assurance Regime for Institutions which Redeem Pre-School Education Vouchers*, HMSO, London.

Department of Education and Science (1972) *Movement. Physical Education in the primary years*, HMSO, London.

Department of Education and Science (1975) *A Language for Life* (The Bullock Report), HMSO, London.

Department of Education and Science (1982a) *Education 5 to 9: an Illustrative Survey of 80 First Schools in England*, HMSO, London.

Department of Education and Science (1982b) *Bullock Revisited: a discussion document by HMI*, HMSO, London.

Department of Education and Science (1982c) *Mathematics Counts* (The Cockcroft Report), HMSO, London.

Department of Education and Science (1983) *Teaching Quality*, (White Paper) Cmnd. 8836, HMSO, London.

Department of Education and Science (1984) *Circular 3/84*, HMSO, London.

Department of Education and Science (1985a) *The Curriculum from 5 to 16. Curriculum Matters 2. An HMI Series*, HMSO, London.

Department of Education and Science (1985b) *Education for All* (The Swann Report), HMSO, London.

Department of Education and Science and the Welsh Office (1987) *The National Curriculum 5-16: a consultation document*, HMSO, London.

Department of Education and Science (1988a) *Report of the Committee of Inquiry into the Teaching of English* (The Kingman Report), HMSO, London.

Department of Education and Science (1988b) *English for Ages 5–11. Proposals of the Secretaries of State*, HMSO, London.

Department of Education and Science (1989) *Mathematics in the National Curriculum*, HMSO, London.

Department of Education and Science (1990a) *Starting with Quality: The Report of the Committee of Inquiry into the Quality of Educational Experience Offered to 3 and 4 year olds*, HMSO, London.

Department of Education and Science (1990b) *Technology in the National*

Curriculum, HMSO, London.

Department of Education and Science (1991) *Mathematics in the National Curriculum (1991)*, HMSO, London.

National Curriculum Council (1990) *Curriculum Guidance 3: The Whole Curriculum*, NCC, York.

Office for Standards in Education (1993) *A Handbook for the Inspection of Schools*, HMSO, London.

School Curriculum and Assessment Authority (1995a) *Pre-School Education Consultation. Desirable outcomes for children's learning and guidance for providers*, SCAA, York.

School Curriculum and Assessment Authority (1995b) *Planning the Curriculum at Key Stages 1 and 2*, SCAA, York.

Literature referred to in the text

Aardema, V. (1981) *Bringing the Rain to Kapiti Plain*, Macmillan, London.

Agard, J. (1981) *Dig Away Two-Hole Jim*, Bodley Head, London.

Agard, J. (1983) *I Din Do Nuttin*, Bodley Head, London.

Agard, J. and Nichols, G (eds,) (1994) *A Caribbean Dozen. Poems from Caribbean Poets*, Walker, London.

Ahlberg, A. (1983) *Please Mrs Butler*, Kestrel/Penguin, Harmondsworth.

Ahlberg, J. and Ahlberg, A. (1977) *Each Peach Pear Plum*, Kestrel/Penguin, Harmondsworth.

Ahlberg, J. and Ahlberg, A. (1981) *Peepo!*, Kestrel/Penguin, Harmondsworth.

Ahlberg, J. and Ahlberg, A. (1989) *Bye Bye Baby*, Heinemann, London.

Armitage, R. and Armitage, D. (1977) *The Lighthouse Keeper's Lunch*, Andre Deutsch, London.

Bang, M. (1983) *Ten, Nine, Eight*, Penguin, Harmondsworth.

Barber, A. and Bayley, N. (1990) *The Mousehole Cat*, Walker, London.

Briggs, R. (1970) *Jim and the Beanstalk*, Hamish Hamilton, London.

Briggs, R. (1978) *The Snowman*, Hamish Hamilton, London.

Browne, A. (1979) *Bear Hunt*, Hamish Hamilton, London.

Browne, A. (1981) *Hansel and Gretel*, Julia MacRae, London.

Browne, A. (1983) *Gorilla*, Julia MacRae, London.

Browne, A. (1986) *Piggybook*, Julia MacRae, London.

Browne, A. (1989) *The Tunnel*, Julia MacRae, London.

Burningham, J. (1970) *Mr Gumpy's Outing*, Cape, London.

Burningham, J. (1977) *Come Away from the Water, Shirley*, Cape, London.

Burningham, J. (1982) *Avocado Baby*, Cape, London.

Burningham, J. (1984) *Granpa*, Cape, London.

Burningham, J. (1986) *Where's Julius?*, Cape, London.

Burningham, J. (1991) *Aldo*, Cape, London.

Butterworth, N. and Inkpen, M. (1992) *Jasper's Beanstalk*, Hodder & Stoughton, London.

Carlson, N. (1982) *Harriet and the Roller Coaster*, Penguin, Harmondsworth.

Causley, C. (1970) *Figgie Hobbin*, Macmillan, London.

Cherrington, C. (1984) *Sunshine Island, Moonshine Baby*, Collins, Glasgow.

Cope, W. (1986) *Making Cocoa for Kingsley Amis*, Faber & Faber, London.

Cowcher, H. (1991) *Tigress*, Andre Deutsch, London.

Cutler, I. (1971) *Meal One*, Heinemann, London.
Dickinson, E. (1959) *Selected Poems* (J. Reeves ed.), Heinemann, London.
Doherty, B. (1992) *Dear Nobody*, Hamish Hamilton, London.
Emecheta, B. (1980) *Nowhere to Play*, Allison and Busby, London.
Foreman, M. and Turnbull A. (1989) *The Sand Horse*, Andersen, London.
Foreman, M. (1992) *Jack's Fantastic Voyage*, Andersen, London.
Foreman, M. (1993) *War Game*, Pavilion, London.
Hamilton, V. (1985) *The People Could Fly: American Black Folk Tales*, Walker, London.
Hayes, S. and Ormerod, J. (1988) *Eat Up, Gemma*, Walker, London.
Hersom, K. (1981) *Maybe it's a Tiger*, Macmillan, London.
Hoffman, M. and Binch, C. (1991) *Amazing Grace*, Frances Lincoln, London.
Holman, F. (1974) *Slake's Limbo*, Scribner, New York (1980) Macmillan, London.
Howker, J. (1985) *The Nature of the Beast*, Julia MacRae, London.
Hughes, S. (1979) *Up and Up*, Bodley Head, London.
Hutchins, P. (1968) *Rosie's Walk*, Bodley Head, London.
Hutchins, P. (1972) *Titch*, Bodley Head, London.
Ingpen, R. (1986) *The Idle Bear*, Blackie, London.
Joseph, J. (1977) *Warning*, in D. Saunders and V. Oliver (eds.) op.cit.
Kaye, J. (1992) *Two's Company*, Penguin, Harmondsworth.
Keeping, C. (1975) *Cockney Ding-dong*, Kestrel/Penguin, Harmondsworth.
Keller, H. (1984) *Geraldine's Blanket*, Julia MacRae, London.
Kent, J. (1972) *The Fat Cat*, Hamish Hamilton, London.
Kerr, J. (1968) *The Tiger Who Came to Tea*, Collins, Glasgow.
Kitamura, S. (1986) *When Sheep Cannot Sleep*, Black, London.
Llewellyn, C. (1992) *My First Book of Time*, Dorling Kindersley, London.
Lloyd, E. (1978) *Nini at Carnival*, Bodley Head, London.
Lord, J. V. and Burroway, J. (1972) *The Giant Jam Sandwich*, Cape, London.
Lurie, A. (1980) *Clever Gretchen and Other Forgotten Folk Tales*, Heinemann, London.
Lurie, A. (1985) *Foreign Affairs*, Michael Joseph, London.
Macaulay, D. (1990) *Black and White*, Houghton Mifflin, Boston.
Magorian, M. (1981) *Goodnight Mister Tom*, Kestrel/Penguin, Harmondsworth.
Mark, J. (1983) *Handles*, Kestrel/Penguin, Harmondsworth.
McAfee, A. and Browne, A. (1984) *The Visitors Who Came to Stay*, Hamish Hamilton, London.
Munsch, R. N. (1980) *The Paper Bag Princess*, Scholastic Publications, London.
Newman, N. and Foreman, M. (1993) *There's a Bear in the Bath*, Pavilion, London.
Nicholl, H. and Pienkowski, J. (1972) *Meg and Mog*, Heinemann, London.
Ormerod, J. (1981) *Sunshine*, Kestrel/Penguin, Harmondsworth.
Ormerod, J. (1984) *101 Things to Do with a Baby*, Kestrel/Penguin, Harmondsworth.
Rayner, M. (1976) *Mr and Mrs Pig's Evening Out*, Macmillan, London.
Rosen, M. (1983) *Quick, Let's Get Out Of Here*, Andre Deutsch, London.
Rosen, M. and Oxenbury, H. (1989) *We're Going On a Bear Hunt*, Walker, London.
Samuels, V. and Northway, J. (1988) *Carry Go Bring Come*, Bodley Head, London.
Saunders, D. and Oliver, V. (1977) *People: Poems and Pictures*, Evans Bros , London.
Scieszka, J. and Smith, L. (1992) *The Stinky Cheese Man*, Penguin, Harmondsworth.
Sendak, M. (1967) *Where the Wild Things Are*, Bodley Head, London.
Seuss, Dr. (1984) *The Butter Battle Book*, Collins, Glasgow.
Showers, P. (1975) *Your Skin and Mine*, A & C Black, London.
Steptoe, J. (1987) *Mufaro's Beautiful Daughters*, Hamish Hamilton, London.

Stoddard, S. and Munsinger, L. (1985) *Bedtime for Bear*, Houghton Mifflin, Boston, Mass.
Storr, C. (1990) *Last Stories of Polly and the Wolf*, Faber and Faber, London.
Swift, G. (1983) *Waterland*, Heinemann, London.
Trivizas, E, and Oxenbury, H. (1993) *The Three Little Wolves and the Big Bad Pig*, Heinemann, London.
Vipont, E. (1969) *The Elephant and the Bad Baby*, Hamish Hamilton, London.
Wagner, J. (1977) *John Brown, Rose and the Midnight Cat*, Kestrel/Penguin, Harmondsworth.
Walsh, J. P. (1972) *Goldengrove*, Macmillan, London.
Walsh, J. P. (1976) *Unleaving*, Bodley Head, London.
Walsh, J. P. (1982) *Babylon*, Andre Deutsch, London.
Willis, J. and Ross, T. (1988) *Dr Xargle's Book of Earthlets*, Andersen, London.
Woolf, V. (1943) *To The Lighthouse*, Hogarth, London.

Sources for traditional material

Alderson, B. (illustrated by Oxenbury, H.) (1974) *Cakes and Custard*, Heinemann, London.
Opie, I. and Opie, P. (1955) *The Oxford Nursery Rhyme Book*, Oxford University Press, London.
Opie, I. and Opie, P. (1974) *The Classic Fairy Tales*, Oxford University Press, London.
Opie, I. and Opie, P. (1980) *A Nursery Companion*, Oxford University Press, London.
Opie, I. and Opie, P. (1985) *The Singing Game*, Oxford University Press, London.
Stones, R. and Mann, A. (illustrated by Jones, D.) (1977) *Mother Goose Comes to Cable Street*, Kestrel/Penguin, Harmondsworth.

Author Index

Subject Index